A MOTHER'S PLEA

"This is my daughter," Janet McGinn said, holding up for television cameras the same photo of Stephanie that she had held the day before. "She's twelve years old. She's about one hundred pounds. She has blond hair. It's long in the back and short in the front. She wears it like this," Janet said, pulling her own hair back, exposing her forehead.

The frantic mother trembled, desperation showing in her blue eyes that were swollen and red from crying. Then, looking directly into the camera, Janet spoke to her daughter as though willing her alive.

"Stephanie, baby, I'm not mad. Please come home." Janet's plea was laced with fear.

"What do you think about your husband being arrested for murder?" the reporter asked.

"I can't for the life of me think my husband did anything wrong," Janet responded. "They do everything together."

Other Books by Patricia Springer

BLOOD RUSH
MAIL ORDER MURDER
FLESH AND BLOOD
A LOVE TO DIE FOR
BODY HUNTER

Published by Pinnacle Books

BLOOD STAINS

PATRICIA SPRINGER

PINNACLE BOOKS
Kensington Publishing Corp.
http://www.kensingtonbooks.com

Some names have been changed to protect the privacy of individuals connected to this story.

PINNACLE BOOKS are published by

Kensington Publishing Corp.
850 Third Avenue
New York, NY 10022

Copyright © 2002 by Patricia Springer

All Kensington Titles, Imprints, and Distributed Lines are available at special quantity discounts for bulk purchases for sales promotions, premiums, fund-raising, and educational or institutional use. Special book excerpts or customized printings can also be created to fit specific needs. For details, write or phone the office of the Kensington special sales manager: Kensington Publishing Corp., 850 Third Avenue, New York, NY 10022, attn: Special Sales Department, Phone: 1-800-221-2647.

Pinnacle and the P logo Reg. U.S. Pat. & TM Off.

First Printing: August 2002
10 9 8 7 6 5 4 3 2 1

Printed in the United States of America

To Bill and Dot Wilemon and Rob Church.
Thanks for everything.

ONE

The last remnants of daylight had surrendered to the darkness by the time the Brown County sheriff's dispatcher took the anxious call from Ricky McGinn.

"My stepdaughter's missing," McGinn said, a hint of panic in his voice. "I've looked and looked for her, but I can't find her anywhere."

McGinn, who had grown up in Brown County, had moved his wife and two stepdaughters to the rural area of May, Texas, with a population just under three hundred, only three weeks earlier.

Moments after taking McGinn's call at 9:40 P.M., the dispatcher alerted deputies to a missing child in the May community.

At 10:09 P.M. Deputy Don Roberts arrived at the McGinn home. Steve Sirois, McGinn's best friend, waited in the front yard for the deputy; he had been summoned by McGinn prior to calling authorities.

"Ricky's in the back looking for Stephanie," Sirois said, nodding his head toward the house.

Sirois led the deputy through the leaning white fence, which was missing several pickets, then through the McGinn house to the backyard.

Roberts's eyes shifted from one side of the dwelling to the other. Stacks of cardboard cartons littered the living room, along with filled black garbage bags. The ceiling sagged precariously overhead. It appeared that the Mc-

Ginns were either moving out or in. A folding bed was open on one end of the room, the thin mattress covered with a gold-colored pad. As the deputy moved through the living room toward the back door, he noticed the kitchen ceiling was in much the same disrepair as he had observed in the living area. The kitchen table was cluttered with dishes and pop bottles, as were the countertops. When Roberts stepped outside the screen door, he noticed a rusted white clothes dryer nestled in the foot-high grass, the door standing open.

In the distance Roberts could hear a male voice calling, "Stephanie! Stephanie!"

A flicker of light caught Roberts' attention. It was the beam of a handheld flashlight moving around the far side of a dirt pond. Roberts started walking toward the light, but as he approached, the light moved farther away.

"Follow me," Sirois told the deputy as he led him to a place at the edge of the water. "Ricky and the kids usually swam here."

There was a small floating platform made of wood. The ground surrounding the area was so hard packed it was impossible to tell if anyone had been in or out of the pond recently.

As Roberts surveyed the area, a man approached. He was dressed in gray shorts, a dark-colored shirt, and white sneakers with white socks. The man was carrying a flashlight and he walked with a pronounced limp.

Sirois introduced Deputy Roberts and McGinn. After a few moments Roberts asked, "What does your stepdaughter look like?"

"She's twelve years old, five feet three inches tall, one hundred pounds," McGinn began. "She has blond hair and blue eyes."

McGinn appeared anxious but in control.

"What was she wearing?" Roberts asked.

"A gray short-sleeved T-shirt with, I think, the word

Hillbilly on the front, green-and-white shorts, and white tennis shoes," McGinn answered.

"When did you last see her?" Roberts asked.

"It was about five-twenty P.M. when she left the yard to take a walk, which was usual for her. When she left, she was going west, past the north end of the pond toward the back of the property. She frequently walked back there and would then return to the house by way of County Road 417. Only this time she didn't return," McGinn said, his voice trailing off.

Stephanie, a sixth grader at Brownwood Central Six, enjoyed searching the wooded field behind their home in pursuit of deer and wild rabbits. There had never been cause for alarm. She had seemed safe in the natural surroundings.

"When did you start looking for her?" Roberts inquired.

"About eight-thirty P.M.. I couldn't find her, so I called the sheriff's office about nine-forty."

McGinn explained that he had been working on his pickup when Stephanie had asked to go swimming at her grandmother's, who lived in the Tamarack Mountain addition, not far from the McGinns' home.

"I told her that I couldn't take her right then; I had to work on the pickup. That was when she told me she was going for a walk," McGinn said, an edge of distress in his voice.

Deputy Roberts, Steve Sirois, and Ricky McGinn continued to look for the missing girl around the pond, in several outbuildings, fenced pens, and in a cellar that was partially fallen in. There was no sign of Stephanie and no answer to their repeated calls, however.

After Deputy Roberts had been at the McGinn place for nearly an hour and forty-five minutes, he decided they needed help. Experienced help. He left McGinn's and headed to the sheriff's office, calling dispatch on the way.

"Contact the REACT Club and try to get a search party

organized," Roberts told dispatch. "The girl's still missing."

The wrinkles in Francis McGinn's weathered face grew deeper as she listened to her son's breathless voice on the other end of the telephone.

"Mama, where are Mike and Lisa?" Ricky McGinn asked, an anxious urgency in his tone.

"I don't know; they're gone with friends. Rick, honey, what's wrong?" his mother asked, recognizing the distress in her son's voice.

"Mother, Stephanie's gone and I can't find her anywhere," McGinn said. "I was working on my pickup and told her just as soon as I got finished I'd take her over to her grandmother's so she could go swimming. She asked if she could take her walk, like she does most every evening, and I told her yes, but not to be gone too long. I knew I'd have the pickup fixed and would be ready to go soon.

"I've been calling and calling her, but she doesn't answer," Ricky continued. "I started looking through the woods, walked all over the pasture, and even went down to the little stock tank where we fish and swim sometime. I can't find her anywhere."

Francis McGinn could tell by the sharpness of her son's tone, his rapid speech, the anguish in his voice, that he bordered on panic.

"Have you called the law?" Francis asked.

"Yes, Don Roberts is here and so is Steve. There's also some REACT people on their way to help search," McGinn responded.

The tension headache that had begun the moment she heard Ricky's voice lessened slightly with the news that Ricky's best friend and the law were already there helping look for Stephanie.

"I'll try to find Mike and Lisa and I'll call Randy," Francis told her son. "And I'll pray."

After a quick Please Jesus prayer, Francis began dialing the phone. She first tried to reach Mike and Lisa, two of her ten children. Lisa couldn't be found until Francis remembered a place in nearby Abilene that Lisa and her friends frequented. When Francis finally spoke to Lisa, she and her roommate agreed to return immediately.

Unable to contact Mike, Francis called Randy, another of Ricky's three brothers. Randy agreed to meet his mother and sister at Ricky's place to aid in the search for Stephanie. She then telephoned her older daughter Verilyn, in Mississippi, to let her know what was happening.

While his mother summoned his siblings, McGinn knew he had a call to make himself.

"I have to call Janet," McGinn told Sirois.

Janet McGinn and Sirois's wife, Robin, were in Arlington, Texas, at a bowling tournament. McGinn was glad Robin would be with his wife when he broke the news that her oldest daughter was missing.

Walking with a severe hitch in his step, the result of an on-the-job injury, McGinn's posture was stooped, as if the burden he carried were as cumbersome as the Sheetrock he nailed at work. The heaviness of informing his wife of her oldest daughter's disappearance hung over him, weighing him down both physically and emotionally.

"I'll make the call," Sirois offered.

Janet McGinn watched the red message light blink on and off on the Arlington motel telephone. As she pushed the "0" on the keypad, the operator's voice came in clear and precise.

"Mrs. McGinn needs to call home as soon as possible."

Janet's brow wrinkled. Before she could make the call,

Steve Sirois telephoned his wife and asked to speak to Janet.

"Steve, what's up?" Janet asked. "Where's Ricky?"

"We can't find Stephanie," Steve uttered nervously. "We've looked everywhere, but we can't find her."

Janet's motherly instincts kicked in. "What do you mean you can't find her?" Janet asked, concern laced with confusion.

"Ricky said she went to the woods. She said she'd be back in an hour. That was several hours ago," Steve replied.

A small sense of relief spread over Janet. Stephanie frequently investigated her new surroundings as well as the abandoned hospital building nearby. She'd probably just forgotten the time.

"Do I need to come home?" Janet asked.

"No, it's late and you don't need to be on the road," Sirois answered, knowing it would most likely be his wife, Robin, who would be driving.

"We can be home in a few hours," Janet reminded him.

"No, I don't want you on the road this late, driving fast and getting hurt. Just come home tomorrow," Sirois insisted.

So Janet remained in Arlington with Robin while their husbands continued to search for her missing daughter.

A short time later McGinn called his wife.

"I just needed to hear your voice," he told her. "I think you should be here, but there are dark clouds forming; looks like a storm's coming in. Just come home in the morning," he said. "I'll keep you posted. And I'll keep searching for Stephanie."

As the night pressed on, it was getting more difficult for searchers to see. Lisa McGinn decided more flashlights and a fresh supply of batteries were needed to help them search through the darkness.

"I'll be back as soon as I can," Lisa said as she climbed behind the wheel of her brother's Ford Escort. Lisa noticed nothing unusual about the red interior of the vehicle.

After returning to the McGinn homestead, Lisa, her friend Brittney Anderson, and her brother Sonny headed for the old hospital. Stephanie had been known to hang out at the once-active rural infirmary. It was an obvious place to look for the missing girl.

Sheetrock hanging from the hospital's walls gave the appearance of sagging ship sails battered by the fierce force of a salty sea. Except for one room, debris littered the floors. That space had been cleared of refuse. In the center of the room was a table, a candle prominently placed in the middle. A small bracelet made from string lay beside the candle. Lisa drew in a quick breath.

"This is just like the bracelets Stephanie makes," Lisa said, holding up the small circular bangle. Their hearts lifted but were soon flattened as they discovered the only habitants of the old building were a few field mice and a large family of spiders.

The trio returned to the McGinn house to tell Deputy Mike McCoy, one of several Brown County sheriff's deputies on the scene, about their findings at the old hospital and to rejoin the search confined to the perimeters of the property. They walked the fence rows looking for any sign of Stephanie, any tracks that might lead to her. They even checked fence wires for bits of clothing or hair.

Verilyn McGinn had been telephoning her mother every thirty minutes. "Have you heard from Stephanie?" she'd asked. The answer was always the same: "No, honey, we haven't heard a word."

Sharon Grimes, president of the REACT Club, advised dispatch that she and her people would meet at the sheriff's office for a briefing with Roberts. Grimes and other members of the REACT Club were trained in search and rescue (SAR), utilizing a number of proven procedures. The search for Stephanie Flanary was made more difficult by darkness; a further hindrance was the size of the property. Grimes decided, since it would be difficult to get onto the grounds, they would carpool rather than drive in a large number of vehicles.

By the time Francis McGinn arrived at Ricky's house, there were approximately one hundred friends and family who had gathered to help in the search for Stephanie.

Francis found Ricky and took him in her arms. "Have they found Stephanie?" she asked, smoothing his brown hair as she had done when he was a small boy.

His softly spoken "No" and the tears that pooled in his brown eyes sent Francis McGinn into a burst of prayer.

After her final "Amen," she studied the people mulling over the McGinn property. Francis asked, "Where's Steve?"

"I don't know where he went," McGinn said.

Sirois was not among the friends and relatives of the McGinns' who had joined the fifteen members of the RE-ACT Club preparing to search for the missing girl.

"Is Janet here?" Francis asked, scanning the faces for the familiar sight of her daughter-in-law.

"No, she's still in Arlington at the bowling tournament," McGinn replied. "She isn't coming home until tomorrow."

Francis McGinn, the furrow of her brow deepening, seemed baffled by the comment. Why wasn't Janet on her way home to help look for her missing daughter?

After a briefing on procedures, the searchers spanned out to cover the property completely. Trudging across the ground uneven with stumps, high grasses, and rocks, the searchers combed every nook and cranny of the McGinn land. They searched from east to west, then north to south. Some people checked out the county roads, the bar ditches, and the culverts near the property, empty buildings in and around the Owens Community and some abandoned buildings and houses on bordering properties. They scoured the interior of the McGinn house, a red Ford Escort parked in the yard, as well as a pickup truck and boat. Any location where Stephanie could be hiding, sleeping—or disposed of.

But there was no sign of the preteen. No clue as to her whereabouts. As searchers were discussing the next step, the dark cloud that had been hovering overhead suddenly opened, releasing a downpour of rain. The heavy, cold precipitation hindered the search efforts to the point that it was finally determined that they would wait until the light of day to proceed with their hunt. It was 4:00 A.M., nearly eleven hours since Stephanie Flanary had reportedly walked away from her home.

Keeping his word, McGinn checked in once more with Janet during the early-morning hours following her daughter's initial disappearance. There was nothing new to report; there was still no sign of Stephanie, no clue as to where she might have gone.

Roberts, Grimes, and some members of the REACT team decided it was time to call for more help. Tracking dogs would be of great benefit in the search, and the best ones for the job, considering the recent rain, were from Rescue One in Dallas. The call was made shortly after daybreak and the dogs and handlers were airlifted by helicopter to the search site where they joined members of Children's Education Search And Rescue and Texas Search Dogs.

Shortly before Roberts went off duty at 6:15 A.M., David Mercer of the Brown County Sheriff's Office Criminal Investigation Division was called in. Then Roberts sent a teletype message to all surrounding regions.

Mercer arrived on the scene and began to question McGinn. McGinn told Mercer that he and Stephanie had been together all day on Saturday. It had been just the two of them.

"How long have you and the girl's mother been married?" Mercer asked.

"About three and a half years," McGinn answered.

"How did you and the girl get along?" Mercer asked.

"Pretty well, with an occasional argument, but otherwise we're very close," McGinn said.

Mercer pledged to keep searching until they found something and promised to keep McGinn advised as to what was happening in the case.

While Mercer questioned McGinn, leads began to filter into the Brown County Sheriff's Office.

Sharon Graham, an E-Z Mart employee, telephoned to inform authorities that she had seen two young blond-headed girls and an older girl, about twenty years old, come into the store between 9:30 and 10:00 on Saturday night. If one of the young girls was Stephanie Flanary, then perhaps she was with friends, or perhaps she was a simple runaway. Authorities knew that two thousand kids a day, 730,000 kids a year, go missing. Some are runaways, some are lost, and some are abducted. In order to help find out what happened to Stephanie Flanary, Ms. Graham would be shown a photograph of Stephanie for identification.

At 10:15 A.M., the day following Stephanie Flanary's reported disappearance, Team Birka and Team Jabo were deployed. Birka, a beginner tracking dog, was initially released to conduct a perimeter search of McGinn's vehicles, the house, and the pond.

Members of the rescue team had been given a search profile of Stephanie Flanary provided by McGinn: white female, twelve years old, five feet tall, one hundred pounds, slender build, shoulder-length curly blond hair, no glasses, no distinguishing marks, no identification, no money. The profile also included the information that

Stephanie was said to be in good physical condition, new to the area, liked to swim, and might have gone to her grandparents' house.

Birka smelled the bare ground where the rust-spotted truck McGinn claimed he had been working on the previous day was parked. He circled the vehicle, moving his head erratically side to side, searching for a scent. The bed of the old brown truck was cluttered with dead tree branches. The roof was white and the back window sported a bumper sticker that said I LOVE MY TRUCK.

As Birka moved away from the vehicle, he sniffed and circled numerous areas of the property. He had shown little interest in the truck, the boat, or the house, but he alerted on the car and at the pond. Jabo, a certified tracking dog who was also cadaver-trained, was working in the same sectors. He confirmed the alerts of Birka. While Birka and Jabo concentrated on the signaled areas, other canine units were used throughout the rest of the morning and afternoon to probe the family home and acreage, as well as areas north and south, a creek to the west, and the grandparents' property at Lake Brownwood.

In addition to the hounds, deputies, friends, and family continued to look in every possible location for the missing girl. They had only come up with two things that might help locate Stephanie. One was a note found attached to a fence post. The partially charred note stated: "Follow Fence To Dirt Road." The second was a ball cap. On the crown of the white hat was SHAW'S LAUNDRY. No one knew if the note and ball cap were significant, but they would be sent to the Department of Public Safety's Austin lab for forensic tests, including fingerprints and hair samples, if any were found.

At noon Bob Grubbs of the Texas Rangers and Brown County investigator Mercer approached McGinn. The stepfather of the missing girl was weary. He had been searching for Stephanie for nearly twenty-four hours. Walking the rough terrain was difficult, at best, with his injured leg. It throbbed with pain and his nerves were equally frayed.

"Several of the dogs have paid particular interest to your vehicle," Grubbs told McGinn, referring to the 1987 Ford Escort four-door hatchback parked between the house and the pond. "We'd like to look in the vehicle."

"That's fine with me," McGinn said, seemingly eager to help.

"We don't know what the dogs are hitting on, but there might be something there to help us locate Stephanie," Investigator Mercer said, watching McGinn's expression closely.

"Sure," McGinn responded.

"In order for us to look in your vehicle, we need you to sign a Permission to Search," Mercer stated.

"You can refuse, if you want to," the ranger said, watching for any reaction from McGinn.

"There's nothing in the vehicle. If you want to look, feel free," McGinn said.

"Oh, we'd like to look in the house as well," Mercer added, almost as an afterthought.

Again McGinn had no objection and he signed a second Permission to Search form.

Then Grubbs stated, "Ricky, we need you to go to the sheriff's office with us."

McGinn had no objection and showed no visible signs of hesitancy. He went with the officers willingly.

As an intense scrutiny of McGinn's vehicle and house began, Ranger Grubbs, Chief Deputy Glen Smith, and Deputy David Mercer continued to query him at the Brown County Sheriff's Office. They asked the same questions time and again.

As McGinn spoke with the lawmen, he was unaware of various calls made to the sheriff's department regarding possible sightings of Stephanie. Neither did he know that

Janet's brother, Joe Bob Talley, a San Saba police officer, had spoken with Deputy Mercer following his initial questioning of McGinn.

"Ricky came into the house and was very nervous and upset after talking with you," Talley had told Mercer. "He said, 'That investigator doesn't need to be here.' "

Talley also told Mercer that earlier that morning, about 5:45, McGinn had left the house and driven down County Road 417. Talley said McGinn had been gone approximately ten minutes.

While McGinn was being interviewed, Investigator Mike McCoy joined fellow deputies at the crime scene. Clad in a denim shirt, blue jeans, boots, sporting a thick handlebar mustache, McCoy resembled a Texas cowboy of a bygone era. McCoy began filming the exterior and interior of the Ford Escort with a video camera.

As deputies opened the Ford hatchback and looked inside, McCoy noticed several red spots that he thought might be blood. The spots were difficult to distinguish on the Ford's red leather seats. McCoy zoomed the camera in closer as he filmed what seemed to be blood spatters in the rear of the vehicle, small splatters on the left rear window, and splatters along the left rear door. McCoy focused the handheld video camera on the back floorboard where additional splatters were recorded on a Lone Star Light cardboard beer case, on a small Igloo Playmate ice cooler, and on the floor of the backseat along the left door. McCoy's camera lingered on what looked like blood in the hatchback area of the Ford, as well as what appeared to be brain matter or flesh. In addition, several strands of what McCoy thought to be hair were stuck to the right and rear side of the hatchback area.

"Get a wrecker out here," McCoy instructed. "We need to impound this vehicle."

McCoy's attention was diverted from the truck by the

roar of helicopters. It was 3:00 P.M., almost twenty-two hours since Stephanie's disappearance.

One Huey and two Apache helicopters had been summoned from nearby Fort Hood to aid in the search. Special heat-seeking equipment on board the aircraft could pinpoint the exact location of the missing girl, if she were in the perimeters of the search zone—and if she were alive.

Within the hour Ramsey Wrecker Service loaded the Escort and towed it to the Brown County Sheriff's Department for further scrutiny. All the while, a Department of Public Safety (DPS) trooper kept a watchful eye on the vehicle until it was secured in the sally port of the sheriff's department. Plans were made to transport the car to the DPS lab in Austin, Texas, the following day to determine if the matter thought to be brain or flesh was in fact just that and if the red spots were indeed blood stains.

TWO

As McGinn's car was being towed to the Brown County Sheriff's Department, deputies began a search of the interior of the house. In a room McGinn had indicated was his bedroom, deputies located a pair of men's white tennis shoes with blue lining. Smeared on the heel of one shoe was a red smudge and traces of ruby-colored spots dotted the second. Officers believed the red substance, like the ones in McGinn's car, were blood stains.

About noon on the day following Stephanie's disappearance, McGinn was taken into an interview room at the sheriff's office. He remained cooperative, although the strain of the past hours was visible on his face. His eyes, weak from lack of sleep, drooped behind his aviator-style glasses.

"Ricky, we want to ask you some questions about some blood we found in the back of the Ford Escort," Chief Deputy Smith began. "First we need to read you your Miranda rights."

After concluding the Miranda instructions, Smith asked, "Do you understand your rights?"

McGinn indicated that he understood and was willing to talk with investigating officers. Smith introduced B. R. Grubbs, a DPS Texas Ranger. McGinn was unaware that Grubbs had been contacted by Brown County deputy sheriff David Mercer earlier that morning in reference to Stephanie Flanary's reported disappearance, or that Mercer had indicated that he suspected foul play. Mercer had requested that the experienced ranger assist with the investigation.

Grubbs, who had been told only the bare facts of the case, wanted McGinn to tell him the events that led him to report his stepdaughter missing.

McGinn initially appeared cooperative and willing to answer all of Grubbs's questions. He would later be described as almost cocky in his responses to their questioning.

McGinn went over events that occurred Saturday, up to the time that Stephanie Flanary was reported missing.

"Janet works at Wal-Mart," McGinn said, in response to inquiries about his wife. He then repeated information told earlier to Brown County deputies—that Janet had left home with other members of her bowling league on Saturday morning to go to Arlington for a tournament.

"Stephanie was awake when Janet left and decided she'd stay home with me. Denise, Janet's youngest daughter, went home with Steve Sirois Saturday morning to stay with him until Janet and Robin, Steve's wife, returned from the bowling tournament," McGinn explained.

McGinn advised the deputies that after his wife left he had given Stephanie a driving lesson along the back roads of Brown County. They had returned home about noon. McGinn stated that Stephanie then went swimming in a dirt stock tank located approximately fifty yards directly behind their house.

"What was she wearing when she went swimming?" Grubbs asked.

"She was wearing shorts and a T-shirt when she went swimming," McGinn said. "She had left her swimsuit at her grandmother's house."

"What kind of bathing suit does Stephanie have?" Grubbs inquired.

"She has two. One is a full one-piece suit, the other a two-piece multicolored suit," McGinn answered.

"How long did she swim?" Grubbs asked.

"Not long, about fifteen to twenty minutes," McGinn said. "When she came back to the house, she put on a gray shirt and went walking in the pasture behind the house."

"What were you doing at this time?" the lawman inquired.

"I was working on a Dodge pickup behind the house. When she came back, she wanted me to take her to her grandmother's house at Tamarack Mountain, near Lake Brownwood, to go swimming. I told her I needed to work on the pickup and couldn't take her over there until I was finished," McGinn said.

Grubbs, Smith, and Mercer studied McGinn quietly, watching him intently, listening closely, scrutinizing each response.

McGinn appeared ready to do whatever the officers wanted, to answer anything they asked, but he later said he wondered why they weren't out looking for Stephanie. He absently extended his left leg straight, massaging it slightly. McGinn was obviously in some physical discomfort.

"What did Stephanie do while you worked on the truck?" Grubbs asked.

"She went into the house and talked on the phone for quite a while. Later she went walking again. It was around five P.M. when I last saw her.

The questioning turned from McGinn's activities and those of his stepdaughter to the vehicle being impounded by the sheriff's department. Grubbs, as well as other lawmen in the room, wanted to know McGinn's explanation for blood detected in the Ford Escort found on his property.

"I don't know," McGinn answered hesitantly. He seemed

to be mulling over the question, searching for the answer. Either he didn't know how the blood stains got into the back of the compact car, he had forgotten, or he was taking his time . . . searching for an explanation Grubbs and the others would consider rational. Believable. The response McGinn gave them was not one Grubbs or the deputies had considered.

"The girls and I used to fish in the tank behind the house. I'd back the car up to the tank dam, open the hatchback, and we'd throw the fish we caught into the car," McGinn said matter-of-factly.

Grubbs's eyes scanned the room for reactions of the deputies.

"Why do you think there was so much blood throughout the car?" Grubbs asked.

McGinn indicated that some of the fish he and his stepdaughters caught were hooked deep in their throats. "We just tossed the fish in the back of the car in different locations," McGinn responded. "We weren't particular as to where they hit."

Grubbs rubbed his chin. When inspecting the vehicle prior to his arriving in the interview room, Grubbs had noted that the blood-spatter pattern in the car indicated that the blood had been directed from front to back, not from the rear to the front as described by McGinn.

"We used minnows for bait," McGinn continued. "We caught about ten fish, mostly pollywog catfish. We cooked them on a grill that's out back of the house."

"We didn't find any fish bones or any other fish remains out there," one of the deputies interjected.

"The cats must have gotten them," McGinn said.

The eyes of the lawmen shifted from one to the other. Each was mulling over McGinn's response.

"How much had you been drinking yesterday?" a deputy asked.

"I hadn't had anything to drink," McGinn responded.

Grubbs studied McGinn carefully. He was dressed in a blue plaid shirt, Levi's jeans, and cowboy boots. Grubbs's attention was drawn to reddish stains on the legs of McGinn's Levis.

McGinn rubbed his rough hands across the knees of his jeans. "I haven't had time to change clothes," McGinn said. "I've been too busy looking for Stephanie."

Grubbs would later learn from Deputy Don Roberts's report that McGinn had been dressed in a dark-colored pullover-type shirt, gray shorts, and white tennis shoes with white socks when Roberts talked to him on Saturday night, shortly after McGinn's call to the sheriff's office reporting his stepdaughter's disappearance.

Grubbs made a mental note: seize McGinn's clothing for testing. The Texas Ranger believed the discoloration on McGinn's pants could be blood stains. Perhaps Stephanie Flanary's blood.

McGinn insisted that he and Stephanie had a good relationship. He was obviously attempting to dispel the implications the lawmen were making regarding his connection to Janet's oldest daughter.

"Janet can tell you what kind of father I've been," McGinn insisted. "She knows I've had a good relationship with both girls. I love Stephanie and I want her found."

McGinn insisted that he'd always thought of the girls as his own children. The entire McGinn family had embraced Janet's daughters as their own.

"Where is your wife?" Grubbs asked.

"I talked to her last night. She's in Fort Worth at a bowling tournament. I told her Stephanie was missing, but I told her to stay there because of the storm that was brewing, that I would let her know what was happening here," McGinn explained.

"Ricky, we'd like for you to let us take some samples from you," Grubbs said.

"What kind of samples?" McGinn asked.

Grubbs explained that McGinn would be transported to Brownwood Regional Hospital for fingernail scrapings, blood samples, hair combings, and semen samples. The biological specimens obtained from McGinn's person would be used in comparisons in the ongoing investigation.

McGinn agreed. He read the Voluntary Consent to Search form, which stated:

> I, Ricky Nolen McGinn, after being duly warned by Glen Smith, a peace officer of Brown County, Texas, that I do not have to give consent to a search of the body of Ricky Nolen McGinn without a search warrant, do voluntarily give my consent to a search of fingernail scrapings, blood, semen, hair combings, without a search warrant to the person(s) who gave me the warning aforesaid.

The document was dated May 23, 1993, at 6:07 P.M..

McGinn signed the instrument, with Glen Smith and Mike McCoy inscribing their names as witnesses. McGinn was then transported to the nearby local hospital for the collection of the designated specimens. McGinn was co-operative, his demeanor calm. The lawmen studied him with interest. Was McGinn anxious to find his missing stepdaughter, making every effort to assist in their investigation, or was he as coldhearted a sociopathic killer as they had ever seen? The lawmen believed the latter.

Janet McGinn arrived at her Brown County home about 5:00 P.M. and found it surrounded by law enforcement personnel and volunteer searchers. The night before, she had completed the bowling tournament in the midcities area of Arlington, which lay between the two diametrically different cities of Dallas and Fort Worth: Dallas, a cosmopolitan telecommunications mecca; Fort Worth, the Western-flavored home of Lockheed and Bell Helicopter, two aircraft production giants. Each city was a far cry from the back-roads country of Brown County, where oil and gas, manufacturing, state prisons, and agribusiness dominated the local economy.

Robin Sirois had driven Janet McGinn from Arlington to May. As Janet stepped from the van, Francis McGinn was there to meet her. Francis wrapped her arms around her daughter-in-law, pressing her soft, pale cheek against Janet's tanned skin. Francis's nose wrinkled slightly as the smell of alcohol assaulted her nostrils. She thought Janet had been drinking, and when Janet stumbled as she climbed from the vehicle, Francis was convinced. The elder McGinn was still overwhelmed that her daughter-in-law had waited nearly twenty hours to come home after learning of her daughter's disappearance; now she was equally dumbfounded that Janet had obviously been drinking heavily.

Janet McGinn did, however, appear overwhelmed by the situation. Anguished confusion distorted her face, her ice-blue eyes glazed with tears as she asked her mother-in-law, "Have they found her?"

Francis hated to answer, but words were not necessary. Janet could tell by the look on Francis's face that the whereabouts of her daughter was still unknown. The two mothers embraced and wept.

By now the news media had ascended on the McGinn property. Normally kept at bay, the reporters had been allowed to film the search, interview investigators, and approach the bewildered mother. With the girl still missing, authorities believed that the media could help by getting the word out, by encouraging everyone to aid in the hunt.

Deputy Scott Martin addressed a TV reporter's questions, his face partially shielded by a sheriff's department billed cap.

"We're going to double back, check all the roads, all the low-lying areas, all the culverts. We encourage anyone

who owns land to search any abandoned barns or outbuildings. Check any areas with birds flying overhead."

Birds overhead? Observers flinched. Martin was talking
about buzzards. A carrion scavenger, feeding chiefly on
the remains of the dead. Eyes turned upward, scanning the
sky for signs of the large birds soaring silently with the
changing air currents. None were spotted, only the search
helicopters.

The female reporter from the Abilene-area station approached Janet McGinn. "Will you talk with us?" she
asked softly.

Janet agreed.

Holding a photo of Stephanie for the camera, Janet's
short blunt-cut brown hair blew gently in the spring air.
The blue shirt she wore intensified the color of her eyes
to a hue of blue topaz. Her shoulders shook gently as she
spoke.

"I just pray she's okay. I can't give up hope," Janet said,
her voice trembling with the pain only a mother could
understand. "I love you, Stephanie."

Janet McGinn turned away, raising her right hand to the
camera. She bent forward, gasped for air, and a rainstorm
of tears poured from her eyes.

While Ricky McGinn submitted to the collection of the
various biological specimens, Grubbs, Sheriff Bill Donahoo, and Chief Deputy Smith met with Brown County district attorney Lee Haney at the sheriff's office. Grubbs and
Smith laid out the evidence they had collected thus far in
their investigation of the mysterious disappearance of
Stephanie Flanary. The evidence found in the car—what
they believed to be the blood, strands of hair, and brain
matter of Stephanie Flanary—and the red-stained tennis
shoes belonging to Ricky McGinn were described in detail
for the district attorney.

Haney, a tall dark-haired man in his mid-forties, stroked his brown mustache as he studied the lawmen and pondered what they had told him. The girl had been reported missing only twenty-four hours earlier; there was no body. And although deputies reported the search dogs had alerted to the suspect's car, no definitive tests on the red blotches believed to be blood had yet to prove that the blood was that of Stephanie Flanary. McGinn had been cooperative, had even agreed to submit to the forensic tests requested by the sheriff's department. However, McGinn had a past, one well known to Brown County law enforcement.

In 1989 McGinn had been convicted of kidnapping and had received a five-year probated sentence. The case stemmed from a December 1987 complaint filed by twenty-seven-year-old Joseph Wade Hardeman of Brown County. Hardeman had claimed that McGinn and another man had abducted him and taken him to a location off rural County Road 135, then had savagely beaten him. Hardeman had claimed the kidnapping occurred on December 20, 1987, when McGinn picked him up on the pretense of needing someone to help him gather pecans.

McGinn was behind the wheel and Hardeman was in the passenger seat as McGinn drove out on Highway 29 to an area near the old Concrete Cowboy nightclub where another man waited.

Ben Freeman had ridden "shotgun" in the front seat of McGinn's vehicle, with Hardeman between him and McGinn. According to Hardeman, McGinn and Freeman beat him, put a handgun to his head, then bound him to a tree. Using a cedar post and a mesquite tree limb, the two assailants resumed their beating of Hardeman while demanding the return of items stolen earlier from Freeman's pickup.

McGinn, originally indicted for aggravated kidnapping, was prosecuted on the lesser charge of kidnapping and given the probated sentence.

The Hardeman kidnapping was an indication that McGinn was capable of a violent act, but there was more. He had also previously been charged with murder.

In 1985 a Concho County Texas jury had heard testimony in the shooting death of McGinn's best friend, nineteen-year-old Jesse Wright of San Angelo, Texas. Wright's bullet-riddled body had been found in a ditch between the Miles and Eola communities. McGinn had been one of the last people to see Wright alive, but jurors found him "not guilty."

There were other accusations as well. In August 1986 a woman in Eastland County had accused McGinn of rape at knifepoint, and then there had been a terroristic-threat charge filed against McGinn by his former wife after their five-year-old daughter had accused him of child molestation.

Latasha McGinn first made the allegations in January 1988. The preschooler had told her mother, "Mama, Daddy stuck these two fingers up inside me." Imogene McGinn was shocked and appalled by the accusation. She called authorities and set out to stop McGinn, who was out of jail on bond for the rape of a twenty-three-year old woman from Rising Star Texas, and for the kidnapping and beating of a man in Brownwood, from his scheduled visitation.

A few days later Latasha had been examined by Dr. Teresa Joseph for a stomachache. The child was diagnosed with a kidney infection. Dr. Joseph also believed that from the redness and irritation inside Latasha's vagina she may have been molested. Ricky McGinn was never charged with child molestation.

Brown County law enforcement personnel were quick to make the association of McGinn with other violent acts. They were convinced McGinn had the propensity to commit murder. Even without the body of Stephanie Flanary, they had physical evidence. District Attorney Lee Haney was ready to act. Haney began to prepare a warrant for

Ricky McGinn's arrest, charging him with the murder of Stephanie Flanary.

Haney wanted everything to go by the book. He didn't want any technicality to taint his case against McGinn. He asked investigators if McGinn had signed a voluntary consent to search in order for rape kit specimens to be drawn. Although deputies told him they had gotten consent from the suspect, Haney instructed them to go back to the jail, have McGinn sign new documentation, and collect the specimens a second time.

McGinn was cooperative, and a second rape kit, with additional blood, hair, nail clippings, and semen, was taken from McGinn.

Haney had tightened at least one potential loophole in his prosecution of McGinn for murder.

THREE

When Janet McGinn heard of the arrest of her husband, she was confused and appalled by the accusations of the sheriff. She knew in her heart that Ricky couldn't have possibly killed Stephanie. He was kind, gentle, and loving. He couldn't even punish the girls without having feelings of guilt. Only three months earlier, after repeatedly threatening to whip them for not obeying, he had told Stephanie and Denise to go to their rooms and change from shorts into their blue jeans. He had taken a belt and given each of the girls two halfhearted swats. Janet remembered he had left the room with tears in his eyes. At the time she thought he was too softhearted. No, Ricky could not have killed Stephanie.

More than anything, Janet wanted Stephanie found and Ricky released. At the request of the sheriff's department, she agreed to answer questions and identify various items at the sheriff's office.

"Can you pick out Stephanie's bathing suit from others?" they asked. "Can you identify this shirt as Ricky's? This pair of pants? These shoes? This ice chest?" The items were varied and numerous.

She answered their questions, then asked, "Why are you keeping Ricky in jail if he didn't do it?" Janet felt as if she were locked in a dark closet, shut out from the truth.

"Well, we just need him here. He's a suspect," they answered.

"Why is he a suspect?" Janet begged to know.

"Well, we've got a reason."

Janet McGinn's anxiety was mounting. Stephanie was gone; Ricky was arrested. It was like a dream sequence in a bad B movie. She didn't know how long it would be before Stephanie was found or Ricky would be released. She didn't know how she would manage without him.

"At some point I'm going to have to go back to work," Janet told the deputies. "My Wal-Mart badge is hanging on the rearview mirror of the Ford. Can I have it back?"

After deputies agreed to retrieve her name badge and after she answered all the questions authorities shot at her, Janet went home. Even though she was exhausted from the emotional stress, she played the events of the day over in her head until the phone rang. It was Ricky.

"Janet, don't believe what they are telling you about me," Ricky said from the Brown County Jail.

"They haven't told me anything, Ricky. I don't know what's going on," Janet McGinn said wearily. "They told me you're a suspect and they told me Stephanie is missing. That's all I know."

"Please don't believe what they're saying about me. I wouldn't hurt you. I wouldn't hurt those girls. But look, I'm in jail and I need some things. I need a package of unopened underwear and a package of unopened socks."

"I'll get them for you, Ricky. I love you," Janet said, unable to hold back the tears. Janet knew she couldn't get Ricky out of jail, but she would make him as comfortable as possible.

The $100,000 bond may as well have been for millions. The McGinns knew they would never be able to raise the bail and that Ricky would be forced to sit in the Brown County Jail until he went to trial. McGinn faced months of confinement away from his family, while Janet dealt with the uncertainty of her daughter's fate and the shocking incarceration of her husband.

After speaking with Ricky by phone, Janet tried to telephone Stephanie's biological father, Steve Flanary. Unable to reach him, she telephoned her former mother-in-law.

"Hi, this is Janet. Is Steve there?" Janet asked. The two women had always gotten along, and during the rare times she had spoken with Flanary's mother following the divorce, Janet had always found the woman to be friendly. Her tone was decisively different in this call.

"Why don't you just leave him alone?" Steve Flanary's mother snapped.

Janet was stunned by the response. Her ex-husband's parents had visitation privileges with Stephanie and Denise; in fact, they were required to be present whenever their son saw his children.

The court-ordered supervised visitation had been implemented when Flanary was charged with molesting his daughters. After learning of the sexual assaults, Janet's feelings for Flanary had changed from love to contempt and she had filed for divorce.

Now, as she dealt with Stephanie's disappearance alone, and suspicions that Steve Flanary may have had something to do with it, she hated him more than ever.

Even with McGinn secured in the county jail, investigators had a great deal of work ahead. The investigation would continue; they needed a motive, a murder weapon, and a body. They set out to get all the evidence they needed to convict Ricky McGinn of murder.

Ranger Grubbs contacted Ron Urbanosky of the Department of Public Safety Laboratories in Austin, Texas. It was late when Grubbs made the call.

"Can you have a crime scene search team available at the Austin DPS tomorrow?" Grubbs asked. "We need to attempt to obtain evidence from the 1987 Ford Escort owned by Ricky McGinn."

Grubbs briefly filled Urbanosky in on the case of the missing girl, the possible evidence inside McGinn's car, and McGinn's arrest.

Urbanosky agreed to accept the vehicle at the state capital office of the DPS and assured Grubbs that the car would be thoroughly scrutinized for any shred of evidence relating to the disappearance of the young girl.

Grubbs hung up the phone, exhausted from the long day that had taken him into the late-night hours of May 23. Stephanie Flanary had been missing for over twenty-four hours. The general agreement of the interdepartmental officers working the case was that she was dead, murdered by Ricky McGinn. However, there was always the fragment of hope that burned in the hearts of everyone who worked child disappearance cases. Hope that the child was still alive and would soon be found.

The search teams had been brought in from the field and the helicopters had been grounded. A briefing session was held with investigators. By 9:15 P.M. the search for Stephanie Flanary was suspended.

Francis McGinn kept vigil by the telephone in her modest trailer home in Rising Star. She had stayed at Ricky and Janet's house most of the day, waiting for word of Stephanie, expecting Ricky to return from the sheriff's office. Finally Francis went home. She tried to rest, and she prayed.

Francis, the widow of a Pentecostal preacher and a minister herself, had implored God repeatedly for the safe return of Stephanie.

At 2:00 A.M. the phone rang. Francis jumped with anticipation. "Please, Jesus," she muttered, hoping it was word that Stephanie was safe.

"Mama." Lisa's voice came over the wire. "Ricky just

called me. He was crying and sounded exhausted. Mama, he's been arrested."

Lisa McGinn had stayed at her brother's house, along with a number of others, at the suggestion of one of the Brown County deputies. "Just in case she has just run off," he had said.

"Arrested for what?" Francis asked, dazed and uncertain of what Lisa was telling her.

"For the murder of Stephanie," Lisa replied.

"Oh, dear Jesus, no," Frances mumbled.

The seventy-year-old mother went to her knees. She now prayed for her son. Head bent, fingers intertwined in a tight ball, she whispered, "Dear Jesus, sweet Jesus, help my baby boy."

The creases in Francis McGinn's pale face deepened. Her eyes reflected the sorrow of a mother who loved her children unconditionally. She didn't doubt Ricky's innocence; no one could persuade her that her son had harmed her stepgranddaughter. She had watched them together, laughing and playing. She could see the love, feel the connection.

Francis had been at Ricky's house for most of the past twenty-four hours. She'd seen the pain in his face, felt the ache in his heart. How could anyone possibly think he had hurt Stephanie? And what evidence could they have that would implicate him?

During the previous day's search, the air rescue team had crisscrossed a twelve-mile radius and had found nothing. One of the helicopter pilots had told Francis they had the capability to detect a dead body, yet they had come up empty. One of the dog handlers had told her much the same story. There was no body. No weapon. Nothing to indicate where Stephanie was, or if she was dead or alive.

Then there was the stranger who had approached her as she had stood by her car outside Ricky's house.

"Are you Mrs. McGinn?" he had asked.

"Yes, I'm Ricky's mother," she responded.

"There's something I think you should know," he said.

The man explained that the evening Stephanie disappeared he had seen an old tannish pickup traveling back and forth along the roadway.

"He was a large guy, curly reddish hair, wearing cowboy clothes," the man said. "My wife said the guy looked like a mental case to her. In fact, the guy would almost stop in front of the yard where our kids were playing and holler, 'You little girls better go in and get on your panties and bra. You don't look good that way.' But his language was more obscene."

Francis remembered seeing the pickup the man described parked along the side of the road when her daughter-in-law had taken her home earlier in the day to rest. Francis hurriedly reached into her purse and jotted down the information the man had given her. She handed the note to Steve Sirois, who had been among the people who overheard the conversation.

"Give this to the cops," Francis had instructed.

Sirois walked over and handed the note to Glen Smith and recounted the conversation with the man.

"We have another lead; we'll look at this later," Smith commented as he put the note in his pocket.

Now, as she sat alone in her living room, Francis wondered, did they even bother to follow up on the man in the tannish pickup? Were they so focused on Ricky that they had instantly eliminated the possibility of any other suspects?

Francis McGinn had an uneasy feeling. She picked up the phone and called a friend who was a private investigator. She told him about Ricky's arrest.

"Tell him not to say a word to anyone until he has a lawyer," the PI advised. But the advice was too late. McGinn had already answered all their questions, had made a voluntary statement, had submitted to DNA testing.

Even without a body or a murder weapon, Ricky McGinn had become the prime suspect in the murder of Stephanie Flanary.

The Monday morning following Ricky McGinn's arrest, the headline blazed across the top of the *Abilene Reporter-News:* MAN CHARGED WITH MURDER OF STEPCHILD.

The story brought West Texas residents a sense of relief. A killer had been apprehended. Yet, they were sickened by the news. Readers could hardly believe that a parent, even a stepparent, could take the life of a child.

But it was true. Sheriff Donahoo confirmed McGinn's custody. "The arrest was made based on physical evidence," he told reporters. He refused to elaborate, not mentioning that the red substance found in McGinn's car had yet to be identified as blood, much less the blood of a girl whom it was uncertain was even a victim of foul play. Sheriff Donahoo only added to his statement that Ricky Nolen McGinn, age thirty-six, was being held in the Brown County Jail. A $100,000 bond had been set by Justice of the Peace Ronnie Lappe.

As difficult as it was for residents of Brown County and Rising Star, in particular, to believe McGinn guilty of murder, Janet McGinn privately and publicly refused to accept the sheriff's justification for detaining her husband.

"This is my daughter," Janet McGinn said, holding up for television cameras the same photo of Stephanie she had held the day before. "She's twelve years old. She's about one hundred pounds. She has blond hair. It's long in the back and short in the front. She wears it like this," McGinn said, pulling her own hair back, exposing her forehead.

The frantic mother trembled, desperation showing in her blue eyes, swollen and red from crying. Then, looking directly into the camera, Janet spoke to her daughter as though willing her alive.

"Stephanie, baby, I'm not mad. Please come home." Janet's plea was laced with fear.

"What do you think about your husband being arrested for murder?" the reporter asked.

"I can't for the life of me think my husband did anything wrong," Janet responded. "They do everything together."

While Janet McGinn spoke to reporters, and Chief Deputy Smith and Deputy Billy Arp were transporting McGinn's car to Austin—along with one rape kit containing DNA samples from McGinn, one pair of his white tennis shoes, white socks, and blue fishnet-type shirt, plus one hairbrush and one polka-dot blouse possibly worn by Stephanie—District Attorney Haney was leaving no stone unturned in his efforts to ensure that McGinn remained in jail. Haney filed a motion to seek the revocation of McGinn's probation.

The petition charged that McGinn, who had received a five-year probated sentence in the 1987 felony kidnapping, had violated five terms of his probation. The motion filed in the 35th Judicial District Court stated that during McGinn's term of community supervision, on or about the twenty-second day of May, 1993, in the county of Brown and the state of Texas, he did then and there intentionally and knowingly cause the death of Stephanie Rae Flanary. That McGinn did violate condition number two of his probation in that on May 22, 1993, he used alcoholic beverages. That McGinn did violate condition number eleven of his probation in that he failed to pay his restitution to Joseph Hardeman in the amount of $1,105 and that he failed to pay his fine in the amount of $500. That McGinn did violate condition number twelve of his probation in that he failed to pay his supervisory fee in the amount of $1,605. And that McGinn did violate condition number thirteen of his probation in that he failed to pay his court costs in the amount of $67.50.

The motion to revoke probation was signed by District Attorney Haney and by Joe Shaw, McGinn's probation officer. The revocation of probation insured McGinn's jail confinement for a minimum of five years in the Texas Department of Corrections. Even if McGinn's family had been able to raise the $100,000 bond on the murder charge, McGinn was now being held without bond, pending a revocation hearing.

Francis McGinn's spirits sank, but her temper flared when she saw a picture of her son in the morning papers. It was a mug shot taken at the county jail, his hair in disarray, his eyes drooping from lack of sleep and worry. When Francis turned on the television, she saw pictures of Janet, Stephanie, and Denise. *It's terrible, just terrible,* Francis thought as she stared at the images of the people she loved splashed across the television screen. But worse than seeing the photos was hearing the hurtful words. Francis put a trembling hand to her quivering lips. "Child killer, dear God, they're calling him a child killer," she moaned.

Later that morning investigators were contacted by Constable Gene Hicks of neighboring Eastland County. Hicks advised David Mercer that McGinn had committed two rapes at an old home place once owned by the McGinn family in Carbon, a small Eastland County community.

"I know McGinn stills comes up to the place," Hicks told Mercer.

Mercer obtained permission to search the property from the leaseholder of the land and from Brooks Gilbert, the landowner.

Searchers, including the canines and helicopters, converged on the Carbon property.

"Take a look at this," one of the investigators said, pointing to a red spot on the sheet of a roll-away bed. "Looks like blood."

Indeed, it was blood, but not from Stephanie Flanary. The blood was from Lisa McGinn, who had been at the farmhouse several days before and had started her menstrual period while sleeping on the bed. Lisa had forgotten to take the sheets home to be laundered.

Tracking dogs brought to the Eastland County property to assist in the search were released inside the abandoned house. The first dog alerted on a framing hammer and a crowbar lying on the kitchen stove. The hammer appeared to have blood on the head and what looked like a blond hair stuck to it.

Deputy Mercer examined the hammer carefully; then he dropped it inside an evidence bag labeled "E-1" to be taken to the lab for further testing. He did the same with the crowbar and soiled sheet. Beer cans scattered near the house and by the gate were also collected. They would be dusted for any possible fingerprints. If McGinn's prints were lifted from the cans, the hammer, or the crowbar, they would be able to put him at the scene. If lab results proved the red stains on the hammer were the blood of Stephanie Flanary, they might well be in possession of the murder weapon. They were convinced the murderer was already in custody.

FOUR

The McGinn family was well known in Brown County. Vernon and Francis McGinn had been Pentecostal preachers in the pulpit of the Rising Star, Texas, church for more than forty years, and at least seven of the nine living McGinn children were popular gospel singers. Ricky himself had enjoyed singing in the church that had been a large part of his life since birth.

Born Ricky Nolen McGinn, March 11, 1957, McGinn was the sixth child born to Vernon and Francis McGinn, their fifth living offspring. A little girl had died at birth prior to Ricky's conception.

Francis had always described Ricky as a loving child who cared more for others than himself. She had embarrassingly admitted that he was somewhat of a "mama's boy." A fact that she neither concealed nor was ashamed of.

The family had moved from small town to small town all across Texas. The McGinns had met and married in New Mexico, pledging not only their love for one another but their love for the Lord. The young couple had dedicated their lives to pastoring in churches across the Lone Star State. Eventually Rising Star became their permanent home.

The McGinn house brimmed with love and was sparse in material pleasures. Although Vernon had worked occasionally as a carpenter, a meat cutter, and a truck driver, he mostly preached from the pulpit to meager congregations. When the McGinns accepted the call to pastor at the Rising Star Church, they made a home for their nine children on a farm in Carbon, Texas. Carbon, named for the mineral deposits found in the area, was populated by just under three hundred. Ricky McGinn attended Carbon High School, where he played football and basketball and took home economics.

McGinn thought the cooking class was all right—after all, he loved to eat—but when the course took a turn in the sewing lab, McGinn decided it was time to leave high school behind. He dropped out during his senior year and took a job as a carpenter and completed requirements for his GED.

At nineteen McGinn fell in love with Virginia, a pretty young girl he had met at his parent's church. The dark-haired, dark-eyed beauty had a loving spirit that touched McGinn's heart and fueled his desires. They were married in the same small church where they had worshiped every Sunday, with Vernon McGinn performing the ceremony. Perhaps their youth, perhaps troubles untold, split the marriage of Ricky and Virginia McGinn. The marriage was dissolved a little over a year after they had taken their vows.

Not long after his divorce, McGinn met Imogene Bible. As much as Francis had liked Virginia, she was troubled by Imogene.

The Protestant Pentecostals stressed the doctrine of perfectionism, or holiness, which states that man has free choice and, while on earth, may become sinless through uniting with God. Francis found it difficult to believe that Imogene would ever reach holiness. The young woman acquired Francis's disapproval when she moved in with Ricky without the benefit of marriage. Then, as if she disregarded the sin altogether, she asked for a church wedding performed by McGinn's father.

It was a tumultuous marriage from the beginning. Francis always suspected that Imogene had a "beam in her eye" for other men, and she moved in and out of Ricky's house with regularity. It was on one such occasion, when Imogene was living with her mother, that she announced that she was pregnant. McGinn had been ecstatic, but his dream of a baby boy was shattered when Imogene called and told him she had given birth to a stillborn son.

McGinn rushed to the hospital, where he found his tiny baby boy lying in what appeared to be no more than a small Styrofoam cooler, a scant blanket tucked around his underdeveloped body. McGinn lovingly lifted the child, still cradled in the box, and rocked him. Francis saw the tears spill down her son's cheeks as he accepted that the son he had wanted so desperately was dead.

Imogene named the baby Albert, after one of her former lovers, and he was buried in Carbon.

The McGinn marriage was on the rocks, but they clung to the hope that it would eventually work itself out. Then, not long after losing Albert, Imogene again acknowledged that she was expecting a child. It was a girl this time, born with beautiful dark hair and twinkling brown eyes. Latasha McGinn was radiant, but her enchantment couldn't help hold her parents together.

One evening after work McGinn returned home to find Imogene and seven-month-old Latasha gone. Once again, Ricky McGinn was alone.

No one knows for certain what event in McGinn's life caused him to take a downward turn. Perhaps it was the death of his son or the dissolution of his second marriage, but McGinn's life unquestionably turned sour. There was the 1985 arrest and trial for murder, the 1986 accusations of rape, his conviction for the 1987 kidnapping, and the 1988 allegations of child molestation against his own child. Ricky McGinn had seemingly gone from choirboy to troubled man.

Then in 1989 a mutual friend, Steve Sirois, introduced Janet Flanary and Ricky McGinn.

Like Ricky McGinn, Janet Talley had been married previously. Janet had wed Steve Flanary on July 24, 1980. Six months after their marriage, on January 11, 1981, the first of their two daughters was born.

Stephanie's birth had been complicated by her mother's toxemia during pregnancy. Baby Stephanie entered the world two and a half months early, weighing a mere four pounds, thirteen ounces. But the staff at the University of Texas Medical Center in Galveston had helped the strong-willed infant to survive. Her sister, Denise, was born twenty-two months later on November 18, 1982.

The Flanary marriage lasted another six years, dissolving in October 1988. Janet knew she and the girls needed a change, and they needed help. She decided to move to Brownwood, near her parents, who had retired near Lake Brownwood in 1985. So Janet left her job as a school-bus driver in Houston, packed up her belongings and her daughters', and headed for a new start. Stephanie was seven and Denise five. The Flanary females adjusted to Brownwood well, making many friends, including Steve and Robin Sirois.

On a hot August day, the Siroises introduced their friends Janet Talley Flanary and Ricky McGinn. There was an instant attraction. Janet was impressed with Ricky's easygoing manner and even more awed by the fact that he hadn't pressured her into an early sexual relationship.

"After we went out the first night, he didn't even want sex," Janet had later told friends. "He's really a nice guy."

The couple saw each other daily, and about a month later Janet and her daughters were living with Ricky McGinn. Four months later, two days before Christmas 1989, they married.

Ricky, Janet, Stephanie, and Denise were close with the McGinn family and even more devoted to Francis after the death of Vernon McGinn in 1989. The entire McGinn family was a tight-knit unit. Ricky's brothers and sisters thought the world of him. "He'd literally, and I do mean literally, give you the very and only clothes he had to his name," his older brother Mike had said. "I can remember too many times he's come to my rescue. And never asked for anything in return. He's been that way all his life."

There were no visible signs of problems. In fact, McGinn's past troubles seemed to be behind him. Janet praised Ricky's role as a father, considering him a good dad. He'd play ball with the girls after work, go fishing, and camping. He had been strict with both Stephanie and Denise, but Janet knew he had their best interests in mind when he didn't allow them to wear bathing suits in public or to go outside without wearing a bra. Ricky McGinn was everything Janet could ever ask for in a stepdad for her children.

And the children seemed to flourish. Stephanie, who had attended five schools in six years, was doing well at Brownwood Central sixth grade, where she played the flute in the school band. Her after-school activities included bowling, swimming, riding three-wheelers, and playing Nintendo, her favorite game. Her younger sister, Denise, was equally well adjusted. Their lives seemed perfect.

McGinn had worked in a number of manual-labor jobs. When he met and first married Janet, McGinn was installing siding and gutters on houses for A-1 Seamless Gutters, then at Shaw's Laundry, repairing machines and doing laundry for customers. He did a stint at a garage and worked various construction jobs. It was while he was working construction that McGinn fell from a ladder, severely injuring his back. The damage caused McGinn oppressive pain and he was unable to work.

After the accident Janet noticed a small change in McGinn's personality. "He got very moody," she had remarked. But even with the minor shift in his behavior,

Janet thought life was good—until May 22, 1993, when Stephanie disappeared and Janet's life took an unexpected turn into an abyss of grief and apparent betrayal.

Janet asked herself, was Ricky McGinn a bad seed that had been growing in the shadow of the church until he bloomed into a killer? Or had Ricky McGinn been falsely accused of the most hideous of all crimes? Brownwood deputies believed the former; his family was certain of the latter.

Brown County investigators were disappointed when they learned that the red substance on the head of the hammer found at the old McGinn farmhouse was paint, not blood as they suspected. Vernon McGinn had developed a habit of marking all his personal tools with red paint in order to distinguish them from others when working with a group. The hammer found at the Carbon house had once belonged to Vernon McGinn.

David Mercer stood outside Janet and Ricky McGinn's house, where Stephanie was last seen. His dark brown hair hung from under the baseball-style sheriff's department cap and blew in the warm spring breeze. The deputy stared at the stock tank in which the Flanary girls had swum and fished. They had been unable to find a murder weapon. Or a body. He knew he had to call Janet McGinn at her parents' home.

"We need to drain the tank," Mercer told Janet. "I need you to come out here and sign a consent form."

"I still don't understand why y'all could press charges against Ricky," Janet said with irritation.

"He's a suspect," Mercer responded.

"Ya'll won't give me enough reason why you're pressing charges. Tell me something," Janet begged.

"Well, we have to protect you," the deputy said. "We can't tell you anything right now."

Janet McGinn's frustration was mounting. When Mercer asked her again to come to the house and sign a search warrant so they could drain the pond, Janet barked out a definitive "No!"

Taking a deep breath, she added, "I can't leave the phone. Stephanie is going to call me. I'm a mama. I'm not giving up."

"Your mother can stay there and answer the phone. Then you and your dad can come out here and sign the warrant so we can drain the pond," Mercer said.

What Mercer hadn't told Janet McGinn was that they were searching for evidence, in particular a murder weapon. Authorities had received preliminary reports on the analysis of McGinn's car, confirming that the blood found in the vehicle came from a human and not a fish as McGinn had suggested to Brown County sheriff Bill Donahoo. What Mercer would never tell Janet was they were also exploring the possibility that her daughter's body might be at the bottom of the mucky water, just fifty yards from her back door.

Janet reluctantly agreed to meet the investigator at the house and sign the forms he requested.

After she arrived at the house, Mercer handed Janet the Consent to Search form; she stared at the deputy blankly, her icy blue eyes pleading.

"Look, you need to be honest with me so I'll know what I'm doing is right. I'm so confused. I want to find my daughter. I want to find her real bad," Janet said, looking into Mercer's eyes. Then her eyes turned skyward.

"I'll tell you what. I'll reach up there and get that sun and put it in your hands if you'll find my daughter. I'm that serious. I'll do whatever it takes," she said.

Janet McGinn quickly scrawled her name across the form. It was sixty-six hours after Stephanie had reportedly walked away from where Janet was standing.

Then began the rhythmic hum of the Brown County

Water Department truck, breaking through the tranquil silence of the rural setting. Large black rubber hoses held
the flow of water from the dirt pond as investigators
watched the reservoir recede. They kept a watchful eye out
for any sign of a weapon protruding from the silt-covered
bottom and any recognition of a human form.

DPS Trooper Gilberto Capuchino cruised U.S. 183,
scanning the grassy shoulders of the roadway for any sign
of Stephanie Flanary. He stopped his cruiser, exited, and
looked under the tin horn of a culvert. Nothing. He was
both disappointed and relieved. Capuchino, as with most
of the searchers who had been looking for the young girl
for the past two and a half days, hoped Stephanie would
be found alive. The experienced trooper knew the odds
were slim, though. He returned to his car and continued
his pursuit.

Less than two miles northeast of the McGinn house, on
Farm-to-Market Road 1467, Capuchino drove slowly, looking for additional tin horns. About one-half mile later he
located another culvert.

Trooper Capuchino pulled his cruiser to a stop. The
morning sun reflected off the DPS emblem as he swung
the door open. Slowly Capuchino moved over the soft
ground, moistened by the recent rains, and through the
brown grass mixed with patches of green. He came to the
opening of an aluminum drainpipe. The three-foot-wide
mouth of the pipe lay parallel to the roadway, about ten
yards from a metal gate that secured an open pasture.
Capuchino cautiously stepped down the rocky incline to
the opening of the culvert, avoiding the twigs and branches
that littered the site.

Holding on to his tan Western-style trooper's hat,
Capuchino bent to peer into the north end of the drain,
looking toward the south. The lawman flinched as his gaze

fell on a motionless body resting inside the far opening of the ridged, tubular-shaped pipe. He knew he had found the missing girl. He ran to the south end of the tin horn to take a closer look.

Stephanie Flanary's body was sprawled lengthwise about three feet inside the metal housing. Her feet were together, her knees wide apart, her left arm bent slightly above her head, her right arm extended from her side. The girl's shirt had been pulled up to cover her face. Her chest was bare, her exposed breasts revealing the early stages of decomposition. Even from his obscured vantage point, Capuchino couldn't overlook the massive injuries to her head. The once-crimson blood stains on her white Keds had turned to a dull pink, most likely from the recent rain. There was a small hole in the crotch of the girl's green and white-striped shorts. It was obvious she wore no underpants.

Stephanie Flanary had either been pushed up into the culvert, causing her body to rest in the genital-exposed position by accident, or she had been placed in the demeaning position on purpose. Killers who know their victims often cover their faces so that they cannot see the death mask of their prey. They position their kill so that others will discover them in demeaning, mocking positions. Yet, most often they leave them where they are sure to be found. Stephanie Flanary had been secretly tucked well inside the metal casing. Either theory of the killer's disposal of the body, whether a haphazard act or a deliberate sign, was possible.

Trooper Capuchino walked back up the rough incline to his car. He radioed the Brown County sheriff that he had found Stephanie Flanary.

The intrusive ring of McCoy's mobile phone broke through the loud hum of the water pump's motor. The deputy, who stood at the top of the dam and watched as gallons of water rushed from the pond to the surrounding soil, answered the incoming call.

Slowly McCoy waved to the pump operator to stop the motor and cease the draining of the mucky water. Moments later sheriff's department vehicles began to rapidly exit the McGinn property.

Janet McGinn watched as one after another of the deputies departed. She ran to the front gate and quickly stepped in front of an exiting auto.

"Tell me everything you know," Janet demanded. "You aren't leaving here until you tell me what's going on." Her eyes flashed with the terror that was inside her.

"We've got a lead," one of the deputies replied. "We think we've found her. Stay right here; we'll be back."

Janet, hot from the noonday heat, suddenly shivered as a cold shroud of impending doom began to smother her.

The justice of the peace, dozens of lawmen, and Stephanie's uncle Joe Bob Talley converged on the site where the girl's body had been discovered. Still photos, as well as a crime scene video, were shot of the body, the culvert, and the surrounding area. Deputies snapped on latex gloves before slowly, carefully, lifting Stephanie's small body out of the narrow tomb and placing her on a metal gurney draped by a crisp white sheet. The men stood back, their stares riveted on the discolored, mutilated body.

The brownish discoloration on her breasts and rib cage were the first stages of decomposition. That garish tincture, as well as the live larva found in her ears, would help the medical examiner determine how long the girl had been dead.

The full extent of Stephanie's wounds would be determined by the Dallas medical examiner, but the lawmen knew without being told that the girl had died from massive blows to her head. The right side of Stephanie's skull was nearly flat, her light brown hair drenched in her own red blood. Her right eye was closed, but her left eye was partially opened. She had seen her killer. Had watched him hit her again and again with a weapon that had ripped into her flesh, penetrated her skull. It was as if her open eye were inviting investigators to see through her and into the face of her killer.

One of the deputies carefully lifted Stephanie's right arm so that a photo could be taken for evidence. Her hand and short fingernails were encrusted with dried blood. An almost burnlike black mark was visible on her index finger between the nail and the first knuckle. Bruising was also apparent. After several minutes the deputy placed clear plastic bags on each of Stephanie's hands, securing them in place. Nail scrapings and other materials would later be collected by the medical examiner.

Joe Bob Talley positively identified the body as that of his missing niece, and Judge Jimmy Cooks, the justice of the peace, pronounced Stephanie Flanary dead at the scene.

Janet McGinn and her father, along with Sonny McGinn and his wife, Wanda, waited for word about Stephanie. As they talked about the events of the past three days, Chief Deputy Glen Smith drove into the dirt drive beside the McGinn house, then joined Janet and her father in the backyard.

Smith walked slowly, his head tilted down slightly. The daunting task before him was one lawmen dread the most.

"It's her," Smith said softly.

Janet screamed a heartsick "No!" as tears spilled down her cheeks. Janet had hoped, prayed, that Stephanie would be found alive. All optimism drained from her body like the water that had rushed from the nearby pond.

Stephanie's grandfather fell to his knees. His chest rose and fell from deep sobs of bereavement. Smith knelt beside the suffering grandfather and held him for several seconds before helping him to his feet.

Sonny and Wanda McGinn moved quickly toward Janet

and her father. Janet, Mr. Talley, Smith, Sonny, and Wanda stood motionless, embraced in a bond of sadness.

"I want to go see her," Janet cried. "I want to see my child."

"No," Smith replied.

"I want to identify her. I want to know that's my daughter," Janet pleaded.

"No, you can't identify her," Smith said, attempting to spare Janet any more pain. "We've got someone else to identify her. You don't need to see her."

Janet looked to her father, his rugged face stained with tears of sorrow, then to Chief Deputy Smith. "Please, don't let this get out. Don't let my mother hear about this until I can go tell her," Janet begged.

"Get in the van. We'll give you a clear light all the way," Smith said.

FIVE

Steve Sirois sat with Chief Deputy Smith at the Brown County Sheriff's Office. He and his wife, Robin, had been best friends with Janet and Ricky McGinn for four years. He would have done anything for Ricky, but Stephanie was dead and McGinn had been arrested. Sirois agreed to cooperate with investigators.

"When did you last see Stephanie alive?" Smith asked.

"My wife, Robin, went to Arlington with Janet McGinn and some other women to a bowling tournament at about eight-thirty A.M. Saturday. I took my wife to the McGinn residence to meet the other women. When I let Robin off, I picked up Denise, Janet's ten-year-old daughter. Denise spent the weekend at my house. After the women left to go to Arlington, Denise and I went home. Ricky told me he'd be over later," Sirois explained.

"What time did you see him?" Smith asked.

"About eight-thirty P.M. Ricky called and told me he couldn't find Stephanie. He said she went for a walk. I asked him how long she had been gone. He said, 'Quite a while. I been lookin' for her for about an hour and a half in the pasture.' I asked him if he had been on the roads looking for her and if she might have tried to go to her grandparents at Tamarack Mountain. I told Ricky I would drive the back roads and I told him to start driving toward the lake on the highway. I told him I'd be leaving in about five minutes. But before I left, Ricky called and said, 'I think I better stay here in case she comes home.' He told me to take the dirt roads."

Smith listened with great concentration to each word of Sirois's statement, replaying in his mind the statements made by McGinn regarding the sequence of events three days earlier, the last time Stephanie Flanary had been seen alive.

"Did you go over to McGinn's house?" Smith inquired.

"After I talked to Ricky on the phone, I drove to his house. When I got there, I asked Ricky if he'd called Janet and Robin. He said, 'No.' I told him to call the sheriff's department. He said, 'You need to call Janet first.' I made the phone call. I basically told her we couldn't find Stephanie and didn't know where she was.

"After Robin and I talked, Ricky and Janet talked. Ricky told her about Stephanie being gone and that he couldn't find her." Sirois thought for a long moment before adding, "When he started talking to Janet, he was very emotional. I'm not exactly sure what time he called the sheriff's office, but I heard him make the call. Deputy Don Roberts came out and he went out to the pasture, where Ricky talked to him. The red Escort was parked in the carport."

Steve Sirois signed his statement at 6:00 P.M. on the day Stephanie Flanary's body was found.

Smith pondered Sirois's statement. It was much like the declaration he had given them earlier. Did he know more than he was saying? Steve Sirois had a past himself. He had been arrested in 1977 and 1982 for possession of marijuana, in 1979 for driving under the influence of liquor; beginning in 1982, he had served a two-year probation for driving under the influence of liquor in Fort Worth, Texas. But Smith knew that Sirois's statement was just a small piece of the jigsaw puzzle that would eventually reveal the total picture of what happened to Stephanie Flanary in her final hours.

Glen Smith next talked to Sirois's father, Stanley. He

had stopped at the McGinn residence on his way home, about 4:15 P.M. on the day Stephanie was reported missing. The elder Sirois told investigators he'd decided to stop when he saw a strange car parked at the McGinn house. He'd known Janet was out of town.

"I knocked on the front door," Stanley Sirois told Smith, "but no one answered. I walked around to the side of the house and saw Ricky McGinn. He was about half-way between where the old boat and pickup were parked and the house. He walked up to me. It was very obvious that Ricky was intoxicated. We talked for a few seconds; then I asked him where Stephanie was. Ricky said she was sick to her stomach and she'd gone inside to lay on the bed. Ricky further said, 'Don't tell anybody about this. Stephanie wanted to try some beer.' He said, 'I went to get her a six-pack.' Ricky said she got sick and threw up. He said, 'Tell Steve that when she wakes up we'll head that way.'

"Ricky's car, a red Ford Escort, was parked near the boat and pickup. I couldn't see the car until I went to the rear of the house. The Escort wasn't visible from the road."

As his son had done before him, Stanley Sirois signed his statement, just after 6:00 P.M. on May 25.

The following day, at 7:00 A.M., medical examiners from the Southwest Institute of Forensic Sciences (SWIFS) in Dallas began conducting the autopsy of Stephanie Flanary. Although interesting and informative, autopsies were never pleasant. When the victim was a child, most medical examiners approached the subject with empathy. This one had been requested by Jimmy Crooks, Justice of the Peace, Brown County, Texas. Homicide was suspected.

Stephanie Flanary was first seen with two white sheets under her slim and badly beaten body by the doctor and Charles Linch of the Criminal Investigation Laboratory. She was clothed in green-and-white-striped shorts. She wore no panties. There was a white and multicolored pull-

over shirt with BEVERLY HILLS UNIVERSITY on the front.
The shirt was on her right arm and around her neck but
not over the left arm. Also on Stephanie's left wrist was
a string bracelet and she wore a string necklace with a
cross. She had on two beige canvas shoes. Her body bore
fragments of plant material.

Stephanie's body was photographed, fingerprinted, palm-
printed, and tagged. Toxicology tests would be run and Dr.
Guileyardo, Deputy Chief Medical Examiner of Dallas
County, would later learn that Stephanie had a blood alcohol level of .03 percent. The twelve-year-old had been
drinking not long before her death.

A standard rape kit was taken, which included blood
samples, oral, anal, and vaginal slides and swabs, pubic
hair, both left and right fingernail clippings, head hair, and
any hair found inside the vagina.

Looking to Linch and nodding slightly, the doctor began
his examination, accompanied by a verbal explanation for
the tape-recorded record.

"This is a normally developed white female of average
build whose appearance is consistent with the recorded age
of twelve years," he stated. "The length is sixty-five
inches, the nutritional status is average, the weight is
ninety pounds. There is early decomposition. Active fly
larvae are present in the mouth and in the right ear. The
abdomen is somewhat swollen and distended with gas,
which is in the bowel. There is early marbling and slight
green discoloration of the lateral aspects of the face and
head. There is some excoriation by ants on the legs bilat-
erally. There is early epidermal slippage of the back. The
body is not embalmed. There is ill-defined lividity of the
back of a normal color. There is no rigidity. The body is
cool."

Stephanie Flanary's corpse had the markings of someone who had been left out in the elements. Her cheeks
and head had a greenish cast. Fly larvae filled her mouth

and right ear. Her legs showed the effects of abrasive ant bites. It was an ugly end to a young girl's short life.

The doctor continued his examination.

"The head hair and eyebrows are brown to light brown. The female body hair is of slight amount. The scalp is unremarkable. Each earlobe is pierced once. The eyes are closed; the corneas are cloudy and the irises are indistinct through the cloudy corneas. The nose and mouth are unremarkable. The teeth are natural. The face, neck, pectoral region, breasts, abdomen and limbs, female genitalia, back, buttocks, and anus are unremarkable except for injury."

The doctor again looked toward Linch. He was about to begin the explanation of the victim's injuries and he knew Charles Linch would be most interested in this area of his examination.

There appeared on Stephanie's scalp a group of irregular wounds covering a four-inch by three-inch area. The wounds extended from the left front to the right back of her head. Abrasions from one-eighth to one-fourth inch were present, some abraded, some sharp. Over the right ear were several one-eighth-inch to one-quarter-inch lacerations directly over fractured bone. In the right area of the head, near the optical bone, were 2 three-quarter-inch lacerations. Another wound group was centered two and three-quarter inches to the right of the midline and one and one half inches below the top of the head. In addition, there were several yellow abrasions on the left side of Stephanie's face and beneath her chin. They were determined to be postmortem abrasions. Whoever had beaten Stephanie Flanary to death had continued to beat her even after she had died.

Hemorrhaging had occurred beneath all the scalp wounds; fractures to the head were most pronounced beneath those wounds. The most severe fractures involved the right side of the girl's head, although fractures were also present in the left frontal region.

The doctor's solemn, clinical evaluation of Stephanie's injuries didn't come close to the revolting, horrific sight of the once-vibrant young girl lying on the cold steel table. The right side of her head had been smashed in with such force that it made her skull appear as if it were half a cone head. The dry blood matted in her light brown hair was a shocking statement of how the life had been prematurely drained from her.

Stephanie's brain was extensively distorted by decomposition, with numerous fly larvae present in the tissue. The brain had a semiliquid consistency.

The contusions on Stephanie's tongue revealed that she had apparently bitten the outside edges of the organ during the violent beating she had suffered.

The doctor's verbal record continued. "There are yellow postmortem-type abrasions on the chest and the left shoulder. In the midright portion of the back is a group of contusions covering a four-inch by two-inch area. Toward the left side of the back are additional yellow postmortem-type abrasions."

The person, or persons, who killed Stephanie Flanary had continued to beat her, not only after the young girl had lost consciousness but even after her death. Profilers of killers know that the accepted theory of "overkill," or the use of excessive violence toward their victim, is an indication that the killer may have known his victim well, or that he was so enraged at the time of the homicide that he could not stop the massacre from continuing. What could have prompted such rage against this young victim? This innocent child?

There was purplish bruising on each of Stephanie's thumbs and a one-half-inch abrasion surrounding a contusion on the right index finger. There were scattered yellow postmortem abrasions on both thighs, a few superficial abrasions on her knees and legs, as well as postmortem abrasions on the backs of her arms. Some of these post-death injuries could have occurred if her killer had dragged her into the tin culvert.

The internal examination of Stephanie Flanary failed to reveal any extraordinary information. There was no urine in her bladder—victims often spontaneously empty their bladders during an attack or the fear of attack—and she was not pregnant. The doctor did remark, however, that Stephanie Flanary's vaginal wall was somewhat lax and could easily admit an adult vaginal speculum. If Stephanie Flanary's small body could readily accept the insertion of a metal instrument used for dilating the passage for inspection, could she have had prior sexual experience? Could she have been sexually violated in the past? These were questions investigators would ponder, especially in light of the doctor's final autopsy conclusion.

Just as Deputy McCoy and others at the Brown County Sheriff's Office had suspected, there was vaginal bruising, as well as purplish discoloration consistent with bruising and inflammation in the rectal/anal area. Stephanie Flanary had not only been murdered, she had been raped.

Sixth-grade students, some faces sprinkled with freckles, others dotted with pubescent pimples, and many streaked with streams of tears, listened to Nadean George, Central Six counselor, tell of the loss of their classmate Stephanie Flanary. On Monday the approximately three hundred students had tried to convince themselves that their fellow student would be found. The news of her death on Tuesday brought a myriad of emotions and an outpouring of passionate sentiment. Some cried. Some felt guilt because they couldn't. George and the six other school counselors encouraged students to express their feelings. While a few scribbled messages across blackboards to their lost friend, "We love you, Stephanie," others wrote poems describing her curly hair, smiling face, and shining spirit. Principal

Gary Chamberlain described Stephanie as a bright and energetic student who was liked by the other students and who would be missed.

The outpouring of sympathy expressed to Stephanie's grieving mother was not limited to the schoolchildren but included mothers, fathers, friends, strangers, the rich, and the underprivileged across Brownwood and neighboring communities. It seemed as if every time the doorbell rang, Janet McGinn or her parents would return to the kitchen laden with another casserole, red-and-white-striped buckets filled to the brim with golden brown chicken, or plates of scrumptious desserts. The foodstuffs were so plentiful that they fed Janet and her family and friends for nearly two weeks.

And there was more than food. Wal-Mart, Janet's employer, held fund-raisers, raising $1,500 the first weekend. As overwhelming as the outpouring was to the mother of the victim, the mother of the accused killer was shunned. Except for her family, closest friends, and devoted parishioners, Francis McGinn was alone like a boat adrift in a sea of despair.

She wanted to set the record straight, to shout from the rooftops that Ricky McGinn was an innocent man. She chose, instead, a letter to the editor of the *Brownwood Bulletin.*

"From a Mother's Heart. To Whom It May Concern," Francis wrote. She began by quoting II Timothy 23:11. Then she wrote:

> I would have the world to know that I committed my children unto God when they were born, and God has promised me my household if I stay faithful. And to God I will stand true, regardless of the situation.
>
> I want to also say, I will stand by my son. I will never believe he did this terrible thing until he tells me, "Mother, I did it." And if by any chance that

should happen, I would know that something snapped within him. My son is not capable of this horrible crime.

Convinced beyond a shadow of a doubt of her son's innocence, the matriarch of the McGinn clan warned her son's accusers by writing, "Judge not, lest ye be judged in the same like manner."

SIX

Residents living near the site where Stephanie Flanary's body was found would need to be asked if they had seen a person or persons in or around the culvert, if they'd observed a vehicle or heard any noises. Ranger Grubbs left the task to Brown County deputies while he and Deputy Valton Posey returned to the McGinn residence to check on the pumping operation at the tank.

The draining of the pond had been suspended when Stephanie's body was found, but the pumping had been resumed in hopes that new evidence, perhaps the murder weapon itself, would be located.

Although the tan-and-white Dodge truck McGinn stated he was working on the evening his stepdaughter disappeared had been reportedly searched by more than one person over the previous four days, Posey walked to the truck for yet another look. He wouldn't be satisfied that the search had been completed until he checked the vehicle himself.

Posey opened the driver's door and glanced about the cab. Reaching up under the driver's seat, the deputy felt the narrow space between the bottom portion of the seat cushion and the top of a speaker box. His hand felt a wooden cylinder-shaped object. He pulled it from beneath the seat . . . and stared at an ax.

Black electrical tape was wound around the wooden neck of the handle near the metal head, and the blunt end was covered in what appeared to be blood, as well as what looked like blond hair encrusted with dried blood.

McCoy and Posey nodded to one another. They believed they had found the murder weapon. One more missing piece of the conundrum. The picture was coming into full view.

"Bag it," Grubbs said as he moved from the truck to a charred plot of ground behind the McGinn house. The ax would be sent to a forensic lab in Dallas for analysis. Meanwhile, Grubbs had other leads to follow.

It had been reported that McGinn had been observed burning a pile of dry grass on the day Stephanie Flanary walked away from her house. McGinn had told them he had burned fish remains after cleaning the pollywogs he and Stephanie had caught, then eaten.

Using a knife, Grubbs, joined by Sheriff Donahoo, sifted through the ashes in an attempt to ascertain what had been burned. There was no evidence of fish having been cleaned at the site, no smell of fish. No definitive determination of what had been burned could be made. Grubbs filled a plastic bag with a portion of the charred debris and the soil under it, sealed the Baggie, and marked it to be sent to the DPS lab for examination.

With what investigators believed was the murder weapon in their possession, Grubbs, Chief Deputy Smith, and Deputy Mercer converged on the county jail. They wanted to talk to McGinn, to once again ask him questions concerning Stephanie's disappearance and ultimate death.

"Ricky, I need to advise you of your rights," Smith said, reading the familiar Miranda warning to McGinn. "You have the right to remain silent . . . ," Smith began.

At the end of the short legal disclaimer, McGinn signed the form indicating he understood his rights, then stated, "I want to talk to a lawyer." At that point the interview was immediately terminated.

Grubbs, Smith, and Mercer were disappointed, yet not

surprised. They had hoped their suspect would cooperate, would even confess to the gruesome death of his stepdaughter, but the only statement they got from McGinn was yet another declaration of his innocence.

The trio of lawmen walked from the jail to the office of the criminal-investigation division of the Brown County Justice Center. They began going over facts of the case and reviewing new information that had come in while they were conducting the field investigations.

"We might need to check this out," one of the lawmen said, holding a note in his hand. "McGinn and a young female were seen in Oleta's Liquor Store in Brownwood on Saturday. The day he reported the girl missing."

Grubbs and Mercer agreed to check out the report. Within the hour they met with Kay Lobstein at the liquor store.

"I know Ricky McGinn because he comes into the store regularly," Lobstein said. "On Saturday he came in and bought a twenty-pack of Lone Star Light and paid cash. It was at eleven twenty-seven in the morning. The little girl stayed in the car while Ricky came in. I gave him some candy to take to her."

"Did you recognize the little girl?" Mercer asked.

"It was the same girl whose picture I saw in the newspaper a few days later," Lobstein replied. "Stephanie Flanary."

The McGinns were a tight-knit family who had no intentions of idly standing by while detectives continued to build a case against Ricky. The family began their own investigation.

Equipped with a handheld video camera, Verilyn, who had come in from her home in Mississippi to help her mother and support her brother, and Lisa, Carol, and

Randy McGinn went back to the culvert where Stephanie's body had been found.

Blood, puddled in the crevices of the culvert, was still red and sticky. Scrutinizing the interior of the drainage pipe closely, Lisa drew in a quick breath. Staring at the metal wall, she pointed at a red imprint.

"Look!" Lisa shouted to her siblings.

Pressed against the metal was a bloody handprint. The impression appeared to have been left by someone whose hands were smaller than an average man's and larger than Stephanie's. The camcorder recorded the print.

The McGinn siblings trudged up the rocky embankment, looking closely for signs of blood, clothing fibers, or anything that would indicate who had brought Stephanie's body to the hiding place. They found nothing.

As they climbed out of the steep-pitched ditch and up to the road, Verilyn remarked, "Ricky couldn't have carried Stephanie's body down there and put it in the culvert. With his injured leg he couldn't have even gotten down there by himself."

Verilyn felt an undercurrent of hopefulness lift her spirits.

The following morning Grubbs and Mercer drove the two hundred miles from Brownwood to Austin to deliver evidence personally to the Department of Public Safety Laboratory for examination. Burned grass and material located in the dirt from behind the McGinn residence was submitted to be checked for possible blood, brain matter, or bone. An ax, with a broken handle covered with blood and what appeared to be blond hair, would be checked for latent prints and then would be compared with the victim's hair and blood type. One pair of gray shorts belonging to McGinn would be inspected for blood, hair, and semen. A hair sample from the body of Stephanie Flanary would be used for comparison purposes, as well as a blood sample from her body. One pair of eyeglasses, belonging to McGinn, would be examined for possible blood spatters. Three beer bottles, located in the ditch where the girl's body was found, would be tested for latent prints of both the victim and suspect.

In addition, one sexual-assault evidence kit with a pubic hair from inside the victim's vagina would be compared against a pubic hair from the suspect. A frontal bone and head hair from the scalp and body of Stephanie Flanary, as well as the clothing she was wearing when her body was found in the rural culvert, were also submitted.

Forensic science had won many a case in Texas and across the country; investigators wanted to be certain that any fragment of evidence, no matter how small, was available to scientists to help in establishing their case against Ricky McGinn.

The small, badly damaged body of Stephanie Flanary was transported from the cold, antiseptic confines of the Dallas Medical Examiner's Office to the funeral home near her home. Janet McGinn hadn't seen her daughter since she kissed her good-bye the morning of Stephanie's disappearance. When she closed her eyes, she could picture Stephanie: her curly light-colored hair, her crystal-clear blue eyes, and her infectious smile. She could hear her laugh, feel her warm embrace. Janet couldn't imagine Stephanie as a lifeless form confined in a box inside a building designed for those who had lived long, full lives, not ones taken too soon.

"I want to see my daughter," Janet told authorities. "I can't believe she's dead. I want to see her for myself. I want to know that it's really Stephanie."

"No, Janet, you don't want to see her. You need to remember her the way she was. You don't want your final memories of your daughter to be the way she looks now. You'd have nightmares the rest of your life," investigators said.

But Janet desperately wanted to touch Stephanie, to say good-bye.

"Please, just a foot. A hand. I'd know if that was my daughter. I have to know it's really Stephanie," Janet begged. But her heartfelt, desperate cry for proof of her daughter's death was denied, as were the requests of Janet's mother, her youngest daughter, and Francis McGinn.

From the Brown County Jail Ricky McGinn expressed his own pain. "I'm hurting just as much over this as any of the other survivors," he told Wilson Craig of the *Brownwood Bulletin*. Those who knew him well and those related by blood believed his expression of sadness, while others doubted his words.

Janet McGinn summoned her strength to make funeral arrangements, and at 2:00 P.M. on May 28, 1993, six days after her disappearance and three days after her body was discovered, Stephanie Flanary was laid to rest.

Janet sat in the pew of the small Pleasant Grove Baptist Church waiting for the angels to appear. She had been eight when she had last seen the heavenly spirits. It had been at her grandpa's funeral. As the pastor was saying the words of grace and adoration for her grandfather, Janet had glanced off to the side of the church. An open stairway had appeared, and her grandpa was ascending the steps, angels surrounding him. Her grandfather had turned and blown her a kiss before disappearing from her life forever.

As an adult Janet realized she had seen the image as a child because she wanted to see her grandfather one more time, to know he was Heaven-bound. She wanted the image to reappear, but this time Janet needed to see Stephanie climb the staircase guided by cherubs. As hard as Janet tried to visualize Stephanie blowing her a kiss from the flight of steps, she couldn't see the image, couldn't feel the peace. Was Stephanie at rest, or was she in a state of purgatory, waiting for her killer to be punished?

Sitting beside Janet in the front row of the rural church, holding her hand, comforting her, was Francis McGinn. Francis, who had thought of Stephanie as a granddaughter, felt as though a part of her rested in the casket surrounded by flowers at the front of the altar.

As Francis scanned the faces of the mourners, she squeezed Janet's hand. She was pleased that so many people had come to pay their respects to a child whose life had ended too quickly. There were friends and family, including all of the McGinn children and Janet's parents and brother.

Francis dabbed a cloth hankie to her damp eyes as her son Sonny preached the funeral service.

At the conclusion of Sonny's moving message, Francis watched Janet as well-wishers paid their respects to her. There were students from Stephanie's school, members of Janet's bowling team, friends of the Talleys' and of the McGinns' and, to Francis's dismay, Mike McCoy and Valton Posey of the Brownwood Sheriff's Office.

What are they doing here? Francis thought. The always kind and normally forgiving mother held deep inside her bitterness and resentment for the men who had arrested her son.

Her anger, however, was transcended by what Francis considered Janet's unorthodox behavior. Her daughter-in-law seemed to have gone from grieving mother to animated hostess, laughing, talking, and seemingly enjoying the attention lavished on her.

Despite the efforts of investigators to persuade her that Ricky McGinn was a killer, Janet McGinn continued to believe in her husband's innocence. Investigators hadn't given her any concrete reason to believe the same man she chose to bring into her family had been the evil that had ripped it apart. Following the burial of Stephanie, Deputy McCoy again approached Janet, making a convincing argument for McGinn's guilt.

"Janet," McCoy said, "the interior of the Ford Escort is covered in blood. We believe it's Stephanie's."

Janet was perplexed. After retrieving her Wal-Mart badge from the Ford Escort parked in the sally port of the sheriff's department earlier, she had discussed her observations with Francis McGinn.

"Janet, did you see any blood in the car?" Francis asked.

"No, Mom. I saw one little spot about the size of a quarter on the back floor, but it looked more like grease than blood."

Now McCoy was telling her the Ford Escort contained a significant amount of blood and that preliminary reports on the analysis of the car confirmed it was human, not fish blood, as officers said McGinn had told them. McCoy told her they further believed it to be Stephanie's blood, left in the vehicle they theorized McGinn had used to transfer the girl's body to the culvert.

Had she not seen the blood stains against the red seat covers of the car? Had she not been able to sense her own daughter's spilled blood when she looked in the vehicle? Janet questioned herself.

Janet also learned that investigators had received a report from the Brownwood Police Department indicating that Jennifer Gray, one of Stephanie's close friends, had talked with them concerning Stephanie's relationship with her stepfather.

Gray reported that Stephanie had talked about being mad at McGinn because he had "tried to mess with her." The young girl indicated that Stephanie had told her that McGinn had touched her and she had gotten mad at him, refusing to talk to him for two days.

"Stephanie's personality changed after that," Jennifer

Gray told the police. "It was about a month before she was killed."

McCoy's words rang in Janet's ears. Stephanie's blood had been found in the family car. Ricky had made inappropriate and unwanted advances toward her daughter. Those revelations, coupled with the newspaper article she had read chronicling McGinn's past brushes with the law, including charges of murder and accusations of rape, which she had been unaware of, were enough to convince Janet she was married to her daughter's killer.

The last time Janet had spoken to McGinn, he was still in the Brown County Jail. He had cried and had sounded seemingly mournful at the loss of her daughter, had bewailed the fact that the sheriff refused to allow him to attend Stephanie's funeral.

"Our baby was buried and they wouldn't even let me out to go," McGinn had moaned.

At the time Janet's heart had been heavy with the loss of her child and the incarceration of her husband. She had wanted Ricky with her, needed him there to support her. After her conversation with McCoy, Janet never wanted to speak to McGinn again. She went home and began to throw away the final remnants of his existence.

Later that night Ricky McGinn telephoned Janet from jail and again moaned and complained that he had not been allowed to attend Stephanie's funeral.

"They buried our baby and they didn't let me come," McGinn said.

"No, and they're never going to let you out of there," Janet snarled. "Now leave me alone! Never call me again, never send me another letter, nothing!" Janet slammed down the phone.

Lisa and Mike McGinn took the video camera used to document the interior of the culvert where Stephanie had been found and headed to their brother's house. They wanted to record for themselves as much of the area in and around the house as they could.

The first thing they noticed was an old toilet that Janet had utilized as a planter, smashed to smithereens. Broken porcelain and damaged flowers were scattered about the area.

Then Lisa emitted a low cry and Mike groaned as they walked around the house and found their brother's personal belongings spilling from a fifty-five-gallon barrel. The siblings began sifting through the discarded belongings strewn among the existing chunks of broken toilet porcelain and rubbish scattered about the yard.

"They just threw all his stuff away. That's sorry," Lisa muttered.

"Yeah," Mike said as he picked away at the barrel's contents with hands covered by heavy work gloves.

"Looks like he got her some flowers," Lisa said, holding a florist card in front of the camera for Mike to record.

"A poet I'm not and the words are few, but I want you to know I'm in love with you, Ricky," the note said.

Lisa dropped the note and picked up the base of an electric coffeemaker. "This is his coffeemaker. It still works, or did," she said, dropping it to the ground. "And that canister he's had for years. This is sorry. It would destroy Ricky if he knew that they had done this."

It was obvious to Mike and Lisa McGinn that authorities had gotten to Janet, had changed her mind, and that she now believed their brother was the killer.

Mike and Lisa salvaged what they could of their brother's personal effects in hopes that he would soon be back home to use them.

But the chances of Ricky McGinn being home with family and friends grew slimmer. On June 10, 1993, McGinn's case was presented to the grand jury of Brown County. The specially called jury was seated to determine whether the facts and accusations presented by the prosecutor warranted an indictment and eventual trial of Ricky McGinn.

Authorities had received confirmation that the blood recovered from the rear of the Ford Escort was the same blood type as the victim's, type A, and that the matter located in the vehicle was probably brain matter. They were also advised that the pubic hair inside the girl's vagina was the same type as that of Ricky McGinn. The district attorney shared this information with the grand jury. He also exhibited the ax as evidence. Grand jurors learned that the blood on the ax and in the car matched the victim's type and that search dogs had "hit" on McGinn's car, which contained blood, hair, and the girl's swimsuit.

Having determined that there was sufficient evidence for indicting of McGinn, the foreman of the grand jury endorsed the True Bill indictment, which stated that "in the course of committing and attempting to commit aggravated sexual assault of Stephanie Rae Flanary, Ricky Nolan McGinn did then and there intentionally cause the death of Stephanie Rae Flanary, an individual, by hitting her in the head with an ax."

McGinn's bond was raised from $100,000 to $1,000,000.

The formal grand-jury indictment was an emotional blow to the McGinn family, a welcome affirmation to Janet McGinn, and a disturbing declaration to the community.

Editorials from the pens of reporters for the *Brownwood Bulletin* called for citizens to remember that under the American judicial system a suspect who has been charged remains innocent until guilt is officially established in a court of law. Commentaries asked, "How much do you really know about the case? Who among us has seen the bloody ax, the blood in the car, or any of the other evidence?" The writer himself cautioned readers to beware of the impassioned details of the case presented in the press, warning them to remember that a man's life was at stake.

Wilson Craig wrote, "Citizens of Central Texas must keep their eyes, ears, and minds open with regard to this case, because there exists the possibility of another senseless murder, that of Ricky McGinn."

SEVEN

Francis McGinn soon learned that the cost of justice came high. She summoned her family together and asked them to give whatever they could to help in their brother's defense. They were able to raise a mere $5,000 to hire Pete Gomez. A month later Gomez, after filing a motion for a change of venue, left the case prematurely. Gomez claimed McGinn fired him; however, Francis was certain that the lawyer quit because the family was unable to raise his $100,000 fee for defending the capital-murder case.

Francis was overwhelmingly distraught. They had given their money, their trust, and their hopes for McGinn's future to a man who failed them. There was no alternative; McGinn would have to declare indigent status and request a court-appointed attorney.

District judge Ernest Cadenhead designated Bob Spence to represent McGinn. The Brady, Texas, attorney had been following the case closely and knew the McGinn family.

While Spence completed a capital-murder case in Fredericksburg, Texas, Francis and Mike McGinn picked up the case files from Pete Gomez and arranged to meet Spence in his office at a later date. It was at that meeting that Francis McGinn found hope. God had answered her prayers.

"I've been watching Ricky's case closely," Spence told Francis during their initial two-hour meeting. "I know he didn't do it."

While Bob Spence and his private investigator, Jim Wright, also of Brady, began work to win an acquittal, Brown County investigators continued to pursue leads that would insure McGinn's conviction.

Ranger Grubbs and Deputy Mercer met with Imogene Bible, Ricky McGinn's second wife, at the Brown County Sheriff's Office.

"Ricky McGinn and I married on May 23, 1980," Imogene said. "We had a daughter, Latasha Ranae, on May 31, 1983, and we divorced in January 1984."

Imogene Bible's next statement captured the attention of the investigators.

"In 1988 I filed a complaint against Ricky for sexually molesting our daughter," Bible told them.

From Bible, Grubbs and Mercer learned that the molestation investigation had been started in Brownwood. It had been determined, however, that jurisdiction in the case was in Eastland County, so the case had been referred to the larger county to the west. No charges were ever filed.

Grubbs and Mercer mentally banked the information and began asking themselves questions. If McGinn could molest his own daughter, would it be inconceivable that he had also molested his stepdaughter? Grubbs and Mercer thought not. It was time to interview Janet McGinn.

Janet was fidgety as she sat with investigators ready to discuss her life with Ricky McGinn. Nervously she lit a cigarette, her hands shaking visibly as she put the flame to the end of the smoke. She had been pummeled by a torrent of emotions for ten long days. Her daughter was dead. She now had to face telling investigators about her life with her daughter's killer. She drew in a deep breath.

Janet explained that she had lived with Ricky McGinn for approximately four months and had married him in December 1989. She told them about changing residences often and living in the Owens Community for only about three weeks prior to Stephanie's disappearance.

Grubbs, Smith, and Mercer listened as Janet explained Ricky's accident while employed at John Manning Construction, which prohibited him from working and caused him constant pain.

"After his accident I noticed a slight change in Ricky's personality," Janet said. "He was moodier and he drank more."

Janet McGinn indicated that her husband had been strict with both Stephanie and Denise while living in the city of Brownwood, making certain that the girls had on a bra when leaving the house and never allowing them to wear bathing suits in public. But, according to Janet, he relaxed his rules when they moved to the country. She said McGinn had even made the girls go swimming topless in the tank behind their house.

The investigators made no noticeable reaction to the statement.

"Did you ever catch fish in that tank?" they asked her.

"We fished in that tank quite often," Janet said. "All the fish we caught were extremely small and we always threw them back. Nothing we ever caught was big enough to eat."

Janet was excused from the interview and deputies began reviewing information obtained from the Department of Human Services Child Protective Services relating to an interview with Denise Flanary, Stephanie's ten-year-old sister.

The blond-haired girl had given interviewers much the same information her mother had related. Denise said McGinn would make her and her sister take off their swimsuit tops while swimming in the tank behind their house. The younger Flanary sister didn't indicate that she had ever been sexually or physically abused by McGinn. She also stated that Stephanie hadn't been sexually abused by McGinn. The interview conducted earlier in the week with

Stephanie's friend Jennifer Gray, though, contradicted Denise's statement.

The questioning of Janet McGinn and Denise Flanary by authorities had only added to Janet's pain. When people pointed fingers at her or stopped her at the Wal-Mart where she worked and asked if she was still on McGinn's side, she could feel a cold chill of resentment run through her body.

"I lost my whole life," Janet told reporters who continually asked the same insensitive question. "I lost my daughter; I lost my home; I lost everything I had except for my other daughter, and now she's all I've got.

"Let me tell you, this is an awful, awful way to learn a lesson."

What Janet didn't talk about them were the times she had driven to her daughter's grave, often with a twelve-pack of beer. She would sit beside the turned earth, talk to her daughter, drink, and scream at the moon. At times she had lain across the grave, thinking of her life, her loss. She had even cried herself to sleep until the early-morning hours.

Janet reflected back on her short courtship with McGinn. She had known he was on probation. McGinn had told her he had beaten someone and had to serve community service for assault. The revelation that he had once been tried for murder, only to be acquitted by a jury, had been shocking news. She had second-guessed herself a hundred times since Stephanie's death and McGinn's arrest, but she knew she wouldn't have done anything differently.

"It wasn't like I could call the sheriff's office and say, 'Hey, I'm Janet Talley; I'm going to start dating Ricky McGinn. Can you tell me about his past?' " Janet said later.

She had believed in McGinn partly because he was a preacher's kid—he had even taken her and the girls to church with him. The day after their first date, he brought flowers to her work and helped her cook supper that night. She once believed no one who treated her that good could possibly have done what investigators had accused him of. She now believed different.

Coping as best she could, Janet had returned to work.

"I've had to pick up and go on with my life, and it's tough. It takes more strength than I ever knew I had," she said.

Part of Janet's dilemma was due to the repeated letters from McGinn proclaiming his innocence, even after she had told him she wanted no further contact with him. He had even sent a preacher to her work to talk with her. The man had told her manager in the layaway department that he wanted to buy Janet a Coke. Janet reluctantly agreed.

As they sat at a small table in the snack bar at the front of the store, the minister said solemnly, "I've been visiting with Ricky. You know he didn't do this."

"I beg your pardon," Janet said in surprise. "I have nothing to say to you."

"But I've been visiting with Ricky and he wouldn't lie," the man said.

"But Ricky has lied!" Janet said angrily. "Ricky's lied so bad. If he didn't do it, why do I still not have my car? Why do I still not have my daughter? Why was her blood on his body? If he didn't do it, who did?"

Janet pushed back her chair and walked away.

Janet McGinn had wanted to file for divorce the moment she accepted that Ricky McGinn had been responsible for Stephanie's death, but on the advice of both the district attorney and sheriff's investigators, she had waited. After the grand jury's indictment had been returned, and Janet had a new man in her life, she took legal steps to sever her relationship with Ricky McGinn forever.

"I'm trying to get my named changed. I'm trying to stand up and be strong. I haven't seen Ricky McGinn or talked to him. I don't want to see him or talk to him. No man is worth me losing a child, especially the one I've got now," Janet commented.

Janet felt like she had already lost part of Denise. The ten-year-old refused to play with a friend whose grandfathers were always at his house. She had fears and nightmares that should never plague children. Denise would be forever altered by the experience of her sister's death, as would Janet, her family, the McGinns, and the entire community.

Both sides of the McGinn murder case were feverishly preparing for trial. Bob Spence requested that the court consider a motion filed by Pete Gomez, McGinn's original counsel, for a change of venue.

At a pretrial hearing held on March 7, 1994, ten months after Stephanie's death, Bob Spence called witnesses in an effort to convince the court that McGinn couldn't get a fair trial in Brown County. His first witness was Everett Deason, the managing editor and associate publisher of the *Brownwood Bulletin*.

When asked by Spence if he felt McGinn could get a fair trial, Deason replied, "I believe it would be difficult for him to receive a fair trial in Brown County. There has been discussion and perhaps conclusions by the general population concerning the guilt of the defendant."

Spence questioned Deason about several articles that had appeared in his paper, citing in particular the headlines: MAN CHARGED IN MURDER OF STEPDAUGHTER, MISSING GIRL'S BODY FOUND, BLOWS TO HEAD SAID THE CAUSE OF GIRL'S DEATH, SUSPECT CLAIMS INNOCENCE, and STEPDAUGHTER STEPHANIE FLANARY RAPED AND BEATEN TO DEATH WITH AX. A booking mug shot of McGinn had been included in the body of many of the stories. Other headlines, other stories, were referred to by Spence in an effort to make his point to the court.

Deason stated that the circulation of the newspaper was approximately ten thousand, five hundred on Sundays and about eighty-five hundred Monday through Saturday in a county with approximately thirty-nine thousand residents.

Spence concluded his examination of Deason by again having the witness state he believed it was not possible for McGinn to gain a fair trial in Brown County. He then passed the witness.

Lee Haney made short order of his cross-examination.

"In any discussions that you may have had outside of, perhaps, discussions at the newspaper about coverage in this case, have you heard anyone discussing this murder within the last month?" Haney asked.

"No, I have not. Not outside our office," Deason replied.

"In the last three months?" Haney asked.

"No, not in the last three months."

"How about the last six months?" Haney persisted.

"I'm not aware of any in the last six months."

"Do you believe that there has been an article since the June twenty-seventh article?" Haney asked.

"I'm not aware of any article since last summer," Deason answered.

Spence countered by presenting a copy of an article that appeared the month before the hearing. The story detailed a change in the legal counsel for McGinn.

Spence's next witness was Joyce Turk, a local resident and Spence's secretary, who testified that the gossip at the local beauty shop she frequented was centered on McGinn and his guilt in the Flanary murder.

"The consensus in the beauty shop is that he is guilty. With the talk I hear there, I can't imagine what kind of talk there can be outside the shop," Ms. Turk stated.

Haney simply asked on cross-examination if Ms. Turk

knew the names of other patrons in the shop. When she said, "No," Haney asked if she knew if they were Brown County residents or if they were registered voters, two criteria that had to be met to be selected in the jury pool. Ms. Turk replied, "No."

Bob Spence called eight additional witness, all testifying that they had had discussions with a number of other people in Brown County concerning the McGinn case. Nearly all of them, under cross-examination by Lee Haney, admitted that they thought it possible to find twelve people out of a population of over thirty thousand who could serve as impartial jurors. Haney then called his own witnesses to bolster his contention that McGinn could indeed obtain a fair and impartial trial in Brown County.

After taking the motion under advisement, Judge Cadenhead denied McGinn's motion for a change of venue.

Ricky McGinn would face trial in Brown County for the murder of Stephanie Flanary, and his day in court was rapidly approaching.

McGinn and his mother were pleased with the work Bob Spence and his investigator were doing on the case. The mother and son shared a hope that McGinn's ordeal would soon be over.

Francis's hopes soared when she received a call from Spence shortly before the scheduled trial date.

"Francis, I'm ready to go on this case," Spence said. "I've got my proof and I've got it narrowed down to two people who are the guilty ones. Don't worry. I can prove Ricky's innocent."

Spence hadn't shared the names of his suspects or given Francis any details, hadn't needed to. She trusted her son's attorney.

Francis had replaced the telephone receiver on her black

desk phone and immediately uttered a "Thank you, Jesus" for Spence and the good news he had given her.

A week later Bob Spence was dead.

EIGHT

Reports indicated that Bob Spence's four-wheel-drive pickup had left the rural roadway in Brown County, rolled from tires to roof and back to tires, before coming to a stop. Apparently the attorney's body had gone through the windshield and he had been killed.

Francis McGinn was devastated by the news. She had liked Spence very much, and most of all, she believed he would be the one to prove her son innocent of murder. She wept for Spence, his family, and her son.

Accompanied by her children, Mike and Lisa, as well as Lisa's friend Brittney, Francis attended Spence's funeral. Viewing the body before the service, the McGinns and Brittney looked closely at Spence's face. They observed no bruises, no cuts, no scratches, no knots. Francis looked at Lisa with a puzzled expression.

"How can that be if he went through the windshield?" she asked.

Lisa shrugged.

Following the service, Francis talked with Jim Wright, Spence's investigator.

"Jim, do you think . . . ," Francis began.

Before she could complete her sentence, Jim spoke. "Foul play? Yes, that's the first thing that came into my mind when I heard he was killed," Wright answered. "But I looked around and didn't see anything."

The McGinns were shattered by the death of Bob

Spence. He had been considered a friend of the family's, as well as Ricky's salvation.

What now? Francis wondered.

On May 2, 1994, Judge Cadenhead answered Francis McGinn's silent question by appointing Ben Doyle Sudderth of Comanche, Texas, to represent Ricky McGinn. Sudderth was best known for defending a suspect indicted on DNA evidence ten years after the murder. Sudderth had argued that DNA testing was a lot like lie detector tests, saying, "Like many, many other things, it's subject to human interpretation. It's much like a polygraph test. The operator has something to do with whether or not it's fool-proof."

In 1990 the Senate Committee on Labor and Human Resources requested that the U.S. Office of Technology Assessment (OTA) undertake a study on the use of DNA typing for forensic purposes. The OTA found that DNA tests were valid and the scientific basis for forensic DNA testing was solid. However, the OTA director, Robyn Nishimi, Ph.D. stated, "As currently performed, forensic DNA tests do not produce positive identification. DNA profiling reduces the pool of possible suspects who might have contributed to the evidence and because DNA assays are so highly discriminating that a pool can be reduced to a very small statistic, creating the misconception that DNA tests offer unequivocal identification."

Sudderth planned to use the same arguments on the validity of DNA testing in the McGinn case.

Motions previously filed by Bob Spence, including the appointment of Jim Wright as investigator and Dr. Richard Coons of Austin, Texas, as an expert in the matters of psychiatry, were approved by the judge.

Wright, a retired Houston police investigator, had been working as a private investigator for the past nine years.

Dr. Coons had been used as an expert witness in capital-murder cases across the state.

After being appointed to represent McGinn, Sudderth visited his newest client in the Brown County Jail.

"Ricky, do you reckon your family could get your teeth fixed before you go on trial?" Sudderth asked.

McGinn, who had lost a front tooth in an accident, simply shrugged, more concerned with the evidence his attorney planned to present to the jury.

Later, knowing that a client's appearance could be a plus or a minus with a jury, Sudderth approached Francis McGinn with the same question: "Do you think you could get his teeth fixed before trial?"

Francis was dumbfounded by the suggestion. In her sweet Texan drawl, Francis replied, "I think saving his life is more important than getting his teeth fixed right now."

In September 1994 Sudderth appeared before the court again. He requested the appointment of a local cocounsel to aid him in the jury selection process.

"I don't want to dance around the issue," Sudderth told the court, referring to allegations of bank fraud that were being investigated in Lubbock, Texas. "I want the record to show that I did discuss the fact with Mr. McGinn that there are accusations pending against me in the federal judiciary, and that has been given some notoriety in this part of the state. It has not caused me to quit trying cases. In fact, I tried a jury case in Comanche County this week and won it.

"I've made Mr. McGinn aware of the adverse effect it could have in dealing with a jury in his case and told him that if he felt like he didn't want me to continue, then he certainly had the right, and he should request I withdraw."

When asked by Judge Cadenhead if McGinn wished to have another attorney appointed to represent him in light of the fact that Sudderth was facing the federal investigation in Lubbock, McGinn opted to keep Sudderth on the case.

Cadenhead appointed Brownwood attorney Dana Smith to assist Mr. Sudderth on a limited basis. Smith's primary function would be to assist with jury selection.

Once appointed to McGinn's case, Sudderth filed a second Change of Venue Motion.

March 10, 1995, the Change of Venue Motion was heard in the 35th Judicial District courtroom in Brownwood. Sudderth's first witness was Jim Wright.

Having established that Wright, during his duties as defense investigator on the McGinn case, had talked with a fair cross section of the people of Brown County, Sudderth asked him if he felt McGinn could obtain a fair trial composed of Brown County citizens.

"No, sir, I don't feel like he could," Wright answered.

"And what is it based upon?" Sudderth asked.

"Well, most of the people, when I start talking to them, they say, 'Is that the fellow that killed his stepdaughter?' " Wright responded.

Sudderth established that Wright questioned a cross section of people in Brown County by xeroxing pages from the phone book, cutting out each column separately, then putting those in a cardboard box and drawing out just one column. Wright had then cut each one of the names up separately, put those back in the box, and drawn out eight to ten names of persons to interview.

Subsequent witnesses, most of whom were those randomly selected by Mr. Wright in his nonscientific poll, were asked about pretrial publicity concerning the McGinn case. In particular, Sudderth wanted to know if they had read an article chronicling McGinn's past criminal record. Each witness confirmed they had read the article and admitted they had been negatively influenced by McGinn's prior criminal history.

Lee Haney defused this barrage of witnesses and their

testimony by presenting evidence that there had been only one article published in the *Brownwood Bulletin* in some eighteen months. In addition, most of the witnesses agreed that it would probably be possible to find twelve impartial jurors in Brown County.

Sudderth ended the hearing by presenting a number of motions. The most significant was the request for blood tests on Steve Sirois, Stanley Sirois, and Joe Bob Talley.

"Have you—without going into details, have you obtained information relating to an alleged relationship involving some of those people with this young lady?" Sudderth asked Jim Wright under oath.

"Yes, sir, I have," Wright responded.

"Would a blood sample test of these three people be very relevant in this lawsuit?" Sudderth asked.

"In this case, yes, sir," Wright answered.

The court ordered that DNA test results be forwarded to Sudderth for blood samples already taken from Steve Sirois. However, the judge reserved the right to withhold testing of Stanley Sirois and Joe Bob Talley until probable cause could be established by the defense.

A motion to take depositions from Steve Sirois and Stanley Sirois was also heard by the judge. The deposition, a method of pretrial discovery that included a written transcribed statement, would allow Sudderth to ask questions of the two men prior to their appearance as witnesses for the state.

Jim Wright testified that both Sirois men had refused to talk to him concerning the case on two separate occasions.

Haney stated that investigators had interviewed both men and those interviews would be made available to Sudderth. The judge denied the requests for defense depositions. Sudderth was disappointed. He had hoped to have an opportunity to question both men on a number of subjects relating to Stephanie Flanary.

Judge Cadenhead set jury selection to begin on April 21, 1995, with the trial to commence the following month.

The all-white petit jury, comprised of seven men and seven women who represented the twelve primary jurors and two alternates, would begin hearing the Statements of Fact on May 17, 1995. It would be the task of the jury to determine issues of fact in the criminal case and to reach a verdict in conjunction with those findings.

On behalf of the state of Texas, District Attorney Lee Haney was seeking the death penalty. No one had been sentenced to death in Brown County since 1974. The McGinn case had drawn the curiosity of a number of local citizens who planned to attend the "high drama" of the courtroom contest.

Ricky McGinn had been restrained in jail for nearly two years. He was anxious to get the trial started and to take the stand in his defense.

Both Francis and Janet McGinn were equally eager for the trial to begin. Francis, hopeful that her child would be coming home; Janet, impatient for her daughter's death to be avenged.

NINE

Ricky McGinn slipped his jail jumpsuit from his shoulders, letting it fall to the floor. He began to dress in civilian clothes. As he buttoned his white dress shirt, stepped into his trousers, then knotted the tie at his neck, he thought of the events of the past twenty-three months: the death of Stephanie, the loss of Janet, the pain he saw on his mother's face.

He wished that the events of May 22, 1993, could be wiped away like the dust on a tabletop. He missed Janet, longed for the closeness they once shared. Each time his mother spoke of his former wife in an angry tone, accusing Janet of forsaking him, he said, "Mama, don't be mad at Janet; it's not her fault. The cops turned her against me. I still love her." And each time his mother visited, he would always ask, "How's my baby?" referring to Janet's younger daughter, Denise. He missed them both.

McGinn slid on his suit jacket and pressed his hands against the fabric of the lapels. He needed to present himself in a favorable light. He knew it was important for the jury—Sudderth had made that clear—but he anticipated seeing Janet and wanted to look his best.

Judge Cadenhead had ordered that he not be required to appear in handcuffs or shackles, a directive McGinn appreciated. He knew his mother would be hurt even further to see her son chained like a mad dog for all of Brownwood to see.

McGinn took one last deep breath and waited for the door of his cell to open and the guard to escort him to the waiting car. Within minutes he would be at the Brown County Courthouse, on trial for his life.

Secured in the backseat of the sheriff's cruiser, McGinn watched as they sped past familiar local landmarks. The Coliseum and Soldiers and Sailors Museum, which was completed in 1923 and was where Elvis Presley performed in 1955; the original Brown County Jail, a four-story historical structure resembling an ancient European castle complete with the third story containing a trapdoor and lever for executions; the Camp Collier marker located on the Brown County Courthouse lawn honoring those Texans who served the Confederacy, along with a marker honoring Vietnam veterans and one honoring all War veterans; and the courthouse itself.

Like in most small Texas towns, the Brown County Courthouse stood in the center of the older part of the city. Surrounded by small shops and an abundance of law offices, the Brownwood courthouse was home to the district attorney's office as well as a number of other district and county departments.

McGinn had taken notes on each jury panelist during jury selection. Armed with a legal pad and pen as he entered the courtroom, McGinn also planned to keep his own record of the trial proceedings.

As Ben Sudderth and Ricky McGinn settled in at the defense table on the left side of the courtroom, facing the judge's bench, Judge Cadenhead announced a change in the jury panel.

It seemed one of the selected jurors was unable to sit through the trial due to a leg ailment. Judge Cadenhead replaced her with the first alternate, another female. The replacement juror moved into the twelfth spot, maintaining the men-to-women ratio balance of the jury panel of six men and six women.

Judge Cadenhead took care of what the court generally called "housekeeping" items, such as letting the jury know that they would be given breaks every hour and a half, the thermostat could be set for their comfort, that the judge would allow no note taking during the court proceedings so that each juror would give their full attention to the testimony, introductions of key court personnel, and the standard warning not to discuss the case with anyone, not even among themselves. The jury was then excused so the court could take care of a number of miscellaneous business items. The first, to swear in witnesses.

Janet Talley (McGinn) filed into the courtroom, along with a number of others. Judge Cadenhead preferred to have witnesses pledge to tell the truth prior to their being called to testify. It made his courtroom and the trial process run smoothly, with fewer interruptions in the flow of the case.

As Janet moved past McGinn, his lips curved upward slightly. He was happy to see her, to have her so close, but his smile quickly disappeared as her gaze deliberately avoided his. Janet and the other witnesses scheduled to testify would not be allowed to sit in on the trial. Most waited in the hall downstairs, anticipating their turn in court, but Janet would wait in the comfort and seclusion of the district attorney's office.

Once the witnesses had taken the oath and proceeded out of the courtroom, the jury returned to take their seats.

District Attorney Lee Haney stood and faced the jury. He was tall and slim, and his mustache was neatly trimmed, as was his thinning dark hair. From the paper in his hands, Haney read the indictment of Ricky McGinn for the murder of Stephanie Flanary. When he had completed the statement, Judge Cadenhead addressed the defendant.

"And how does the defendant plead to the allegations in the indictment?" he asked.

"Not guilty," McGinn said emphatically.

"All right, the plea is noted," Judge Cadenhead responded. "Is the state ready for an opening statement?"

"We are, Your Honor," Haney replied.

Haney moved to the railing of the jury box. The district attorney began his opening remarks by telling the panel that the burden of proof rested on the state and how he intended to prove the state's case.

"There will be typical fact witnesses, the individuals who were witnesses to some of the events or circumstances in the case, ordinary citizens who know something that may be relevant in the case. There will be investigating officers who participated in the investigation of the disappearance and murder of the victim. There will be some witnesses who we would call chain-of-custody witnesses. All that they may have done in the case is see that a particular item of evidence gets from one place to another. And finally there will be witnesses who are experts in their particular fields, whether scientific evidence or whatever. So that's the types of evidence that we expect will be presented during the state's Case in Chief," Haney said.

Most of the jurors hadn't heard many of the technical aspects of the trial Haney described, but one juror was very familiar with the terminology—she was an experienced court reporter.

Haney then gave jurors a brief chronology of McGinn and the victim. He began with Stephanie's premature birth and the birth of her sister, the divorce of Stephanie's parents, and her mother's marriage to McGinn. The district attorney continued with a synopsis of the events of May 22, 1993, beginning with Janet's departure for a bowling tournament in Arlington, Texas. He told the six men and six women that at 11:30 A.M. Kay Lobstein, a clerk at Oleta's Liquor Store, had seen McGinn and Stephanie.

"I believe the evidence will be that no one saw Stephanie alive after that point," Haney said for emphasis.

The prosecutor explained briefly Stanley Sirois's visit to the McGinns' house at 4:00 in the afternoon and McGinn's phone call to Steve Sirois at 8:30 that night, stating that Stephanie had been missing several hours. Jurors were told they would hear about McGinn's call to the Brown County Sheriff's Office reporting the missing child and the arrival of Deputy Don Roberts on the scene.

Haney described search efforts made in an all-out attempt to find Stephanie Flanary, including the deployment of cadaver-trained search dogs and heat-sensitive helicopters.

"The dogs are trained in such a way that they detect the odors that dying or dead bodies give off," Haney explained. "And the dogs alerted on the McGinn vehicle."

Ricky McGinn, sitting at the table beside his attorney, listened to the prosecutor's litany of proposed evidence. He stared straight at Haney; according to his personal notes of the trial, he was contesting in his mind each statement being made. However, he remained calm, knowing he would eventually get his chance for rebuttal.

As he paced in front of the jury box, Haney continued with a brief description of the hair, blood, and brain matter found in the car, the seizure of the vehicle, and the retrieval of some of McGinn's clothing for evidence. As part of the usual autopsy, Haney explained, samples of the victim's head and blond hair, scrapings and tapings of her skin and fingernails, and of course examinations of all parts of her body were taken.

"It was included among other finds that there was a pubic hair found inside Stephanie's vagina and that there was tearing or contusions or some trauma caused to the interior of her vagina. Also collected were swabs or slides of the fluids that were inside her and all those were sent off for analysis," Haney explained.

A few members of the audience squirmed in their seats. The sexual assault of the young victim was not something easily heard or understood. But the pubic hair and semen samples to be introduced later were the strongest link between the victim and the defendant that the state could produce.

"There may be testimony about what is called DNA evidence," Haney said. "I can't tell you what DNA stands for. It's one of those real long words."

The remark garnered some snickers from audience and jury alike.

"Some expert will have to tell you exactly what it is, but it's my understanding that DNA fingerprinting is a generally accepted scientific principle in the field of genetics. DNA is a genetic blueprint that is distinct for each individual, except for identical twins."

Haney continued by telling the jury that the head hair found in McGinn's car and on the ax located in his truck exhibited the same microscopic characteristics as Stephanie's head hair. He claimed the DNA experts would also testify that the blood found in those areas also belonged to the victim.

"I believe that, based upon the evidence, the state will ask you to find the defendant guilty of this offense," Haney concluded.

The prosecutor took his seat at the state's designated table, next to the court clerk on the right of the courtroom. Haney took in a deep breath. He had covered a lot of material in a short span of time. He could only hope the jury had grasped the significance of the evidence he intended to present and appreciate the magnitude of a case involving the death of a twelve-year-old child.

"Thank you, Mr. Haney," Judge Candenhead said, acknowledging the district attorney's opening statement. "Mr. Sudderth?"

"Your Honor, we will reserve our opening statement until we begin putting on our side of the case," Sudderth said.

"All right. Mr. Haney, will you call your first witness, please," the judge instructed.

Lee Haney rose to stand before the court again.

"We call Earl Kimbrell at this time, Your Honor," Haney announced.

Earl Kimbrell had been on duty at the Brown County Jail the evening Ricky McGinn had called to report his stepdaughter missing.

"The call came in at approximately nine-thirty and the caller identified himself as Ricky McGinn. He said that his stepdaughter had got mad about five o'clock and walked off in the woods and hadn't returned," Kimbrell told the jury.

Ricky McGinn picked up the pen lying on the yellow legal pad in front of him. Under the heading he had written when the proceedings began, "Witness Called 5–17–95," he wrote:

1—EARL Kimbrell—Now he is lying about times and what I said. I wonder if he is still an alcoholic.

McGinn's attention returned to Kimbrell as he explained that he had told McGinn that he had only one officer on duty that night and he would have to dispatch him from Bangs, a community about thirty minutes from McGinn's location. Kimbrell said he then notified Deputy Don Roberts of the situation.

As Haney announced he had no further questions, Ben Sudderth stood. He sauntered to the witness-box to begin his cross-examination.

"Did you subsequently have occasion to overhear deputies discussing matters relating to who was probably responsible for the girl being missing?" Sudderth asked.

"No, sir."

"You have made the statement to at least one person that the first reaction of the deputies was that Ricky

McGinn was responsible for her being missing, have you not?" Sudderth probed.

"No, sir, not that I know of," Kimbrell coolly responded.

Sudderth tried repeatedly to get the former jailer to admit overhearing a statement in reference to McGinn's possible involvement on the night of Stephanie's disappearance, but to no avail. Kimbrell held firm to his testimony that he didn't recall such a statement being made.

Sudderth's intention had been to show that McGinn had been targeted as a suspect from the moment he called in to report his stepdaughter missing, but Kimbrell hadn't flinched. Perhaps Sudderth would have better luck with the state's next witness.

Don Roberts had been in law enforcement for nearly thirty-one years, and was the Brown County deputy on duty the night of May 22. He had an easygoing manner and sat comfortably in the witness chair as Haney began questioning him concerning the events after he received the call from dispatch that a child was missing.

"What does the property look like?" Haney asked in reference to the McGinn home.

"Well, the property is located on the west side of Highway one eighty-three North, and it would be just south of County Road four-seventeen. As near as I can recall, there is a house and possibly three or four outbuildings behind the house. The property is maybe a quarter of a mile wide, north and south, and approximately a quarter to a half mile, east and west. There was a barbed wire fence all the way around it and a stock tank, or pond of some sort, west of the house, which would be behind the house, probably about three to four hundred yards. In the unimproved area there were a few mesquite trees, maybe a live oak or two, and heavy brush or weeds," Roberts explained.

Haney handed Roberts a map and asked if it clearly

depicted the property he had described. Roberts confirmed it as the McGinn tract.

"When you saw Mr. McGinn, do you recall how he was dressed?" Haney asked.

"He had on a dark pullover shirt, shorts, white tennis shoes, and white socks. It just hit my mind that it was like 'Pistol Pete' Maravich. I don't know if people know who he was or not, but his socks was hanging down loose over his shoes," Roberts replied, referring to the former NBA star known for his outside shot and sloppy socks.

He told jurors about returning to the sheriff's office to call the REACT team and send out a missing-person teletype to fifteen or twenty counties with a description of Stephanie and the clothing she had been wearing, provided by McGinn. He had then joined the volunteer searchers at the McGinn property.

"The REACT president briefed all the people about how they was going to conduct their search, not only of the property but also the roads, the culverts and bridges, and bar-ditches," Roberts said, using the local term for a roadside gully.

"Were all of these areas that were included in this search located to the west of U.S. one eighty-three?" Haney asked.

"Yes, sir. They searched everything west of one eighty-three, with the exception of some empty buildings in the Owens community itself, right there on the highway," Roberts answered.

"Is there any reason why y'all didn't search to the east of U.S. Highway one eighty-three?" Haney inquired.

"Yes, sir. Because Rick stated that Stephanie never went across the highway. She always went to the north or west," Roberts answered.

It was nearly eleven o'clock in the morning. Court had been in session nearly two hours when Judge Cadenhead, surveying the stirrings of the jurors, decided it was time to take a fifteen-minute break.

When court resumed, Roberts was back on the stand. He described the downpour of rain that had halted the search for the missing girl, the decision to call in specially trained dogs out of Dallas for tracking in the rain, and his departure from the scene between 5:00 and 5:30 in the morning following the reported disappearance.

Haney passed the witness.

Ben Sudderth approached Roberts with an air of controlled defiance. Roberts had made his client look as if he had deliberately steered the search party in the wrong direction in order to conceal the location of Stephanie's body. Sudderth intended to set the record straight.

He began his cross-examination calmly. "I want to visit with you just a few minutes about some of the matters relating to your testimony," Sudderth said. "When you arrived at the McGinn place that evening, he told you that the mother of this child had left about nine A.M. to go to Fort Worth to a bowling tournament, did he not?"

"Yes, sir," Roberts replied.

"The mother hadn't planned to return that night, according to what you were told," Sudderth stated.

"No, sir."

"You found that to be consistent, did you not, as things developed?" Sudderth asked.

"Yes, sir."

"Then, of course, Stephanie had a little sister named Denise. He said that she went to stay with friends?" Sudderth asked.

"Yes, sir."

"And you found nothing to indicate that wasn't correct, did you?" Sudderth asked.

"No, sir."

"And he said that he and Stephanie had a good relationship, and you found nothing to indicate that that wasn't correct, did you?"

With each question Sudderth's voice rose louder.

"He said Stephanie had gone swimming that afternoon, and you found nothing to indicate that was incorrect, did you?" Sudderth almost snarled.

"I didn't find anything either way," Roberts said calmly.

Sudderth continued to fire questions at the deputy, each time indicating that McGinn had not misled them during the initial investigation. Then, in the middle of his inquiry concerning McGinn's Dodge pickup, Sudderth asked, "Are you friends with Bob Tally?"

Roberts remained composed. "I know Bob Talley, yes," Roberts answered.

"I asked if you were friends," Sudderth snapped.

"Yes, sir."

"Are you friends with the Talley family?" Sudderth asked, a hint of contempt lacing his voice.

"Yes."

Either Sudderth didn't know or chose not to bring out in court that Janet Flanary had dated Larry Roberts, Don Roberts's son, for a brief period of time prior to her marriage to Ricky McGinn.

Returning to his inquiry concerning the truck, Sudderth asked, "Did you look in the Dodge pickup?"

"No, sir, other than just curiosity, curious inspection to see if maybe Stephanie was in the pickup. I looked in the cab, then the bed. That's it," Roberts explained.

"You didn't see anything, did you?" Sudderth asked.

"I didn't see anything," Roberts answered.

"Mr. Kimbrell has testified in this court," Sudderth stated, changing the subject. "He was asked, did any of the deputies say, 'Old Ricky McGinn is probably responsible for her being missing; he is a criminal.' And he replied by saying, 'I didn't say it in those exact words.'

"Now, did you overhear any statements made by any of

the deputies that were supposed to investigate this matter of a similar import?"

"No, sir," Roberts said simply.

Sudderth's frustration level was beginning to rise. He wanted to show the jury that Ricky McGinn had become the prime suspect at the onset of the investigation. Even though his client had cooperated, had given authorities no reason to suspect him, Sudderth believed that, because of his past troubles, McGinn had been intentionally pegged as a target.

"There would certainly be no cause for any deputy to be making a statement on Saturday evening the twenty-second, when there wasn't even a body, that Ricky McGinn had been guilty of any kind of misconduct, was there?" Sudderth asked.

"Not to my knowledge, no, sir," Roberts said in a slow drawl.

"And you say you didn't do that?" Sudderth shot back.

"I don't recall doing that." Roberts shrugged.

Sudderth walked to the defense table, picked up papers, and returned to the witness. He held a copy of the report filed by Deputy Roberts regarding his part in the investigation of the disappearance of Stephanie Flanary. Sudderth covered each step point by point.

"Show me in this report here," Sudderth said, holding up the papers, "where you said that no search was conducted east of Highway one eighty-three."

"I probably didn't state it in that report," Roberts said.

"Why are you telling this jury about Ricky saying, 'She never walks east of one eighty-three,' if you're not trying to infer that you didn't search over there because of him?" Sudderth asked, nodding toward his client.

"Because that's probably why I didn't search," Roberts said.

Sudderth again covered the manner in which the volunteer searchers covered the property and surrounding area.

"Did you feel like you were under a great amount of pressure to assist in solving this problem with this missing girl?" Sudderth asked.

"No, sir. I was concerned because I knew them and knew the family, but I had my regular patrol duties to take care of," Roberts said.

"Isn't it a fact, Mr. Roberts, that the entire Brown County Sheriff's Office felt like it was under extreme pressure to solve this mystery and charge somebody with capital murder as quickly as possible?"

"I have no idea what they were thinking," Roberts replied.

"Were you not aware of the fact that there were four unsolved slayings involving females?" Sudderth asked.

Haney immediately objected to testimony concerning any other cases. The judge sustained the objection and Sudderth passed the witness back to Haney.

Haney established that Roberts had written the report Sudderth referred to in court the night following the initial investigation of the missing girl. Roberts stated that he had written the report prior to the discovery of the girl's body. Both Haney and Sudderth on subsequent questioning established that the Dodge pickup had been searched for evidence; however, Haney emphasized that searchers at the time were looking for the girl, not evidence. He indicated that the method of search would have been different if they'd been looking for evidence, such as a murder weapon.

Sudderth had two final questions for the deputy.

"I want to ask you if the real reason you felt pressured to charge somebody with a crime was that in 1989 there were two girls of about the same age who went missing and turned up murdered. In 1992 there was still a third girl who went missing and turned up murdered, and at that time there was already one unsolved murder involving a female on the books in this county. And that none of those have ever been solved, and that's the reason you had to charge somebody with this hastily, isn't that correct?"

"No, sir," Roberts said. "I did not have any reason to be attempting to charge anybody with anything because the only report I had was of a missing person at the time."

"Isn't it a fact that when you found out there was a twelve-year-old girl missing, that these other murders and missing girls came through your mind?" Sudderth pushed.

But Roberts held firm. "It's possible. I'm sure it did, but not to the extent that I immediately started thinking that I was looking for a murdered girl."

TEN

The anxiety of both the mother of the victim and the mother of the accused killer rose with each tick of the clock. Neither Janet Talley nor Francis McGinn was allowed in the courtroom and each longed to know what was happening in the trial. Only one McGinn family member would be granted permission to sit in on the trial, and Ricky McGinn chose Verilyn Harbin, his older sister. During the noon recess friends and family of each of the grieving mothers filled them in on the events of the morning session.

The afternoon proceedings began with testimony from Deputy Billy Arp concerning the search for Stephanie Flanary on Sunday, May 23. Sudderth asked Arp, as he had Kimbrell and Roberts, if he had overheard deputies comment on Ricky McGinn's probable responsibility for the girl's disappearance and his past criminal record. When Arp responded, "I don't recall," Sudderth retorted with, "You can't recall?

"No, sir," Arp said.

"And Don Roberts said that he couldn't recall it. And now you say you can't recall it. Is that correct?" Sudderth snapped.

"Yes."

"You're not saying it's not true; you're just saying you can't recall it?" Sudderth asked.

"I don't recall it," Arp answered.

Sudderth let the statement slide, hoping jurors would see through what he considered a veiled admission that his client was a suspect before any evidence had been gathered, before any body had been found.

At least one male juror had been in trouble with the law himself as a juvenile. No one knew how his theft conviction and probated sentence would affect his opinion of McGinn's prior run-ins with the law. Or, how the prejudice that the defense attorney was trying to show authorities had for McGinn from the beginning could taint his conclusions.

Gilbert Capuchino walked into the court following the dismissal of Arp. McGinn watched the DPS trooper closely as he raised his right hand to be sworn in. He had not been present when other witnesses had taken the oath earlier that day. McGinn wondered if Capuchino planned to tell the truth, the whole truth.

A friend of the McGinn family's had reported seeing a news segment on television that featured an interview with Capuchino. In the interview Capuchino allegedly stated that he had first seen the body of the victim while glancing in his rearview mirror. The McGinns, based on their own amateur investigation, knew that it would have been impossible for him to have seen Stephanie's body by driving past the culvert, since the corpse had been pushed at least two to three feet into the tin horn.

McGinn picked up his pen and twisted it between his fingers.

Capuchino explained his role in escorting the wrecker that carried the Ford Escort to the Brown County Sheriff's Office for eventual transfer to the DPS lab in Austin.

"After that, were you later involved in the continuing search for Stephanie Flanary?" District Attorney Haney asked.

"As far as the search is concerned, on May the twenty-fifth, 1993, at approximately eleven-twenty A.M., I was searching for this missing child on U.S. one eighty-three, just north of Owens, Texas. I stopped at one of the tin horns off of one eighty-three. From there I turned right and continued on over the crest of the hill. As I came down to the bottom of the crest of the hill, there was another tin horn. At that point I pulled over and stopped, and I walked to the north end of the tin horn and I looked through to the south end and I noticed a body on the other side," Capuchino stated, making eye contact with the jury as he spoke.

"And what did you do at that time?" Haney asked.

"At that point I came back up and ran across the road to look into the tin horn. I noticed legs sticking out, just barely, what appeared to be a child. I ran back up to the patrol car and radioed in for the Texas Ranger to come to the scene. They were unable to locate him, so we contacted Brown County Sheriff's Office by radio. Shortly thereafter Deputy David Mercer and other units arrived at the scene," Capuchino explained, again looking to jurors.

McGinn scribbled on his legal pad: "Knows how to play to the jury."

After the trooper had identified maps of the area and photos of the victim's body as it appeared when he discovered her, Ben Sudderth began his cross-examination.

It took Sudderth no more than a couple of minutes to get to the question the McGinns had been asking since their friend had told them about the news report.

"Have you ever told anybody that you were driving down the highway and you saw this body through your rearview mirror?" Sudderth asked.

"No, sir," Capuchino said.

"Indeed, it would be impossible to see this body through your rearview mirror, would it not, Mr. Capuchino?" Sudderth probed.

"Yes, sir, it would," Capuchino stated.

Then Sudderth broke new ground.

"Do you have any knowledge of DPS or the sheriff's office receiving any anonymous tips as to where this body was located?" Sudderth inquired.

"No, sir."

Sudderth moved to questioning relating to the position of the body in the culvert, establishing that Stephanie stood five feet five inches and that her body was found at least a couple of feet inside the tin horn. Sudderth asked, "And if the body weighed about one hundred pounds, would it take somebody with some strength to place the body that far up in the culvert?"

"Yes, sir," Capuchino said.

"And you wouldn't expect a person who was disabled and did not have the use of their back or their legs to be able to do that, isn't that right, Mr. Capuchino?" Sudderth asked.

"I suppose," Capuchino said, noncommitted.

Sudderth probed the witness concerning the state of the blood at the time Capuchino found the body, with the trooper stating that he hadn't noticed if the blood was wet or if it had dried. He also testified that he didn't recall seeing any blood in the area outside the culvert.

Later Sudderth asked, "Have you found any officer who has told you that they questioned anyone living in any of the houses around this body?"

"No, sir. The investigation was Brown County Sheriff's and the Rangers," Capuchino said.

As Capuchino left the courtroom, McGinn scribbled an additional line under Capuchino's name: "He can lie good anyway."

Justice of the Peace Jimmy Crooks spent limited time on the stand describing his role in pronouncing Stephanie Flanary dead and ordering an autopsy, as did Andrew Foxcroft, an emergency medical technician who helped load the body into the ambulance for transport to the Southwest Institute of Forensic Sciences in Dallas.

Judge Cadenhead watched jurors as Crooks and Foxcroft gave testimony. Heads had begun nodding forward, then jerking back, in an effort by jurors to focus their attention on the testimony.

"Are y'all about ready for a recess?" Cadenhead asked.

The relieved looks on the faces of the jurors confirmed the judge's suspicions. He excused them for a fifteen-minute break.

When court reconvened, Deputy Mike McCoy was called by the prosecution.

McCoy, a seventeen-year law enforcement veteran, was questioned concerning the impounding of McGinn's Ford Escort.

"Do you know why the car was impounded and taken to the sheriff's office?" Haney asked.

"Two of the dogs alerted to the back portion of the car. Deputies Mercer and Smith got consent to search the car," McCoy explained.

McGinn jotted on his pad "The dogs did not alert on the car," then pushed it over for Sudderth to read.

Sudderth was on his feet. "Now, Your Honor," Sudderth said, "we want this witness to testify to what he knows and not what he's been told. And I believe that this stuff about the dogs alerting on the car—"

"Okay, I'll grant your objection to hearsay," Judge Cadenhead ruled.

"And what, if anything, did you do back at the sheriff's office with the automobile?" Haney asked.

"We went through the automobile, found various items of what appeared to be blood stains and hair," McCoy answered.

Haney presented a number of photographs of the Ford for McCoy to identify. "Now this isn't a photograph that you took, is it?" Haney asked.

"No, it's not. It was taken by Scott Martin," McCoy said.

Sudderth immediately objected to McCoy testifying to photographs taken by Martin, citing the hearsay rule since McCoy was reading the notes of Martin on the back of each exhibit, rather than relying on his own notes or recollections.

The judge allowed the photos, with the understanding that McCoy was not to refer to notes made by Martin in an attempt to interpret the photographs.

As McCoy identified each section of the car and pointed out what was believed to be blood stains, McGinn added to his notes:

Showing him photos not taken by him and asking him to say this is what he saw. Naturally he is gonna say what the D.A. wants to hear. I believe someone threw blood all over the car after I seen the car and opened it for the cops. (Glen Smith, David Mercer, Bobby Grubbs.) Sure hope the jury will keep an open mind. This guy really knows how to play up to the jury. Where did all the blood come from that he is supposedly showing the jury?

McCoy identified spots on a Lone Star Light carton, a phone book, some beer cans, and assorted trash in the backseat, as well as the seat itself and the doorposts. He pointed out in the trunk a water can, a battery, and run marks on the wheel well. He noted spots on the front seat and the door panel. On the left back door, the photo reflected spots and a big clump of human material. There were spots on the side glass in the back of the car, spots on the fender, and splatters on the passenger-side back door between the seat and the doorpost.

When McCoy was asked what he believed the spots to be, the deputy answered, "Blood stains."

After the prosecutor entered a videotape into evidence, and as he began to set up the television and VCR for the jury to view the tape, the judge summoned Sudderth. "While we're getting ready for show time, Counsel, will you approach the bench?"

The side-bar discussion was simply in reference to Sudderth's earlier request to have the backs of Martin's photos, which showed his notes, covered before being presented to the jury.

The TV in place and the VCR keyed to go, Haney started the tape as McCoy began his narration. In addition to the items spotted or splattered that McCoy had described earlier through the still photographs, the video showed an Igloo cooler in the backseat, tennis shoes that appeared to have been spotted with blood, a roll of painter's masking tape, and the headliner of the car.

Quick breaths were audible from some members of the jury as the video presentation quickly and without warning changed from the red Ford Escort to the culvert and a portion of Stephanie Flanary's body. The men and women of the jury could see the child's lifeless form, her feet together with knees apart, one arm up and the other to her side. The girl's shirt had been pulled over her face and her discolored chest was exposed.

The gruesome scene intensified as the camera caught glimpses of the child's body being lifted from the thirty-six-inch tin cylinder and laid on the rocks outside the opening. As the camera zoomed in, the massive head trauma of the victim was a graphic documentation of what the young girl had suffered in death. It was difficult for jurors to watch the screen. Some tried to mask their reactions; others were visibly shaken. All were relieved when the camera clicked off and the next image was that of a rural area and a run-down house.

McCoy continued his narration, pointing out each area of the McGinn property, beginning with the mailbox and half-circle drive.

"That's a carport that attaches to the house," McCoy

said, referring to a dilapidated shed caught on film. "That's another barn there. It's kind of like a shop, not so much like a barn."

The tape ended and Haney turned off both machines.

"At this time, Judge, I would like to pass this witness, subject to recall at a later time," Haney announced.

Sudderth first had McCoy agree that Ricky McGinn had been arrested and charged with capital murder before a body or a murder weapon had been recovered. He then drilled McCoy on various pieces of evidence collected during the investigation. A hammer, a crow bar, a beer can and a blood-spotted sheet found at the old farmhouse in Okra on Monday, May 24. Each item had been seized because it was believed that they were key pieces of evidence in the Flanary murder. McCoy had to admit, though, that they were unrelated to the case.

"You were almost reaching the panic stage in finding something to support the charges that you had leveled against him, weren't you, Mr. McCoy?" Sudderth asked.

"No, sir, I don't believe," McCoy said with a country twang.

"You didn't have any evidence, did you?" Sudderth said accusingly.

"Not at that particular time, other than what was in the car and Mr. McGinn's statements," McCoy said.

"And what do you say that he said about that blood in the car?" Sudderth asked.

"It came from catfish blood," McCoy replied.

McGinn shook his head as he jotted notes on his pad.

I never told the cops that this was fish blood. Now he is lying about things he said when all this began. To be such a big investigator, he sure doesn't know much.

McGinn's attention returned to his attorney and the investigator.

"And you thought that was sufficient to charge him with capital murder?" Sudderth asked.

"I didn't charge him," McCoy said.

"Well, on Sunday afternoon, the twenty-third of May, you certainly weren't qualified to analyze those stains, were you?" Sudderth inquired.

"Not professionally, no, sir," McCoy admitted.

When Sudderth stated that investigators didn't know if it was human blood or animal blood, McCoy said the blood appeared to have human hair in it. But Sudderth countered that allegation with the fact that the Ford had been the McGinns' family car and it would be natural for hair to have been found in the automobile, even his own hair and that of his stepdaughter.

Verilyn Harbin and McGinn family friends nodded in agreement. Stephanie was known to brush her hair a lot, and of course there would be hair in the car she had often ridden in.

"Now, Mr. McCoy," Sudderth said, "do you know anything about the DPS or the sheriff's office in Brownwood receiving an anonymous tip on Tuesday that a body was in a culvert on that Farm-to-Market Road between one eighty-three and Blanket?"

"No," McCoy stated flatly.

"Have you heard anything about Mr. Capuchino saying that he was driving down that Farm to market Road and saw that body in his rearview mirror?"

"No, sir."

"You will admit that that's a physical impossibility, wouldn't you?" Sudderth asked.

"It would be, yes," McCoy agreed.

Sudderth suggested that the motive for covering up any anonymous tip would be that Ricky McGinn had been in the Brown County Jail since Sunday, charged with a capital murder without any evidence.

"So he couldn't have put the body under the culvert, could he?" Sudderth asked.

"I believe the body was . . . ," McCoy began.

"You think the body was put there on Saturday night or Sunday morning?" Sudderth questioned.

"It's just my best guess, yes, sir," McCoy stated.

Sudderth began firing questions at McCoy in rapid-fire succession. "You guessed you had some weapons and you didn't have them, did you? You guessed that he had buried a body up at Okra, but it didn't happen, didn't you? You guessed you found some weapons up at Okra, but you didn't? You guessed you found a beer can he had thrown down out there, but it didn't happen, did it? You guessed that you found a bloody sheet evidencing the scene of the crime, didn't you? And immediately after Ricky McGinn reported this young lady missing, you guessed that he was up to some kind of mischief, didn't you? You guessed that he did it and charged him with capital murder, didn't you?"

With each question McCoy attempted to explain the department's actions, but Sudderth continued to hammer away at him on what he believed to be the investigators' preconceived speculation of McGinn's guilt.

"Mr. McCoy, this pickup where this hatchet was found that you now say was the weapon, it had been searched three times before it was found, hadn't it?" Sudderth questioned.

"I don't believe so, because I think they would have found it if it had been there. If you looked good, you could have found it," McCoy responded.

"You would have to do two things," Sudderth said. "You would have to look good and, second, it would have to be there, wouldn't it?"

"Yes," McCoy said.

The defense counsel then went into a series of questions about where the pickup had been during the three days

McGinn had been in custody and why it hadn't been searched or impounded, as the Ford had been. Sudderth again asked why, against normal investigative procedures, McGinn had been arrested before the weapon had been located in the truck.

"The bottom line is that you and the rest of the officers that were investigating this murder were under heavy pressure to charge somebody with murder because of the unsolved murders involving young women in this county, isn't that right, Mr. McCoy?"

"I don't believe that's true," McCoy said calmly.

"Did you observe the blood on the victim there in the culvert?" Sudderth asked.

"Yes, the blood was dried," McCoy said.

Sudderth ended his questioning of Deputy McCoy by asking if he had talked to a number of persons during the course of his investigation, including the reported blondish redheaded man who was seen traveling up and down the road, Stephanie's thirteen-year-old boyfriend, the occupants of a mobile home near the culvert, and a lengthy list of friends who had been involved in searching for Stephanie. To the mention of each name, McCoy admitted he had not questioned them in relationship to the Flanary murder.

Sudderth, having made his point that the investigation of Stephanie Flanary's murder was done less than thoroughly and that Ricky McGinn had been charged with murder prematurely, passed the witness.

Lee Haney had no further question of the deputy but reserved the right to recall him at a later time. The prosecutor called Dr. Joseph Guileyardo, Deputy Chief Medical Examiner in Dallas County.

Jurors who had been uncomfortable when the crime scene video was shown would certainly be sickened by the doctor's upcoming explanation of the young girl's horrifying death.

ELEVEN

Dr. Joseph Guileyardo's professional demeanor, dress, and speech were a distinct divergence from the "good old county boy" manner of Mike McCoy, as was his educational background.

"What's your background and training?" Lee Haney asked the Dallas County Medical Examiner.

"I graduated from medical school at the Louisiana State University School of Medicine, I completed my training programs in pathology at Charity Hospital in New Orleans and also at Southwest Medical School in Dallas. I'm licensed to practice medicine and surgery in Mississippi, Louisiana, and Texas. I'm certified by the American Board of Anatomic, Clinical and Forensic Pathology. And I'm currently on the faculty of the Department of Pathology at Southwest Medical School," Dr. Guileyardo answered.

Once Haney had established that the doctor had performed thousands of autopsies in the course of his career, Haney turned his attention to the examination of Stephanie Flanary.

Explaining the usual procedure in his work, Dr. Guileyardo stated that his office normally received a call when the body of a person who was killed would be coming into his office. He would take investigative information from various sources; then, when the corpse had been accepted at the institute, it would be given a case number and the body would be tagged. No other corpse would have an identical number; then a list of articles that were present with the body would be inventoried. Dr. Guileyardo stated that photographs were taken at that time.

He told the court these were the identical procedures followed when Stephanie Flanary's body was received at Southwest Institute of Forensic Science.

"Tell the jury what was the first thing you observed," Haney instructed.

"She had on some clothing that was not in the usual position," the doctor answered.

Dr. Guileyardo then described how he had looked for evidence of any hairs or fibers that might be present on the body that could link the crime with a particular person.

"Was there any indication of the length of time that the body had been dead?" Haney asked.

"We can give an estimation of how long a person has been dead, not like you see on television down to the minute or second of how long a person has been dead; that's not possible," the doctor said, his mouth curving at the corners slightly. "But there are ways to estimate how long a person has been dead. A person develops rigidity, or rigor mortis, after they die as one indication. A person also develops a purple discoloration in lower parts of their body. Other changes take place. So in general we can give a rough estimation of how long a person has been dead from an examination of the body."

"Your examination of Stephanie Flanary took place on May 26, 1993. Were you able to estimate the length of time her body had been dead?" Haney asked.

"The length of time after death is somewhere around two or three days, as an approximation," the doctor replied.

"Based on what?" Haney asked.

"On the fact that there was no rigidity remaining in the body, that there was a large amount of insect activity present on the body, that the body was decomposing and had begun to undergo the changes that we see in decomposition, and that there was some slipping of the skin and some green discoloration of the body. It's my opinion that the condition of this body was consistent with about two or three days," the doctor explained.

Janet Talley's friends and family were glad she had been sequestered in the district attorney's office and unable to hear the vivid description of her daughter's condition. They understood more fully why authorities had denied Janet access to Stephanie's body, sparing her the grief of what must have been an incredibly morbid sight.

As Dr. Guileyardo's grim testimony continued, he explained how cotton swabs had been placed in the child's mouth, vagina, and rectal area. The swabs were left there for a period of time and then glass slides were made from the swabs so that crime lab analysts could look for the presence of sperm on the slides.

"And in gathering the evidence for the sexual-assault kit in this case, did you recover anything from the victim's vagina?" Haney prompted.

"Yes. When we removed the cotton swabs from the vagina, there was a hair that was stuck to one of the cotton swabs," Dr. Guileyardo said.

Murmurs could be heard throughout the courtroom. Stephanie Flanary had been raped.

Ben Sudderth picked up a piece of paper, glancing at the information from the Texas Department of Public Safety Crime Laboratory Services in Austin, dated seven days earlier.

The report was an analysis of hair submitted for comparison. The results of the analysis indicated that hair recovered from the victim's vagina exhibited different microscopic characteristics than the pubic hair from Steve Sirois, Stanley Sirois, and Joe Bob Talley. Sudderth laid the report down and redirected his attention to the testimony.

"She had several large gashes, or lacerations, at the top

of her head, approximately four separate defects that extended down through the scalp. The scalp was torn open, the bones under those defects were completely shattered and portions of those bones had been knocked away from the skull and were absent from the skull," the medical examiner testified. "It was difficult to evaluate the brain itself because it had undergone decomposition with the rest of the body and had become almost a liquid consistency. But the most severe injuries that she had consisted of about a four-by-four-inch area of defects at the top of her head that were consistent with being struck with some type of heavy object, probably something with some kind of edge to it, because some of these gashes had fairly sharp edges.

"In addition to this massive injury at the top of the head, she had two additional impact sites on the right upper part of her head where the skin was also torn open. So those were the main head injuries.

"She had some tearing of the skin at places where the bones were fractured, and that was probably because as the bones fractured on the inside, they jutted or poked through the skin from the inside. Almost the entire top of her skull was shattered into fragments. And even at the base of the skull, the very heavy part at the bottom, that was also shattered and fractured," Dr. Guileyardo said.

The other significant injury the doctor mentioned in his testimony was a scrape across the back of her right index finger, which Dr. Guileyardo described as a defensive-type wound. He stated that they often occur when a victim tries to ward off, or block, a blow. In addition, there were yellow-colored scrape marks across her back. The color of the wounds indicated they had been made after death since pumping blood through her system would have made the marks pink or red in color. The marks could have been made when someone dragged her body after her death.

In Dr. Guileyardo's final opinion, Stephanie Flanary had

died of multiple head injuries caused by some type of heavy instrument.

Spectators shifted uneasily as Haney raised a hatchet for the jury and the doctor to see.

"Are the injuries that you have described consistent with being caused by a hatchet such as this?" Haney asked.

"Yes."

Lastly, Haney had the medical examiner explain the chain of custody of evidence collected during autopsy; then he turned the witness over to Ben Sudderth for cross-examination.

Sudderth immediately began an attack of the estimated time of death as previously stated by Dr. Guileyardo, citing another physician from the institute who had testified in a pretrial hearing that they didn't estimate times of death.

Dr. Guileyardo responded by saying, "Probably what they meant is that they can't specify an exact time of death."

But Sudderth was not content.

"What time of the day did you conduct your autopsy on the twenty-sixth?" Sudderth asked.

"I began at seven A.M.."

"So, if we back up the time two days, that would be the twenty-fourth at seven A.M., wouldn't it?" Sudderth inquired.

"Yes."

"And then three days would be seven A.M. on Sunday, the twenty-third, would it not?"

"I believe so, yes."

Sudderth knew that his client had been in the custody of Brown County sheriff's deputies since approximately noon on Sunday, May 23. In the defense attorney's mind, Ricky McGinn couldn't have possibly had time to place the body of his stepdaughter in the culvert.

Sudderth changed gears and questioned the doctor concerning the amount of blood normally lost during a head

injury, comparing it to the amount of blood found at what
authorities believed to be the crime scene, which was
McGinn's car. But the doctor refused to give a definitive
answer, saying the amounts varied from crime scene to
crime scene depending on a variety of variables. As hard
as Sudderth pressed, the doctor's answers remained vague,
until the defense counsel moved on to the blood alcohol
levels found in the body.

Dr. Guileyardo explained the fluid tested for alcohol levels in the body was taken from the liquid of the eyes,
since it was less likely to be contaminated by other body
fluids. When asked to explain how much alcohol Stephanie
would have had to consume to have a blood alcohol level
of .03, as indicated in the autopsy report, the doctor explained, "Well, in this case, with the body decomposed,
alcohol is produced by decomposition. So this could have
come from decomposition alone up to .03. It's been recorded much higher than this just due to decomposition.
So I don't know if this came from drinking a certain
amount of alcohol or simply because she was decomposing."

"So you're not suggesting to the jury then that she had
consumed any alcohol at all?" Sudderth asked.

"Not necessarily," the doctor responded.

At the conclusion of day one of the trial, Ricky
McGinn's notes reflected his thoughts on the proceedings.
He wrote on his tablet under his previous notes:

I believe this guy (Dr. Guileyardo) is telling just
what the DA has instructed. Doesn't answer questions
as good for Ben as he did for DA.

I hope this jury keeps an open mind. It appears to
me that the D.A. has done convinced them with just
the opening statement.

TWELVE

Courtroom observers who had been present the first day of the McGinn murder trial watched closely as the accused entered the courtroom the following morning. The previous day the defense had asked Trooper Capuchino if he thought a person with limited use of his legs and back could carry a ninety-pound body down the rugged incline where Stephanie Flanary's body had been discovered in the culvert.

Now, as the trial began again and McGinn was escorted into the courtroom, the audience studied McGinn as he listed sharply to the right, his left hip rising dramatically as he made his way to the defense table. It was obvious the defendant was impaired, but to what degree had yet to be established.

Lee Haney had suspended Deputy Mike McCoy's questioning the first day in order to get the medical examiner on the stand and back to work. On the second day of the trial, McCoy entered the courtroom and made his way back to the familiar witness-box.

The sheriff's deputy explained the taking of samples from McGinn for the first rape kit at the Brownwood Regional Hospital emergency room.

"And would you tell the jury what a rape kit or sexual-assault kit is," Haney instructed.

"It's a standard kit that is used all over the state of Texas. It's a box about this big," McCoy answered as he held his hands apart to simulate the size. "And it has different bags and glass vials and stuff in it that the technicians take the samples and put them in, and then seal the box."

"And then, after they seal that box, do they put their initials or signature or something on the container?" Haney asked.

"Yes, they do," McCoy responded.

As before, McCoy explained to the jury that he was part of a team that had gone to the former McGinn farmhouse in Okra to search for evidence, but that items seized at that location didn't pertain to the Flanary murder. McCoy indicated the investigative team continued to pursue any lead in an effort to locate evidence. Haney asked if that was why investigators had decided to drain the pond on the McGinn property.

"We got the aid of the Water Board, and they brought their big pumps out and was pumping out the tank. We were still looking for Stephanie, and we were still looking for anything that would be evidence in the case of her missing," McCoy said.

On the second page of his tablet McGinn wrote:

DAY #2 Trial 5–18–95
1—Recall Mike McCoy—They pumped the tank looking for a weapon before they found a body.

McGinn's focus returned to the witness.

Once the deputy had completed his brief rundown of the remainder of his part in the investigation, he was passed to the defense for cross-examination.

Sudderth wanted the deputy to clarify why his department sent evidence to the Southwest Institute of Forensic Science rather than the Bexar County lab in San Antonio. He cited the Flores case, another case based on DNA findings, that had been sent to the county to the south. McCoy admitted that he was unaware of the reason for the choice of Southwest's lab over the Bexar County lab.

"Isn't it a fact that the Bexar County lab is in total disgrace in law enforcement in the Southwest, and that is the reason you changed and went to Southwest in Dallas?" Sudderth asked, more or less answering his own earlier inquiry.

"I don't have any information on that," McCoy said.

Sudderth's questioning was puzzling. It was as if he were focusing on the Flores defense, which he also spearheaded rather than the McGinn case.

"You're aware that an examiner in the Bexar County lab is under indictment in this state and the United States today for filing false reports?" Sudderth continued.

Haney objected to the line of questioning, and once the judge had ruled, Sudderth changed his line of scrutiny.

McCoy admitted that McGinn had been taken to the hospital at about 6:00 P.M., and had not been charged with the murder of Stephanie until sometime between 8:00 and 9:00 P.M., prior to authorities receiving the test results performed on the rape kit. As in the previous day's testimony, Sudderth wanted to know what evidence investigators had to charge his client with murder so prematurely.

"All I know is the inconsistent stories with the fish blood and the blood that we believed to be in the car is about all I know," McCoy said.

Angrily McGinn scribbled across his pad:

The cops have made up a story about fish blood. I never told this guy it was fish blood in the car. I didn't see any blood in the car. This man is lying.

"How could the fish blood be determined inconsistent? You hadn't even conducted any test on it, had you?" Sudderth questioned.

McCoy fumbled momentarily before he stated that

McGinn's story couldn't be proved, but Sudderth countered with the fact that it also couldn't be disproved, reminding the deputy that McGinn had offered the explanation that cats most likely had carried off the evidence.

"Because you couldn't chase down the cats and find the fish heads, that was inconsistent, and you charged him with murder, is that correct?" Sudderth said, his voice rising as he challenged the witness.

McCoy explained that they were unable to find any heads, blood, guts, or any evidence that fish had been cleaned at the location McGinn had shown them. McCoy stated that they would have expected to find some remnants of the fish in the hay or surrounding area, but nothing was discovered.

McGinn wrote:

> He keeps changing his story now. It makes me wonder who he talked with after trial yesterday. Now McCoy can't look me in the eye. How could he keep from seeing cats?

"Do you know that out in the country, we're being completely eat up with these cats? They're destroying the quail population. Are you aware of that?" Sudderth fired.

"No, I'm not aware of that," McCoy said.

On redirect McCoy also stated that the car didn't smell of fish, another contributing factor in their belief that the defendant's story was false. On recross Sudderth asked how McGinn could have repeatedly struck the victim in the head with a hatchet, with blood found in several locations in the interior of the car, and not have blood on himself or his clothes.

"I don't have any idea," McCoy replied. "You know, I suppose he could have went and cleaned up."

The defense had almost finished their questioning. Then Sudderth asked, "The doctor that you called yesterday placed the time of death of this young lady somewhere between seven o'clock Sunday morning and seven o'clock, two days later. If his testimony is correct, the crime hadn't even been committed during Saturday night when he was looking for her. Are you aware of that?"

"No, sir, I'm not," McCoy said simply.

But Haney retorted on redirect, "If the pathologist's testimony was that his estimate was that the body he performed an autopsy on had been dead for two to three days, and that the other testimony in the case was that the ambulance delivered the body to the hospital the previous afternoon, it was refrigerated there, and the doctor's testimony was that the refrigeration slows that rate of deterioration, would it not then appear that the time of death could have been from any time Saturday evening up until about the time the body was found, based on his testimony?"

"Yes," McCoy said simply.

As McCoy was excused, McGinn's eyes followed him across the courtroom. McCoy avoided his stares.

The name of Tina Burkhart rang out as the state's next witness. Burkhart, as part of the Search One Rescue, informed jurors of the team's function and how they operated.

"We have different specialties within our search dogs," Burkhart responded to a question from District Attorney Haney. "We have trailing, to find missing people who have walked away and leave a trail. We have air-scenting specialties and also cadaver specialties. My dog has been trained for all three."

When asked if her dog had alerted on Mr. McGinn, the trainer looked toward the jury before answering, "No."

Burkhart told jurors she had been given an article of clothing belonging to the missing girl, which allowed her dog to sniff for a scent. She had then started the search command about ten feet from the car. As is usual, the dog went to the closest object, and her dog had gone straight to the Ford Escort. Burkhart said that before the animal got to the rear of the vehicle, the dog was jumping up and "indicating" on the hatchback.

"She jumps up and does her dig alert," Burkhart said, explaining what "indication" and "alerting" meant.

The "dig alert" indicated a cadaver, or dead body, Burkhart explained as she looked again at the jury. She told them that she informed her flanker of the alert, who, in turn, notified investigators. The dog continued to work but failed to alert at the house and displayed only mild interest at the pond.

When Sudderth began his cross-examination he asked, "Tell me, as a professional dog trainer, why those dogs didn't alert on that pickup?"

"If we assume the pickup was checked, the dog would have alerted," Burkhart said, knowing what was believed to be the murder weapon had been found under the truck's front seat. She added that she believed the pickup had not been searched by the canine units.

After several questions Sudderth remarked, "I noticed when the district attorney was questioning you that you look at the district attorney and then you turn to the jury when you give your answer. Have you had training in how to testify and impress juries?"

"No, I've never done this before," Burkhart said.

"Have you been told to look at the district attorney when he asks the question and then to turn and look at the jury when you answer?" Sudderth asked accusingly.

"No."

"You haven't been told that?" Sudderth persisted.

"No. I watched O.J.," Burkhart replied with a nervous laugh.

Most of the spectators and jurors joined in the snickers, giving a much needed lightness to the intensely morbid mood of the courtroom.

Sell your books at
sellbackyourBook.com!
Go to sellbackyourBook.com
and get an instant price
quote. We even pay the
shipping - see what your old
books are worth today!

Inspected By: Lolymar_Castro

00061658860

0006165 **8860** S

"Do you find this proceeding funny this morning?" Sudderth asked critically.

"No, sir, I'm nervous. I'm just trying to relax. I'm sorry," Burkhart replied, dropping her chin slightly as if embarrassed.

"Do you understand a man is on trial for his life?" Sudderth admonished.

"I do," Burkhart said softly.

"Do you find that somehow hilarious?"

"No."

"Or taken lightly?" Sudderth continued to drill.

"Of course not," Burkhart said in her own defense.

Sudderth, having successfully humiliated the witness, established that at least one abandoned building east of Highway one eighty-three had been searched during the time the trained dogs were assisting in the effort. Burkhart was excused.

During the exchange of witnesses, McGinn jotted on his lined pad:

> She was told to check the car and house and perimeter. This woman is lying out her teeth. This is the woman who jerked her dog to get the dog to jump on the car. The pickup was searched by dogs and people. Why is this woman lying about what was searched? She's saying no dogs searched by and around the Dodge pickup. Just a big liar and really no reason why.

Vicki Truman, a second search-dog leader, testified that her dog's nose had gone immediately to the seam of the hatchback. When he hit on the tail end of the car, his nostrils flared, he began sniffing, and his breathing became louder. At that point he had jumped up on the car and wanted to start digging at the car. Truman stated she had pulled the dog back and moved on to a second car on the premises.

Verilyn Harbin's lips were pressed together tightly as she struggled not to speak. Ricky had told her the dogs had made no unusual movements when sniffing around the car. She wondered how the dog handler could possibly say the animal had indicated anything of evidentiary value.

Sudderth tried to cast a shadow of doubt on the effectiveness of the air-scent-trained search dogs by asking if the results would have been the same if the personal item, supposedly belonging to Stephanie, had in fact been worn by Denise Flanary or Janet McGinn.

Ms. Truman simply replied, yes, because it was the scent the dog was asked to find. She had merely taken the word of an unknown family member who had supplied the item that the hair ribbon belonged to the twelve-year-old victim. Unlike the former witness, Ms. Truman remained unflappable in her testimony and she was excused just before a recess for lunch.

Lisa McGinn helped her mother to her feet and assisted her as she left the courthouse. They would be meeting Verilyn for a quick lunch before returning for the afternoon court session. At the same time Joe Bob Talley was with his sister, making certain she exited the court building without incident. The trial was wearing on both mothers. Each wishing she could be inside, listening to the testimony; each supporting her child through an ordeal that would forever bind them together.

Jurors scattered to various restaurants around town, not worrying about returning early to secure a parking space near the courthouse. Judge Cadenhead had made certain that a designated parking area had been roped off for their convenience.

Ricky McGinn was whisked back to the Brown County Jail, where he ate lunch and mentally prepared for the afternoon session, which began with Glen Smith, a nineteen-year veteran of law enforcement.

The chief deputy of the Brown County Sheriff's Office reiterated what McCoy had said concerning the condition of the interior of the Escort, including the trash found, along with what he also believed to be blood and brain matter.

McGinn's head dropped as he rested his arm on the defense table to write:

> All these pictures that they have of supposedly blood were taken after the car was taken to town. He never told me blood was anywhere except right at the back of the car.

Smith also remarked on the story McGinn had told them about catching, cleaning, and cooking fish from the tank.

"Are you yourself a fisherman?" Haney asked.

"I fish occasionally, over the last thirty years," Smith said.

"Have you ever had occasion to go fishing and throw fish into the back of an automobile?" Haney asked.

"Never."

"Have you ever seen or heard of anyone doing that?"

"No."

"Have you yourself ever cooked and eaten pollywog catfish?"

"No, sir."

McGinn's pencil flew across the page:

> I told him Steph would throw the fish, not me. I said I cleaned the fish. I never told him the fish wouldn't be there. I also showed him the grill where the fish were cooked. All I told him was that the car might smell like fish. I never said there was fish

blood in the car. He has never been a country boy. The D.A. always wants to bring up fish blood. I guess this is all he's got.

McGinn's writing stopped as he listened to Haney and Smith.

"Why did you ask him to go to the sheriff's department?" Haney asked.

Smith told the court that, because there were numerous officers, volunteers, and family members at the house, he had decided to take McGinn to an office setting where he could be questioned further and "make sure that we had the correct details on what occurred regarding her disappearance."

McGinn quickly wrote another line on his pad: "He is now telling another lie about why he asked me to come to town."

Judge Cadenhead requested both attorneys to approach the bench.

"I will ask both of you to make your questions as short and to the point on all of your witnesses. I mean, I'll try to play fair, but, Ben, you know, if he has got a legitimate objection and you're leading the witness, we have to sustain it. At the same time, if he does, Mr. Haney, I'm going to sustain it. Y'all shorten the questioning," Cadenhead said.

Haney, attempting to comply with the court's request, asked Smith to tell the jury the process they went through in obtaining samples for the rape kit.

"After we got to the sheriff's office, I continued to interview Ricky, and during that interview I asked him if he would submit to an examination to take samples for a rape kit. And of course, at that time, before he submitted to a written permission, his rights were read to him before he signed the consent to search his body," Smith replied.

Again McGinn jotted down his thoughts: "I don't remember any rights being read to me before consenting to have the rape kit on me."

Smith explained that after they had questioned McGinn, they took their assumptions to the district attorney, requesting a probable-cause warrant, which consisted of facts and circumstances sufficient to believe that a crime had been committed.

Smith cited what appeared to be tissue, blood spatters, and a glob of blond-looking hair in McGinn's vehicle. He also mentioned McGinn's tennis shoes and blue jeans, which they believed to show signs of blood spatters, as probable cause to request the warrant. Smith added that they believed that there had been foul play and that McGinn was the last known person to be with the missing girl.

McGinn had been staring at the chief deputy throughout his testimony; then he wrote:

> All the blood was discovered after the car got to town. This man can't look me in the eye either. I keep trying to make eye contact with him but he won't. He can lie.

When asked why they had requested a warrant to arrest someone in a murder case when they hadn't recovered a body, Smith replied, "We were fearful that the body would not ever be found if he hadn't been arrested at that time."

On cross-examination Ben Sudderth asked, "Did Ricky McGinn ask you several times to take him back to his house when he was down there on Sunday afternoon talking to you?"

"No, sir, he didn't," Smith said.

"Did you promise that after he went to the hospital, you thought, you would take him back to his house?" Sudderth asked, implying that his client had been held against his will.

"No, I don't think it was ever mentioned," Smith said.

"Now he says I never asked to go back to the house. Can remember what I didn't say but can't remember the important things," McGinn wrote.

Sudderth's questioning moved to the body found in the culvert, suggesting that the position of the body would indicate someone up in the culvert pulling from one end while someone else was pushing from the other. Smith agreed that the scenario was possible but denied that only a person with a great deal of strength, with full use of his back and legs, could possibly have placed the body in the tin horn.

Sudderth concluded his cross-examination by asking Smith if McGinn had demanded an attorney, even though he had been questioned on and off for almost twelve hours. Smith agreed that McGinn had not asked for an attorney and that he had been totally cooperative in their investigative efforts.

"Knowing that anything he said might and would be used against him, he went right ahead and talked to you, didn't he?" Sudderth asked.

"He did," Smith admitted.

Sudderth covered the time table of events, estimating that his client had been up nearly thirty-six hours when he was being questioned at the Brown County Sheriff's Office. He made a point of the fact that, from the time he first reported his stepdaughter missing until he was officially charged with murder late on Sunday evening, McGinn had been without benefit of sleep or legal counsel.

By the time Judge Cadenhead announced court in recess for the day, Chief Deputy Glen Smith of the Brown County Sheriff's Office had spent three grueling hours on the stand. Prompted by the prosecution and hammered by the defense, Smith had endured the day in court. Only time would tell if the chief investigator on the case would fare as well the following day.

THIRTEEN

Lee Haney and Ben Sudderth stood at the front of the Brown County courtroom sifting through evidence. Evidence essential in convincing the jury of the state's facts. Sudderth quickly made notes on a pad, preparing for examinations of witnesses yet to be called.

A cardboard box from the Austin Department of Public Safety laboratory, shipped by Airborne Express, remained sealed until Sudderth opened it in court.

"I'm the one that opened those packages," Sudderth admitted when the judge asked.

"Very artfully, I might say," the judge commented.

"Yes, sir, had a good knife, furnished by Mr. Haney, an heirloom," Sudderth remarked.

The comments brought smiles and a few chuckles from the people near the front of the courtroom.

Once the evidence had been logged in and all jurors and alternates were present and accounted for, District Attorney Haney began calling witnesses to establish the chain of custody of the previously tagged exhibits. Chain of custody was essential in establishing the integrity of the evidence.

Pat Thiemann of SWIFS indicated that she had accepted from Dr. Guileyardo forensic items, including the pubic hair found inside the victim, tagged them, and eventually turned them over to Pat Mahoney, a Brown County constable, on May 27, 1993.

Pat Mahoney testified that he had received the evidence indicated by Ms. Thiemann in a sealed box, which he in turn released to Investigator David Mercer.

The state's next witness was Lonnie McCarty, a licensed vocational nurse at Brownwood Regional Hospital. McCarty stated that he had used a standard commercially developed rape kit when taking nail scrapings, facial and pubic hair, as well as semen samples from Ricky McGinn on May 23, 1993. He indicated that, if blood had been drawn, it would have been done by a lab technician, not himself. McCarty stated he had placed the samples in the evidentiary kit, sealed it, and turned it over to Mike McCoy, who had been in attendance while the procedure was being performed.

For the first time in the day's proceedings, Ben Sudderth rose to ask questions of a state's witness. Dressed in a dark suit with striped tie, Sudderth approached the witness.

"You refer to Exhibit Number ninety-six as a rape kit. Of course, that's just a convenient name that has been attached to that particular item, isn't it?" Sudderth asked.

"Yes, sir, that's correct," McCarty said.

"And that doesn't mean that there was a rape or there wasn't a rape; but, to determine or to assist in helping to determine, these items are gathered by you and placed in a box. We could just as easily refer to them as a box with a hair and samples in it, couldn't we, and fingernail scrapings?" Sudderth asked, ignoring the judge's earlier instruction to keep his questions short.

"Yes, sir," McCarty said.

As McCarty was excused and left the courtroom and as James Florey entered, McGinn wrote in his self-styled journal:

> Pam Thiemann—Evidence reporter and storer. Released some evidence to Pat Mahoney identifying some of the State's evidence from the lab. Why was

she really here? Unless it was just to show some of
the stuff the State has for evidence. All she really
done was to show what she marked.

Lonny (*sic*) McCarty—Works for hospital to take
rape kits. I don't think he could have identified me
in a crowd. The woman was taking blood while he
was in the room.

Florey, a registered nurse in the emergency room at
Brownwood Regional Hospital, told jurors that he had collected hair samples from Steve and Stanley Sirois, as well
as Joe Bob Talley; he had then handed the unsealed enve-
lopes over to David Mercer to be sealed.

Before Sudderth began his cross-examination, he approached the bench.

"If we are going to take a recess, I suggest we do it
now. I want to turn that blackboard around so I can get
ready to use it, and we will also go through the file and
find some documents. It will take me three to five minutes," Sudderth informed the judge.

Judge Cadenhead announced a ten-minute recess, giving
Sudderth ample time to prepare for his cross-examination
of Florey.

At least one of the female jurors was thankful for the
break. The testimony concerning rape kits was distressful.
Before moving to Brownwood, she had been on the board
of an abused women's shelter. She had heard references to
rape kits and understood the physical and emotional trauma
those women had felt.

During the recess McGinn wrote:

James Florey—Nurse from hospital who took the
rape articles from Steve Sirois, hair from Stanley Sirois
and gave to Mercer unsealed. Hair from Joe Talley given
to Mercer unsealed. Why didn't he take a full rape kit
from Stanley and Joe Bob? Why just hair?

Sudderth indicated to Florey that he had only a few questions and began by asking what date he took the hair sample from Steve Sirois.

"On Steve Sirois, the date was April 12, 1994," Florey said.

Sudderth wrote the date on the blackboard.

"What about the other two?" Sudderth asked.

"The other two were both done April 28, 1994," Florey answered.

Sudderth wrote that date under the previous entry on the board and asked Florey if he knew why, almost a year after Ricky McGinn had been indicted and charged with murder, that he had been requested to gather the samples from the Siroises and Talley. Florey indicated that he hadn't been told the purpose; he only complied with the request.

As Florey exited the witness-box, a man of medium height, with short brown hair, entered from the rear of the courtroom. McGinn's eyes locked on the man, a hint of contempt on his face. McGinn's glare followed the man until he was seated in the witness chair.

Valton Posey had been with the Brown County Sheriff's Office his entire fifteen-year law enforcement career. Posey had been the deputy who found what was believed to be the murder weapon under the front seat of McGinn's truck.

After identifying photos of the interior of the Ford Escort, indicating what had been believed to be blood stains throughout the back portion of the car, Posey told the jury that on the day after the reported disappearance of Stephanie Flanary, he had gone to the property to aid in the search.

The soft-spoken deputy said, "I went and helped search a trash pile in a pasture. I believe there was a helicopter out there that day, that they had gotten some kind of a heat reading on that pile. We went to that pile to see if there was anything there." Posey indicated nothing had been found, however.

Posey had also been part of the search team that had explored the farmhouse in Okra and the scene where the girl's body had been found. He had been responsible for videotaping each area.

Lee Haney asked what other duties Posey had performed during the investigation, leading the deputy to the point of locating the ax.

"On Wednesday Texas Ranger Bob Grubbs and I went back to the McGinn residence. Pumps were still pumping the tank. We went to see if the tank had been dry, so we could search the tank for any possible evidence," Posey said.

"Were you able to obtain any evidence from the tank?" Haney asked.

"No, sir."

"What else did you do there at the scene?" Haney inquired.

"We searched the outside of the residence around the property. I found an ax that had blood and hair on it, and it was under the seat of an old Dodge pickup behind the house," Posey explained.

McGinn's eyes flashed with anger. He had told his mother that Posey had lied about finding the ax. She had seen the videotape showing the deputy reaching up under the seat and producing the weapon. Posey had commented to others that the ax had been far up under the seat, between the underside of the cushion and the top of a speaker box. To Francis and others who had seen the tape, it looked like Posey had had no difficulty in producing the weapon. Francis believed Posey had reenacted the event for the video camera.

From a brown paper bag, Haney produced the implement for the jury's inspection. He held the menacing object up so everyone could see. The ax handle appeared to have been broken off or cut off to approximately ten to twelve inches and tape had been wound around it.

Some in the audience shifted uneasily in their seats.

From the medical examiner's testimony, they knew that the girl had been struck repeatedly, and now they were looking at what might prove to be the murder weapon. They could only imagine the fear, the pain, Stephanie must have felt at the moment of impact.

"Did you observe anything else relevant to the investigation that day?" Haney asked.

"Yes, sir. Under the carport we found a spare tire, jack, tire tools, other items that appeared to have been taken out of his car," Posey said.

As the courtroom television was being moved so that the jury could have a full view of the screen, Sudderth and McGinn made their way to an area of the courtroom that would allow them to view the video as well. The state agreed to mute the sound in case there were any inadvertent comments made during the taping of the crime scene.

Haney had established through Posey's testimony that Posey alone, and to his knowledge, no one else, had searched the Dodge pickup prior to his discovery of the ax. He indicated that because they didn't know initially the cause of death, they didn't know what type of weapon they were looking for. But by Wednesday, three days after the girl's disappearance, Posey had seen the massive head wound and had a better idea of the kind of instrument used to murder the victim.

Haney passed the witness.

Ricky McGinn wrote furiously on his notepad:

Valton Posey—This is the man who found the ax under the seat of the old Dodge pickup. After the body had been found. The day after.

The manner of Sudderth's cross-examination was fierce from the beginning. He fired question after question in rapid succession regarding the fact that no one had seen McGinn driving the Ford Escort or the Dodge van after noon on Saturday, the day McGinn reported Stephanie missing. He emphasized the fact that dozens of people were on hand from about 11:00 o'clock on the evening of May 22 until McGinn's arrest on May 23.

"There is one thing that you know would be a physical impossibility, and that is for Ricky McGinn to place the body of Stephanie Flanary in that culvert, isn't that correct?" Sudderth asked, having established that McGinn was at the Brown County Sheriff's Office during that time period.

"That's right," Posey responded.

Sudderth drilled Posey on the position of the body when found in the culvert, arms outstretched and knees drawn up. He asked the deputy if it would make sense that one person was pulling the body and one pushing for the corpse to have been positioned in that manner. Posey agreed that it was a possibility.

When Sudderth asked if he inquired as to how McGinn had injured his leg and back, Posey responded by stating that it wasn't his place at the time.

"Well, Mr. Posey, I am having a hard time finding anybody with the Brown County Sheriff's Office that felt like they had a place in this investigation. Tell us what was going on."

"I've told you what mine was," Posey said.

"You said earlier that when you first went to work for the sheriff's office you just did everything. Now you apparently don't do anything. Is that correct?" Sudderth said sarcastically.

"No, sir, not at all," Posey said.

Sudderth asked Posey if he had investigated and learned that the only way for McGinn to haul water to the residence, since it had no running water at the time, was in thirty-gallon containers in the back of the Ford hatchback. When Posey answered no, Sudderth asked if that would not have been significant. Posey admitted it could have been.

McGinn sighed, and again wondered why investigators hadn't asked Janet or anyone in his family why the back end of the hatchback had been emptied. Everyone knew that they were required to haul water from town. Janet and the girls commonly took baths at the Talleys' house, while he most often sponged or bathed in the stock tank.

The defendant's attention returned to his attorney and Valton Posey.

The deputy established that he had never observed anyone search the pickup, and if they had and hadn't seen the ax under the driver's seat, then that could be significant to the investigation.

"Was the ax handle dusted for prints?" Sudderth asked.

"I kind of doubt it with the kind of tape that was on the handle. It would be very hard for any prints to be found on it," Posey answered.

Sneering, Sudderth asked, "That's no task for an old boy that has been at it fifteen years, is it, Mr. Posey?"

"I didn't fingerprint it at all. It was sent to the lab for examination," Posey said, remaining calm.

Posey then admitted to the jury that he had reached under the seat and taken hold of the handle before he realized what it was, contaminating the weapon with his own prints before bagging it for evidence.

"Now, at the scene, down there at the culvert where the body was found, there were two sets of tire marks. Did you attempt to get any plaster casts of those tire marks?" Sudderth asked.

When Posey responded in the negative, stating that he didn't believe the tracks were good enough to cast, Sudderth reminded him of the previous heavy rain, which normally would produce excellent tire marks. He also reminded the witness that the rain occurred at 4:00 A.M., therefore the tire tracks had more than likely happened after the rain.

Judge Cadenhead decided it was time to take a lunch break and excused the jury until 1:15 P.M.

When the trial reconvened, Sudderth looked at Posey and smiled. "Mr. Posey, you can relax."

The astute defense attorney then asked if Posey had interviewed anyone living near the culvert.

"I don't think I did," Posey said, sounding somewhat confused. "I went to a house or two, I believe, and nobody was home at the time."

"Well, normally if you will just go back, sooner or later you'll find somebody at home, won't you?" Sudderth said with a sly grin.

"That's true. I didn't go back. I'm not sure if other officers did or not," Posey said.

"Didn't talk to people behind the place," McGinn wrote, shaking his head slightly.

As with witnesses before him, Sudderth asked Posey if he had received information about a man with reddish blond hair seen in a van nearby. He also asked about a number of people who had been involved in the search and whether Posey had not felt pressured to charge someone with the crime. To each inquiry Posey responded, "No."

On redirect Lee Haney handed Posey a photo of Stephanie Flanary's body resting in the drainage tube.

"What do you observe between the bottom of the photograph and Stephanie's tennis shoes?" Haney asked.

"Quite a bit of blood, and maybe blood and water, mixed," Posey said.

"Based upon your experience as a criminal investigator, do you have an opinion as to whether that indicates that the body was there before or after the rain that has been referred to?" Haney asked.

"It looks like the body was probably there before the rain," Posey answered.

Posey, later, in response to a recross question from Sudderth, stated that there was no blood found outside the tin horn. His explanation: the heavy rains could have possibly washed it away and still left water mixed with blood standing inside the culvert itself.

It was midafternoon when District Attorney Haney called his final witness of the day.

Investigator David Mercer walked to the stand; his collar-length hair had been trimmed, as well as his dark mustache. He began his testimony with a recap of the events that led him to the McGinn house on Sunday, May 23, and his initial discussions with Ricky McGinn. He described the search that took place for the missing girl and indicated that the helicopters used to aid in the search had flown over the majority of the countryside not immediately adjacent to the McGinn property.

Mercer looked down at his hands as he told them about first one, then another of the SAR dogs "hitting" on the Ford Escort parked behind the McGinn house.

"I opened the left rear door, being the driver's side. The first thing I observed was what appeared to be some kind of flesh lying on the armrest with some blood," Mercer said.

He elaborated on other signs of blood throughout the car and his ultimate decision to seize the vehicle and get it to a lab for further interrogation.

McGinn wrote:

I am the one who told Glen Smith, yes, he could take the vehicle to town. This man can't look me or anyone in the eye. When he is talking he looks down at the floor.

Mercer said he boarded one of the helicopters for an aerial view of the area, instructing the pilot to fly low enough to blow the brush around. They also checked creek beds for any sign of the missing girl.

In reference to questions concerning the location of the tin horn where Stephanie's body was found, Mercer told the court that deputies had blocked the site off with police tape to help insure the integrity of the scene. The inside and the top of the culvert had been dusted for latent fingerprints—prints not visible to the naked eye. He told the court that no prints were found.

Mercer estimated that if the victim's feet had not been drawn up near her body, as they were when she was discovered, more than likely her feet would have been sticking out of the end of the culvert.

Concerning the tire tracks, Mercer testified that they were on the north side of the road, seventy-one feet from where the body had been located on the south side. He indicated that the tracks were not discernible, as they were in thick grass that had more or less been mashed down. The second set of tracks, seventy-seven feet from the body, was not identifiable, either.

"Do you recall any residences in the area that you observed?" Haney asked.

"Not in the immediate area, no. To the east of the location of the body, there is a house at the next county road, a couple of hundred yards to the north. And there was also a residence a couple of hundred yards to the south on the dirt road. There was one at the intersection of the highway. I believe it was a trailer house, but it was on the opposite side of the hill. I believe it was checked, but they didn't know anything," Mercer said.

After identifying a number of pieces of evidence marked for exhibit by the prosecution, Mercer told the jury that on June 3, 1993, an evidentiary search warrant was obtained for blood, hair, and pubic hair from the defendant. He said that Dr. James Piccione had secured the samples from McGinn, sealed them, and handed them to Mercer and Bob Grubbs to be transported to the DPS lab.

As jurors cleared the courtroom for a welcome fifteen-minute bathroom/smoke break, McGinn was escorted to the bathroom himself. He straightened his light blue jacket and blue tie before again taking his place beside his attorney at the defense table. Mercer's testimony frustrated McGinn. He was refuting every issue Sudderth had brought up during other testimony. McGinn believed Mercer had been coached prior to his testimony.

Mercer continued his testimony by telling the court that he had personally observed the taking of a pubic hair from Steve Sirois and had seen the sample sealed into a kit.

Mercer had also observed blood samples taken from Janet McGinn at Brownwood Regional Hospital and had personally delivered the blood to the DPS lab in Austin. In addition, he had traveled to Donaldsonville, Louisiana, to the Ascension Parish Prison on September 7, 1994, where he met with Stephanie's biological father, Steve Flanary. He obtained a blood sample from Flanary.

Finally, Mercer said that he had taken samples from the DPS lab in Austin to Gene Screen in Dallas for DNA testing on behalf of the defense.

Ben Sudderth took on an immediate offensive as he approached on cross-examination.

"Ricky McGinn was charged with murder in this case on May 23, 1993. On September 7, 1994, you got around to getting a blood sample from Stephanie's father, is that correct?"

"That's correct," Mercer said.

Sudderth began to escalate his attack by asking short, pointed questions concerning the lack of investigative time spent in pursuit of Steve Flanary. He asked why Flanary had not been a suspect when it was reported that Stephanie had told a friend that she intended to run away and live with her father. He drummed in the points that Flanary had not been in prison, but rather living in Houston at the time of the murder, and that he could not be located immediately following the death of his daughter.

"You weren't interested in what connection he might have, if any, to the tragedy that fell to Stephanie Flanary, were you?" Sudderth asked accusingly.

"No, sir," Mercer said simply.

"Why did you overlook Steve Flanary?" Sudderth asked.

"For quite a while we had not been able to locate him," Mercer replied.

"Wouldn't that be the best reason why he needed to be located? Here, his daughter goes missing, is killed, and he goes missing. Wouldn't that be the very best reason in the world for finding him and questioning him?" Sudderth asked, his voice increasing in volume with each question.

"Under some conditions, yes," Mercer said.

McGinn picked up his pen and began to write: "They never questioned or suspected anyone in this case but me. They always bring it back to me."

Sudderth was able to establish that the Dodge pickup belonged to Joe Bob Talley, not McGinn, and the Ford Escort was registered to Lisa McGinn, Ricky's sister.

"So we've got two vehicles here that are evidence, neither of which is even owned by Mr. McGinn, don't we?" Sudderth said in a calmer tone.

Mercer agreed.

The deputy then testified under oath that he had seen McGinn move the Ford about one hundred feet from the back of the house and park it beside the road.

Sudderth was irate. He told Mercer that no other person who had testified was able to put McGinn in that car. He then went one step further when he said, "Did you discover that somebody needed to have to put this man in this vehicle that he didn't even own? Did you learn that?"

Mercer denied the charge.

Then Mercer exploded a bombshell. When questioned about the failure to interview residents in the vicinity of where the body was located, Mercer announced that they had indeed been interviewed by a deputy named Scott Martin.

Sudderth was incensed. Scott Martin had been acting as a runner for the jury during the McGinn trial and could not be called as a witness.

"Is there any record, written record, that you won't have to pump up in the sheriff's office that will show that Scott Martin interviewed those people near this culvert?" Sudderth asked with a touch of venom in his voice.

"No, sir," Mercer said.

Sudderth went point by point down his list of inconsistencies regarding the McGinn case. Mercer remained consistent in his answers, maintaining his belief that Ricky McGinn was the killer.

On redirect Haney established that Steve Flanary had not been seen or heard of in the area for some time and that he had not visited with his children in more than two years. As he continued his redirect, he attempted to clarify a number of issues brought up by the defense, including why everything investigators did on the case was not written in a file and why Mercer indicated to the Texas Rangers that foul play had occurred the day after Stephanie was reported missing. As Mercer continued to answer questions, McGinn wrote:

The D.A. is trying to shut witness off short. The only way the D.A. can come up with good questions is after Ben Sudderth questions the witness. My life is at stake and this detective doesn't want to use too much paper. The D.A. asked the same questions as my lawyer does and mind you, these are his witnesses. They give different answers to the questions. There was foul play after this guy made it that way.

David Mercer was excused and the jury retired for the night. It had been a difficult day for McGinn, emotionally draining, but the worst was yet to come.

FOURTEEN

On day four of the McGinn trial, in anticipation of presenting his case, Ben Sudderth called sixteen people to be sworn in as defense witnesses. Each raised a hand and swore to tell the truth, the whole truth.

Twelve witnesses had failed to show and Sudderth informed the court that he intended to call for *capias pro fines,* or arrest papers, to force them to appear. He then began to take the home and work phone numbers of each of the defense witnesses so that he would be able to notify them of when they would need to be available to testify.

McGinn watched each of the potential witnesses with a puzzled look; then he wrote in what had become his trial journal, an account of the trial he hadn't shared with his attorney.

DAY #4 TRIAL 5–22–95

Start off with swearing in witnesses for defendant's side. Not sure of some of these witnesses though, need to make sure of Tonya Holbrook and her mother before they take the stand. The cops have already talked to them a lot.

McGinn had started to write in the third person, disconnecting himself from the ordeal of the proceedings.

Following the familiar roll call of the jury members, Lee Haney called Texas Ranger Bob Grubbs, who had been with the Department of Public Safety for twenty-six years.

Grubbs told the jury that his involvement in the Flanary case began on Sunday morning, May 23, 1993, with a call from David Mercer. Mercer had told the ranger that a little girl was missing, that they had been hunting all night, and that he suspected foul play.

"I got there approximately ten o'clock, I guess. I came in right behind a dog team that had been called in, and they were conducting a search for the little girl," Grubbs reported.

McGinn scribbled quickly:

> Bobby Grubbs—Texas Ranger—He says he got there to the house after the dogs started the search, which is not true. He got there before the dogs ever started.

Grubbs described talking with McGinn, who had given him much the same information he had presented to Brown County deputies. During that conversation, Grubbs said, he was advised that the dogs had hit on the vehicle that McGinn drove.

"We opened the rear hatchback of the vehicle, and at that time we could see what appeared to be blood in the rear of the vehicle and some strands of what appeared to be blond hair," Grubbs said.

"He says he examined the car before they took it to town, which he did not," McGinn wrote.

Grubbs was shown photos of the interior of the car and he identified the spots and splatters as the way the car appeared when he first saw it at the McGinn property.

Verilyn Harbin shook her head. She had reviewed the photographs and had been unable to distinguish any stains on the red interior of the car. She didn't see how anyone could testify that they observed red blood on the red seats of the Escort.

Then Haney moved on. "What did you do next?" Haney asked.

"I went into the bedroom that had been identified as Mr. McGinn's bedroom, and I located a pair of white-looking tennis shoes that appeared to have blood stains on them," Grubbs said.

Haney displayed the shoes for Grubbs to identify and for the jury to see.

"What if anything else did you do there at the scene at that time?" Haney asked.

"We went back into the house and looked around some more. We received a T-shirt and some shorts. I believe, a pullover-type shirt and some shorts," Grubbs responded.

As Haney displayed the fishnet-type T-shirt, shorts, and a pair of socks that had also been confiscated, McGinn bent over his tablet and wrote:

> He went straight to the shoes, he did not search for anything. I don't know when they got the shorts they are showing, or the shirt. I'm sure the socks came from the bedroom too, as all of the other must have.

The seasoned Texas Ranger explained that he had locked McGinn's vehicle and returned to Brownwood after it had been towed to town, where he met with Chief Deputy Glen Smith and Sheriff Donahoo.

"Do you know what a pollywog catfish is?" Haney asked.

"I guess it could be described as a mud cat or pollywog, kind of. It's a member of the catfish family. It's a rough type of fish," Grubbs explained.

"Is it a fish that you would normally eat?" Haney inquired.

"No, sir."

Again McGinn bent over his writing: "This man doesn't know much about fish or fishing. But of course he is going to say exactly what the D.A. wants him to say."

There was at least one fisherman on the jury panel. Only time would tell if his experience with pollywogs would influence other jury members.

Haney asked what other evidence had been seized from McGinn while he was at the Brown County Jail and Grubbs told him they had taken McGinn's eyeglasses and the clothing he was wearing at the time.

Haney took a brown paper bag from in front of the prosecution table and asked Grubbs to identify the items inside. First there was a pair of blue underwear, a pair of blue jeans, and a plaid Western shirt.

As Chief Deputy Smith and Deputy Mercer had previously testified, Grubbs told jurors that the McGinn car was inspected in the sally port of the Brown County Sheriff's Office before being transported to the DPS lab in Austin. He also stated that Janet McGinn had given permission to drain the tank, and that Trooper Capuchino had located the body.

After Grubbs explained that he had gone to the location where Stephanie's body had been found, Haney asked, "Did you observe what appeared to be blood on the clothing of the body that you saw there?"

"Yes, sir, I did," Grubbs said.

"Was that blood like wet or dry, or what was its consistency?" Haney asked.

"Dry," the Ranger responded.

On Wednesday, the day after the body had been discovered, Grubbs had accompanied Valton Posey to the McGinn property to check out an old cellar. Grubbs told the court that it was after that when Posey had discovered the ax under the seat of the Dodge pickup.

"Did you do something else?" Haney prompted.

"We had information at that time Ricky McGinn had burned something the night before, or Saturday anyway, I believe," Grubbs said.

Sudderth stood to object. "Just a second," he interrupted.

"We looked through the burned debris," Grubbs said before the judge stopped the testimony.

"Just a second," Sudderth repeated. "We move that that be struck. That is hearsay obviously, and this throwing in Saturday-night is just a low lick. There is no evidence in the record at all about anything. No witness has testified about any Saturday night stuff. We move that that be struck. We object to it as being hearsay."

Haney told the court that he wasn't asking if McGinn had burned anything, just why his attention was drawn to the pile.

Judge Cadenhead overruled Sudderth's objection and ordered the proceeding to continue.

Frustrated, McGinn wrote: "Now this man wants to say without knowing, that I had burned things on Saturday."

Following a brief description of the procedures taken to send samples of the burned material to the Austin lab, Haney asked, "What did you do next?"

"On Thursday, May 27, 1993, we attempted to question Ricky McGinn. At this point Ricky advised he wanted to terminate, and we terminated the conversation," Grubbs said.

Sudderth was back on his feet, asking to approach the bench.

"This is no rookie highway patrolman. He knows well and good that he can't testify as to whether or not this man refused. The very fact that he terminates the conversation is not admissible because it violates my client's Fifth Amendment rights. This man is throwing this stuff in here knowing well and good what he's doing, purposely, and we object to it," Sudderth said with passion.

The experienced defense attorney knew that knowing McGinn had stopped the investigators' interview and asked for an attorney could be prejudicial. The jury might think only a guilty man would ask for a lawyer. Sudderth had to stop the testimony concerning McGinn's questioning by authorities.

Judge Cadenhead sustained the objection and instructed the jury to disregard the answer of the witness.

Angrily McGinn wrote:

Now he's said things that shouldn't be said. The judge has instructed the jury to disregard but tell me how someone is going to disregard? What they have heard is already stuck in their minds. How are they gonna remove it?

After establishing that Grubbs had been with Mercer when evidence samples were taken to the Austin lab and when blood was drawn from Steve Flanary at the Louisiana prison, Haney passed the witness.

Sudderth stood and walked toward Grubbs. He was on the assault, hammering Grubbs as to his inadmissable answers to the prosecutor's questions.

"I believe one of the deputies that worked with you in this investigation has testified that the Dodge had been searched two or three times prior to finding the ax. Do you have any knowledge of that?" Sudderth asked.

"No, sir, I don't."

"In your investigation, did you learn that or have you just heard about it the first time this morning?" Sudderth continued.

"You will have to back up just a second. I don't understand where you're coming from," Grubbs said.

"It doesn't make any difference where I'm coming from," Sudderth shot back. "Can you answer my question without worrying about where I'm coming from?"

In the audience eyebrows went up at the defense attorney's strident tone.

Grubbs asked Sudderth to repeat the question, then said, "I don't know how many times the vehicle had been searched."

"Does it make any difference?" Sudderth asked.

"Not to me, no, sir," Grubbs said.

Sudderth spent several minutes trying to establish if Grubbs had any knowledge of water containers being found anywhere near the Ford Escort. Grubbs's answer of "I don't recall" obviously displeased Sudderth, who continued for several minutes to ask the ranger about the containers.

"You asked to search the house, and Ricky readily consented, didn't he?" Sudderth asked.

"Yes."

"You asked to search the vehicle, and he readily consented?"

"Yes, sir, he did," Grubbs admitted.

The attorney was obviously trying to convince the jury that a guilty man wouldn't agree to such actions.

After Grubbs indicated to the court that McGinn had told investigators that the blood in the car might be fish blood, McGinn wrote: "I never told them it was fish blood in the car."

"Just because *you* don't go fishing at a little old tank dam like that, back a vehicle up there and throw the fish in the back of the vehicle, does that make it wrong for him to do it?" Sudderth asked.

"I don't guess it would make it wrong," the ranger replied.

"The old saying 'Different strokes for different folks.' Some people might back their vehicle up, catch a fish, and throw it in the back of it; some may not. Is that right?" Sudderth questioned.

"I guess that's right," Grubbs said.

The defense began to question the Texas Ranger about the condition of the culvert and the position of the body.

Grubbs said that some of the blood inside the culvert was still "tacky" to the touch; then he explained that it had been blood that had congealed, indicating that it was not fresh blood. On the position of the body, Grubbs admitted that Stephanie's arms had been extended over her head and her knees had been pushed up as if her body had been pushed into the confined space. When Sudderth asked how that could happen, the ranger merely stated that he didn't know that it could, unless the killer exited out the other side.

"It would suggest someone was pulling and someone was pushing, wouldn't it, Mr. Grubbs?" Sudderth asked.

"Not necessarily. Not this instance; I don't think so, no, sir," Grubbs said with assurance.

"Because you choose to believe that Ricky McGinn put the body there, don't you? That's the only reason, isn't it?" Sudderth fired.

"I do."

Grubbs denied accusations from the defense attorney that leads or indications that someone other than McGinn could have killed Stephanie were ignored because authorities had already decided McGinn was guilty.

On May 1, 1995, just days before the trial began, Sudderth had written a letter to his investigator, Jim Wright. In the letter Sudderth had asked Wright to determine when Bill Donahoo had taken office as the sheriff of Brown County and to determine how many unsolved murders existed since that date. Sudderth knew there were two or three murders other than a young girl killed south of Brownwood and another girl found murdered in a west Brownwood cemetery.

Sudderth told Wright that he believed there had been "tremendous pressure" to solve the Flanary murder, and when his client was charged, it was prior to finding a body or weapon. "We need to try to take a look at this thing and see just what evidence they did have when they charged him Sunday evening. I believe that they had none," Sudderth had written.

But, as had others before him, Grubbs denied the charge and allegations that they were under pressure to solve the crime.

Grubbs admitted, after the defense had brought it to the attention of the court, that neighbors living in close proximity of the culvert had not been interviewed prior to trial. He then stated that he had gone out to speak to them only days before.

Then Sudderth chastised the ranger for failing to consider Steve Flanary a viable suspect.

Judge Cadenhead interrupted the proceedings to announce a fifteen-minute recess. Before he released the jury, he admonished the audience for the loud discussions of the case that had been heard by the court on numerous occasions.

"I want to say something to the members of the audience at this time. These jurors have been instructed that they are not to talk with anyone about this case, and I don't want any member of the audience at any time, whether they are in this room or out in the hall, to make any remarks in the hearing, presence, or sight of these jurors. Is that clear with everyone in this courtroom?"

When Judge Cadenhead was satisfied that the audience had understood his instructions, he lowered his gavel to signal the morning break.

During the recess McGinn jotted down additional notes relating to Grubbs's testimony:

> I sure must have been a powerful man back then. Everyone just seems to do what they say I told them to do. Even the cops. These cops don't understand anything, except for what they want to.

Grubbs was on the stand only a few minutes following the midmorning recess. As Haney announced his next witness, McGinn took in a deep breath and turned to watch his ex-wife walk into the courtroom.

McGinn had not seen Janet since the morning she had left for the bowling tournament and Stephanie had disappeared. He had not spoken to her since the Sunday night following his arrest. He had been amazed at how quickly she had turned from the loving, supportive wife to the bitter accuser. It had hurt him when she filed for divorce and surprised him when she took back her maiden name of Talley.

Near the bottom of his page, he wrote the name he'd known her by when they met: "Janet Flanary." Then he sat back and waited to hear what Janet had to say.

FIFTEEN

Janet Talley had been waiting for three days in the office of the district attorney for her chance to testify. She felt frustrated at not being allowed to hear what was being said in the courtroom. It had been two years to the day since she had last seen her oldest daughter and she still had so many unanswered questions. She had hoped the trial would give her the answers she needed, but once again she had been shielded from the facts.

McGinn's gaze followed Janet all the way to the witness stand, but she refused to look at her former husband.

Lee Haney established that Janet had once been married to Steve Flanary and that two children, Stephanie and Denise, had been born of that marriage.

"Do you know Ricky McGinn?" Haney asked.

Looking at the prosecutor, Janet replied, "Yes, sir, I do."

"Do you see that individual seated here?" Haney asked.

"Yes, sir, I do. Right there," Janet said, pointing to McGinn but looking at the friendly faces of her supporters in the audience.

"Can you describe either where he is sitting or what he is wearing?" Haney asked, forcing Janet to look at McGinn.

Janet's gaze drifted to the defendant. He smiled broadly. *I'm not smiling back,* Janet thought. *I'm not giving him the satisfaction.* Her face remained rigid, her eyes narrow.

Focusing her attention back on the prosecutor, Janet

said, "He is sitting beside Mr. Ben Doyle Sudderth, and he is in a blue jacket, slacks, and dress shoes."

Janet Talley relayed how she had met McGinn through mutual friends Steve and Robin Sirois, dated almost every day thereafter, moved in together within a month, and married four months later.

She told the jury that McGinn had worked on at least seven different jobs in the nearly four years of their marriage and that they had lived in at least eight different residences. Talley had worked as both a home health-care provider and a child-care provider and was currently employed at Wal-Mart.

Haney asked her to describe the house they lived in at the time of Stephanie's disappearance.

"It wasn't a very nice house. It had four bedrooms, a bathroom, a living room, and a kitchen. There was a pond out in the back. There was some old barns, and it was all fenced completely in. It was a white color, and we had started painting it gray," Janet said.

Janet Talley told the jury and the audience that there was no running water, that they had to haul water from town in a fifty-five-gallon black trash can and five-gallon jugs for drinking water. She described helping her husband unload the cans from the car.

Many in the audience grimaced and asked themselves how anyone could live under such primitive conditions.

Janet kept her eyes on Haney, carefully avoiding McGinn. She told the court that they had taken over the payments on the red Ford Escort from Lisa, McGinn's younger sister, who was buying a newer car. The McGinns had been paying $150 a month to the car lot that carried the note. The Dodge pickup, which was sporadically operable, McGinn was buying from Janet's father.

Since it had been near the end of the year when the McGinns moved to the May Community, Janet Talley said that they had opted to leave the girls in their Brownwood schools. She told the court that most often it had been McGinn who had taken them and picked them up from school each day, just as he had regularly taken her to work.

Haney had Janet tell the jury about her marriage and ultimate divorce from Steve Flanary. She said that Steve seldom exercised his visitation rights and never took the girls out without his parents present. Prior to the divorce Steve had hidden the girls in an effort to convince Janet to go back to him. He'd finally given up and told her he would sign the divorce papers and she could pick up the children.

In describing her life with McGinn, Janet said he had been a strict stepfather, requiring the girls to do chores, but they appeared to get along well. The family had backyard barbecues and played baseball. "I thought it was a pretty good thing," Talley said somewhat sadly.

Haney asked if anything unusual had ever happened while they had been swimming at the pond on their property.

"Yes," Janet said. "After we moved out to the country, Ricky would tell me and the girls that we could take our bras off, which wasn't even like him. And one day we were out at the pond swimming, and he told me and the girls that we could take our tops completely off and swim without them, if we wanted to, which we didn't until he left, or we stayed down under the water. I raised my children to be proud of your body, but not to show it off."

When asked if they had ever fished in that same tank, Janet said yes, but that they seldom caught anything. The little catfish they occasionally caught tasted muddy. She denied ever catching fish from the pond, cleaning, and eating them.

Haney switched from fishing to bowling, asking Janet Talley how often she bowled and if she regularly participated in out-of-town tournaments.

Janet explained that she bowled in two leagues a week,

one with Ricky, and that he also bowled in two leagues a week. Together they normally attended an Abilene tournament, taking the girls with them when they went. She had bowled in the 1992 women's state tourney in Amarillo and again in 1993, in Arlington. Stephanie and Denise had stayed with Ricky on both those occasions.

It was noon. Judge Cadenhead called for an hour and fifteen-minute lunch break and court was recessed.

As Janet left the stand, she looked toward friends in the gallery while McGinn's stare locked on her face.

Before leaving for his own noon meal, McGinn wrote beside Janet's name:

> She has sure been reading up on information. She says she helped unload the water and that she never done. She has sure been schooled on what to say and how to act. But she sure has gotten good at lying, or maybe she has always been good at lying. I'm wondering just what this D.A. has promised this woman. Whatever has happened, she is lying a lot. I do know this woman has been told how to act.

When court reconvened in the afternoon, Judge Cadenhead inquired of the jury, "Members of the jury, what is your decision about Monday, the twenty-ninth?" The judge needed to set the court schedule so that both the prosecution and the defense would have witnesses ready.

With all jurors indicating a negative response to the possibility of working on Memorial Day, Judge Cadenhead announced, "Let the record reflect that all of the jurors made a simultaneous motion, drawing a flat hand across the front, which I assume that means we're not going to see you Monday."

Members of the audience laughed and were somewhat relieved that they would have a three-day break from the intensity of the capital-murder trial.

"That breaks our heart, folks," Cadenhead said in his folksy manner. "We will not, then, meet on the twenty-ninth of May, 1995.

"Did you folks know there is a new grandfather amongst you?" Cadenhead asked the jurors.

Mr. Hammond, one of the six male jurors, grinned broadly. "He is about that big," Hammond said, gesturing with his hands. "He's a keeper. He's nineteen inches long. I know he's legal, weighs about five pounds six ounces," the juror said, sounding like a real fisherman.

His fellow jurors smiled. Many chuckled at his fish analogy, while members of the gallery wondered if Mr. Hammond knew if pollywogs were edible and how that would influence other members of the jury during deliberations.

Judge Cadenhead rapped the gavel and called the afternoon session of the McGinn murder trial to order.

Haney wanted Janet Talley to tell the jury what plans had been made for Stephanie and Denise while she was to be away at the bowling tournament. She explained Denise had asked to stay with Steve Sirois, along with some other kids, while Stephanie had requested to be left at home with McGinn.

"He told her if she would stay home with him that weekend that she could drive him around while he drank his beer. She loves to drive," Janet said.

Sudderth objected, with the judge sustaining and instructing the jury not to consider the statement.

Janet told the court that after eating at Poncho's Mexican Restaurant in Arlington, she had returned to her room after 9:00 P.M. to find the light blinking on the motel telephone. When she talked to McGinn he told her that Stephanie was missing. "He sounded real funny," Janet said.

Friends of the McGinns' attending the trial looked at

one another. One said softly to another, "Of course he sounded funny; the girl was missing."

Janet then testified that McGinn had told her that Stephanie had gotten mad at him and stomped off through the pasture.

"What else did he tell you?" Haney asked.

"I asked him if we needed to come home, and he told me that there was nothing we could do, [that] it was dark, that we didn't need to get in a hurry and come home and have a wreck and maybe get someone hurt. So we should just stay there, finish our bowling the next day, and then come home. So we did," Janet said.

Janet Talley had spoken to her husband again thirty minutes after the first call, learned that nothing had changed, and that the police had been notified. She said she had talked to McGinn a third time, about six o'clock the next morning. When she asked again if she should return home, she testified that McGinn had once more told her there was nothing she could do, that people were there searching, and that dogs and helicopters had been brought in.

"So I took my shower and went to the bowling alley, where I called back to the house and I called my parents' house, a little after eight," Janet explained.

Although Francis McGinn was not in the courtroom, she had heard Janet's story before. Francis, as a mother who loved her children unconditionally, had often asked how Janet could have stayed away when she knew that her child was missing, when she didn't known her fate.

"What did you observe when you arrived in Brownwood?" Haney asked, referring to the number of searchers that had convened on their property.

"The worst nightmare a person could ever look at," Janet answered in a shaky voice.

"That's the stuff we object to," Sudderth interrupted. "She can tell us what she saw without trying to inflame the jury or prejudice the rights of this defendant. We object."

Judge Cadenhead overruled the objection and Janet continued. "I saw, I would guess, seventy-five to a hundred people standing in my front yard. I saw people with dogs. I saw police officers. I saw REACT set up. I saw another search and rescue. There was cars parked all up and down the highway, people driving by, five, ten miles an hour, staring over there at the people and the dogs. And I got out of the Suburban, and nobody knew nothing," Janet said. Visibly shaken by the memories that played in her mind, Janet wiped her eyes and took in a deep breath.

Having established that both Janet and Ricky drank, Haney asked Janet to make a comparison between the two.

"Two to one, three to one. My one to his two or my one to his three, sometimes," Janet answered.

Later, when Francis McGinn learned of Janet's response to the court, she was furious. She would never believe that Ricky consumed more beer than Janet. After all, it had been Janet whom Francis had often seen with a beer in her hand, not Ricky.

Haney passed the witness to Ben Sudderth, and he rose to meet Janet Talley.

Sudderth wanted to know who she was currently living with, and Janet answered with her daughter, and with a friend and his son.

Sudderth asked if she had been married or engaged to be married since her daughter's death in May 1993, and Janet replied, "I was kind of engaged, but it's passed."

"When did you start going with him?" Sudderth asked.

"August of 1993, after my daughter's accident."

A couple of court observers looked at one another questioningly. Accident? Had Talley yet to accept the true fate of her oldest daughter?

After the aggressive lawyer tried to show Janet as a woman who led a loose lifestyle, he continued his personal attack, one that displeased not only Janet's friends in the audience but some townspeople whose hearts went out to the victim's mother.

Sudderth didn't simply question; he interrogated Janet Talley on her indulgence of alcohol. Janet denied Sudderth's allegations that she had a drinking problem or that she had anything to drink the day she returned home from the bowling trip. Janet admitted that she enjoyed a beer every day when she got in from work, sometimes two or three, sometimes five or six, sometimes a case. She also admitted that she occasionally drank vodka and orange juice, but she continually denied any addiction.

When asked if she allowed Stephanie to drink regularly, Janet dismissed the charge, yet she admitted that she would let the girls take a sip of her beer or Ricky's from time to time.

"I didn't allow my daughter a whole beer," Janet proclaimed.

Francis McGinn would later disagree with Janet's statement. "I've seen Janet let Stephanie get a beer from their fridge and drink the whole thing," she retorted.

In response to Sudderth's questioning concerning her tendency to intoxication, Janet stated that she would not get drunk on five or six beers, but she would indeed be intoxicated after consuming a case.

"Who would be caring for the children during those times you drank a case?" Sudderth questioned.

"Myself and my husband, Ricky," Janet Talley responded.

"You've never had any treatment in connection with alcohol abuse?" Sudderth asked.

"No, sir," Janet replied, her straight light brown hair swinging slightly as she shook her head.

"You never tried to hide your drinking, did you?" Sudderth asked.

"No, sir," Janet said matter-of-factly, obviously believing her drinking habits were not unusual.

"But there is one place you didn't take your drinking and that was into the McGinn home, the Francis McGinn home," Sudderth stated.

"That's very correct," Janet said, remembering the McGinn rule of no alcohol inside Francis's home. If she had been drinking a beer on the way to her mother-in-law's trailer home in the tiny town of Rising Star, she would remain outside while she finished the drink. She had had no trouble respecting the standard Francis had set, but she had also seen no reason to hide the fact that she enjoyed an occasional drink.

When Sudderth moved on to the subject of Stephanie's biological father, Steve Flanary, Janet told the defense attorney that her daughter had no contact with him and, in fact, had no idea where he was at the time. He never called while Janet was home and, to her knowledge, had never written.

"Do you think she may have contacted him or been able to call him some of those nights when you had drunk that case and went to bed drunk?" Sudderth asked.

"No, sir," Janet Talley said, her blue eyes narrow, her lips tight.

Sudderth brought to the attention of jurors that Flanary had not been present at his daughter's funeral, claiming he had not been informed. However, he showed up unexpectedly the following day at his sister's house in Alvin, Texas. The defense attorney was attempting to spread a veil of suspicion over the father.

"And did you ever become concerned because your daughter was spending too much time with her thirteen-year-old boyfriend?" Sudderth asked, enlarging the potential pool of suspects.

"To my knowledge, sir, she was not spending time with her thirteen-year-old boyfriend," Janet answered.

She further explained that Stephanie didn't have boys at the house when she was home, but she added before Sudderth could object, "She did when Ricky was home, and he got mad."

Establishing that Janet had to rely on others to tell her what had transpired between the time Stephanie went missing on Saturday afternoon and when Janet returned home the following afternoon, Sudderth asked, "You don't know who was there, who wasn't there. You don't know where Ricky was or wasn't. You don't know where Stephanie walked, do you?"

Janet definitively responded, "No."

"You don't know whether she walked west of the highway or east of the highway, do you?"

"The kids never went across the highway," Janet answered, explaining that she had instructed both Stephanie and Denise to stay within the fence line of their property to avoid a number of dump trucks whose route went along the dirt road by their house.

"Is that the only reason that you didn't want her walking on the county road?" Sudderth asked.

Bordering on an angry outburst at the insulting way in which the attorney was questioning her, Janet Talley replied with a snappy "Isn't that reason enough?"

Not responding to the witness's question, Sudderth went through a litany of questions that again indicated that Janet hadn't been present when certain events had taken place in the course of the investigation. She admitted knowing of a mobile home parked at the back of their seven-acre tract of land, but she stated she had never met the man and his son who lived there and was unaware of when they had moved. She told the court she had no knowledge of a reddish blond haired man driving a tan van in the vicinity of the house during the weekend of her daughter's disappearance. And she admitted that she had been aware that Stephanie had played in the old abandoned hospital nearby. Sudderth was doing all he could to show the jury that someone other than his client could be responsible for the death of Stephanie Flanary.

"Did you sell the Dodge pickup about a week after May twenty-second or twenty-third?" Sudderth wanted to know toward the end of his cross-examination.

"No, sir, I wasn't allowed out there on the property until a week after my daughter's funeral. His family helped theirselves before I was allowed to touch the property; thank you," Janet said with a scoff.

McGinn, who had hung on every word of Janet's testimony, picked up his pen to write:

> This woman has really turned cold or is just following someone's instructions. I believe she is scared of someone. Janet thinks she is really doing something by giving smart answers.

The defense asked if law enforcement had an opportunity to go over the vehicle carefully, looking for evidence prior to the sale of the truck.

"Yes, sir," Janet snapped.

"How do you know they went through the vehicle?" Sudderth asked, annoyed that the defense had not been afforded the same opportunity.

"They told me they did," Janet declared.

Janet Talley was excused. She kept her eyes, glazed with resentment and contempt, on friendly faces in the gallery. She avoided, as before, the gaze of her ex-husband, now looking less yearning and more embittered.

The jury took a breath and twisted in their seats to improve their level of comfort. Everyone in the courtroom had felt the intensity between the ill-fated mother and the willful defense attorney. An almost inaudible sigh went through the courtroom as Steve Robertson approached the stand. Robertson, a chemist and supervisor of the Criminalistic Section of the DPS crime lab in Austin, had been called to testify. Most thought Robertson would be just another dry, factual expert witness identifying photo after photo, as others had before him.

Robertson's explosive testimony, however, would have more of an impact than any other they had heard.

Denise and Stephanie Flanary well before their mother Janet's involvement with Ricky McGinn. *(Courtesy Janet McGinn Roberts)*

Twelve-year-old Stephanie three months
before her murder. *(Courtesy Janet McGinn Roberts)*

The McGinns' home. *(Courtesy Verilyn Willis)*

Vernon McGinn and his six sons. Ricky is on the far right.
(Courtesy Francis McGinn)

Ricky McGinn prior to his stepdaugher Stephanie Flanary's disappearance.
(Courtesy Francis McGinn)

Heat–seeking helicopters were used in the search for Stephanie Flanary. *(Courtesy Brown County Sheriff's Dept.)*

Searchers find Stephanie's body.
(Courtesy Brown County Sheriff's Dept.)

The opening of the metal culvert where Stephanie's body lay.
(Courtesy Brown County Sheriff's Dept.)

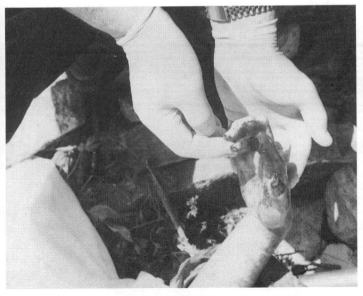

An investigator examines Stephanie Flanary's hand
after the body was removed from the culvert.
(Courtesy Brown County Sheriff's Dept.)

Blood spots on a beer carton in Ricky McGinn's car.
(Courtesy Brown County Sheriff's Dept.)

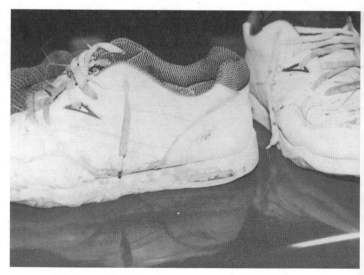

Ricky McGinn's blood-stained tennis shoes.
(Courtesy Brown County Sheriff's Dept.)

McGinn's pickup where the murder weapon was found.
(Courtesy Brown County Sheriff's Dept.)

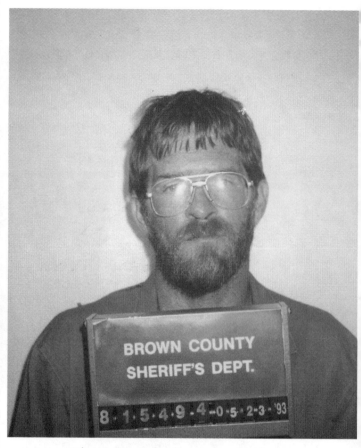

Ricky McGinn is booked on murder charges.
(Courtesy Brown County Sheriff's Dept.)

Brown County Sheriff's Deputies
Byron Thompson and Mike McCoy.

Investigator Tina Church is interviewed while waiting
for Governor George Bush's call, June 1, 2000.

Francis McGinn talks with reporters following the announcement of her son's stay of execution, June 1, 2000.

Verilyn McGinn Willis addresses the media after McGinn's last minute reprieve, June 1, 2000.

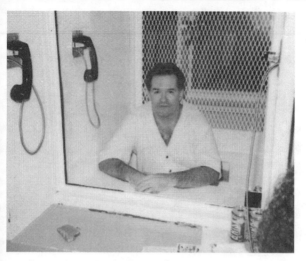

Ricky McGinn on death row. *(Courtesy Francis McGinn)*

The McGinn family visits Ricky in his final days.
Francis McGinn (front, center), Mike, Darlene,
Sonny, Ricky, Verilyn, Randy, and Lisa.
(Courtesy Francis McGinn)

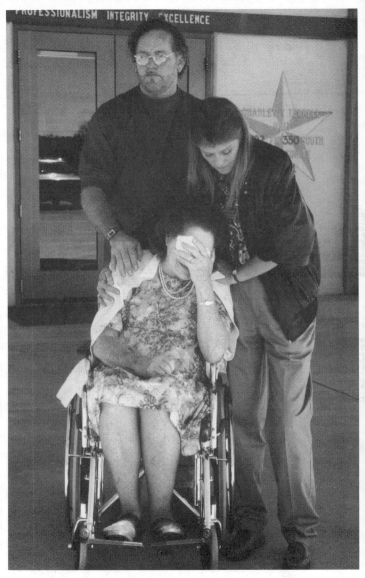

Mike and Lisa McGinn comfort their mother
after her final visit with Ricky.

An unidentified demonstrator before McGinn is put to death.

Christi Jo Egger's grandfather awaits McGinn's execution in Huntsville.

Anti-death penalty protesters demonstrate outside the Texas death chamber preceding McGinn's execution.

McGinn is transported from death row to the Walls Unit.

Janet McGinn Roberts and Denise Flanary at Denise's high school graduation in 2001. *(Courtesy Janet McGinn Roberts)*

SIXTEEN

For eighteen years Steve Robertson had been a chemist for the Texas Department of Public Safety. In May 1993 Robertson, along with a serologist who types blood stains and examines items in sexual-assault cases for semen, a fingerprint expert, and a photographer, examined McGinn's Ford Escort for evidence.

Using arrows on photographs submitted into evidence, Robertson had noted both the direction and the size of the stains found in the vehicle. In addition, hairs found in the car were marked for state's evidence.

Robertson explained to the court in simple terms that hair comparisons are done by taking a hair from the crime scene, a loose hair that is normally called a questioned hair. That hair is compared with a sample from a known individual. The scientist then looks in the microscope at the internal structure of that hair and sees how it is put together. The internal structure will vary from person to person. It will vary enough, most of the time, that two people's hair can be distinguished apart, one from the other.

Unlike a fingerprint, if the questioned hair matches the sample, then it could be concluded that the hair could have come from the person who gave the test sample or from somebody else who has hair just like that person's. Most of the time scientists can distinguish people's hair, but it is never unique and individual like a fingerprint.

Hair has three main parts—a wooden pencil is a good illustration of how a hair is made. The paint on the outside of the wooden pencil corresponds to a layer of scales on the outside of the hair, similar to fish scales. It is thick or thin, clear or cloudy.

The lead part of the pencil corresponds to what is called the medulla of a hair. It may be unbroken from root to tip, or it may be broken into pieces. The medulla may even be absent.

The wooden part of the pencil is the part of the hair called a cortex. That's where the color is found. Subtle changes in shades of color can be seen microscopically. The individual pigment granules that make up the color, the size, and the shape run along the shaft. They are studied to see if the granules are equally distributed across the width, or if there is more color on one side of the hair than the other, or if there is more color on the outside edge or more toward the inner part of the hair.

If the questioned hair and the sample fall within the range of variation, it can be concluded that the questioned hair could have come from the person providing the sample hair or from another person with hair just like that.

Head hair can also be distinguished from pubic hair or from hair from some other part of the body. Often times race can be determined from head hair as well, or if the hair has been artificially colored, either bleached or dyed, cut with scissors or shed naturally, or pulled out with some force. Diseases or deficiency in the person's body and lice can also be detected.

The confused looks on members of the audience softened and showed signs of comprehending the scientist's explanation.

Robertson told the jury that the first hair he tested was taken from the ax believed to be the murder weapon.

"And what conclusion, if any, did you draw by comparing that hair?" District Attorney Haney asked.

"There were many hair fragments, showing that the root had been broken off. Many of those fragments stuck to the blood on one side of the ax. I mounted a sample of those hair fragments and they had the same microscopic characteristics as Stephanie Flanary's head hair," Robertson said.

"Did they have the same microscopic characteristics as the defendant's head hair?" Haney asked.

"No."

In the opinion of Robertson, as well as a second examiner who had looked at the samples, the hair on the ax belonged to Stephanie Flanary or someone with hair just like hers.

"What other comparisons did you make?" Haney asked.

"A hair was submitted to us and identified as coming from inside Stephanie Flanary's vagina. I determined that it was a Caucasian pubic hair. I compared that hair to pubic hair from Stephanie Flanary, Mr. McGinn, Steve Sirois, Stanley Sirois, and Joe Bob Talley," Robertson replied.

He explained that hair has a normal growth cycle, it grows and then matures. At the end of the cycle, the skin around the hair root pulls away from the root and the root hardens into a bulb shape and becomes dry. Then it is shed naturally. The hair found inside the vagina of the young girl was approaching that point. It was almost ready to shed and had come out without much force.

Robertson reported that the pubic hair had not come from Stephanie Flanary herself, but that it had the same microscopic characteristics as the one taken from Mr. McGinn.

Furthermore, Robertson said, the hair hadn't come from Steve Sirois, Stanley Sirois, or Joe Bob Talley. Those three men could be eliminated as a source.

Murmurs could be heard throughout the courtroom as onlookers grasped the implication of Robertson's testimony. More than likely, the pubic hair found in the Flanary girl's vagina was from Ricky McGinn. It was definitely the most damning evidence to have been presented. The speculation of many was, if he had been the one to rape her, he must have been the one who killed her as well.

Robertson added that hair found stuck in blood inside the Ford Escort also had the same microscopic characteristics as Stephanie Flanary's hair. The hair inside the ball cap discovered near a fence line on the McGinn acreage could have belonged to either Stephanie or McGinn, explaining that their hair was similar. This statement elicited interested looks from the audience.

Ricky McGinn sat motionless for a time, thinking about the incriminating testimony; then he wrote in his trial journal:

> Steve Robertson—He says the pubic hair from Steph's vagina is same as mine. Then the hair from the cap he says could be mine or Steph's either one. Says our hair is the same.

Testimony for the day stopped, with Robertson to return another day for cross-examination. It was a somber moment for the defense. The jury had twenty-four hours to ponder Robertson's scientific implications without benefit of any defense rebuttal.

The next morning Lee Haney entered the courtroom with renewed confidence. He was certain Steve Robertson's testimony had damaged the defense, and the witness he had planned for this day's proceedings should be just as incriminating.

In contrast, McGinn looked as if he were carrying a weighty burden, one that was beyond his capacity.

The jury filed in, taking their seats at the front of the courtroom. Most avoided looking directly at McGinn, focusing their attention on Judge Cadenhead.

Following the testimony of two lab technicians and a Brownwood emergency-room doctor who had taken samples from McGinn for testing, Oscar Kizzee was called to the stand.

Kizzee, a latent-fingerprint examiner for the Department of Public Safety, explained that a latent print is made when the fingers or palms touch an object. There is perspiration on the ridges of the fingers, and when the fingers touch an object, the residual from those fingers is left behind, unseen.

The prints are retrieved through different processes. Some of them are chemical, some physical, such as dusting the area with fingerprint powder.

Kizzee stated he was unable to lift any prints made in blood found on the beer carton or a beer can found inside the Ford Escort. He was also unable to lift any prints from the broken ax handle, explaining, "As you can see, the wood is old and looks like it has been out in the weather. The whole thing is purple. That's what I used to try to get prints on it. And instead of it just showing the prints itself, the whole thing discolored, the background and everything."

In addition, the print expert was unable to raise prints from the black electrical tape wound around the ax handle or from three Miller Lite beer bottles submitted for testing. Prints were obtained from the note found in the field. However, the prints didn't match those of McGinn, Joe Bob Talley, or Steve Sirois. The automatic fingerprint-identification system utilized by the DPS, limited to about three and a half million persons in Texas only, was unable to come up with any match.

On cross-examination Sudderth established that Kizzee hadn't been asked to go to the crime scene in an attempt to lift any prints that may have been on the inside of the metal culvert.

"If you had gone to that culvert and looked in there and saw a handprint in blood on the inside of that culvert, do you think that is a print that you could have lifted?" Sudderth asked.

"Well, usually prints in blood we don't lift. We take photographs of them because of the nature of the way they are," Kizzee stated.

He added that if a photo had been taken that displayed enough precise definition, he would have been able to identify the print directly from the photo.

"You and I can agree that if you had been called to the scene and had been shown that handprint that I've described, it would have been a valuable piece of evidence for you to work with, wouldn't it?" Sudderth asked.

Kizzee concurred, adding that he had not heard of the existence of the handprint until Sudderth had asked him about it that morning in court.

Kizzee was excused. While the next state's witness walked toward the yellow witness chair to be sworn in before her testimony, McGinn wrote:

Oscar Kizzee—D.P.S. Finger Printing. Examined stuff on May 24–93. No finger prints in blood. None on beer carton. No prints on beer can. This guy is really a good one. No prints on ax. No prints on beer bottles. My prints were not on the note. Nor was Steve Sirois's or Joe Bob Talley's on the note.

Michelle Lockhoof, a DPS biologist, was next to testify. Lockhoof had been with Robertson and Kizzee when the Ford Escort was brought into the DPS body shop in Austin. Her main responsibility had been to look for blood specimens. When Lockhoof had collected the individual blood stains off the car, she had isolated each stain, one from another, in small coin envelope so she could keep track of them individually.

During tedious-sounding testimony Lockhoof identified photos of where each blood sample had been taken from the Ford Escort. Although a numbering system had been used for each sample, jurors and audience members alike had difficulty keeping track of where each numbered stain had been collected. At 10:30 A.M. Judge Cadenhead announced a needed break.

Many of the jurors looked weary. The testimony had been technical and tiresome; some had had difficulty concentrating on the witness. One juror, a woman who was accustomed to rising at 3:00 A.M. each day to milk the cows on her farm, still appeared bright-eyed and attentive.

In the journal McGinn wrote:

> Michelle Lockhoof—D.P.S. Lab Austin. Collected blood from car to test for D.N.A. D.A. had had this woman to go into detail about where she got the blood samples from in the car.

While McGinn was jotting down his own notes, his defense attorney was before the bench arguing the admissibility of State's Exhibit Number 95. Sudderth contended the exhibit, which was the second rape kit taken from McGinn, was in violation of the Code of Criminal Procedure. The rule expressly prohibits more than one search and seizure being conducted in any case.

Sudderth, as he had done a number of times during the McGinn trial, cited the case of the *State of Texas* v. *Flores,* in which the court suppressed all evidence obtained and all items attained in the second search and seizure because it violated the Code of Criminal Procedure.

In rebuttal Haney argued that the cases were dissimilar in that the Texas Code refers to cases where two search warrants had been issued. In the McGinn case, Haney debated, the first rape kit had been obtained by consent of the defendant.

Judge Cadenhead took the defense motion to suppress

under advisement, then exited the courtroom for his own midmorning break.

When court resumed fifteen minutes later, Judge Cadenhead told Sudderth, "I'm going to overrule your motion. Motion denied."

Haney smiled, feeling another small triumph. Again Sudderth was on his feet, approaching the bench with another evidentiary objection.

The defense waged the same objection to State's Exhibit Number 132 if it, too, contained any reference to the prior exhibit.

"Is it the same objection?" Haney asked.

"Same objection," Sudderth replied.

"Same ruling," Judge Cadenhead stated, then ordered the state to continue with their case presentation.

Sudderth asked for an early lunch break to afford his own blood expert time to arrive for the afternoon session.

"Members of the jury," the judge began, "do any of y'all have any objections if we break for lunch at this time and come back at twelve-thirty? Any member have a pot roast cooking or anything like that?"

Jurors shook their heads as smiles crossed their faces at the judge's homespun humor.

When court came back into session, the judge remained in a humorous mood as he ordered the bailiff to call the jury back into the courtroom with a Western flair.

"Head 'em up and move 'em out," Judge Cadenhead instructed.

After Haney had asked Ms. Lockhoof to explain how she went about recovering evidence and analyzing it, Sudderth commented that he was having trouble hearing the witness due to the noise in the hall.

The people outside the courtroom had been rebuked a number of times throughout the trial for the disruptive level of their voices, as well as their resounding discussions of the case.

Ms. Lockhoof continued by answering the D.A.'s question in a more audible tone.

"The first test that we do is called a presumptive test for blood. And, in this case, I used two different methods.

"One is called a phenolphthalein, which all it is is a color-indicator reaction. If it's positive, you're going to see a color pink, and if it is negative, you will see no color change at all.

"And the second testing I did was called Luminol, which you actually have to conduct in the dark because if the blood is present, or something similar to blood, then you will see a glowing on the material.

"In this case I used both of those techniques on different items, depending on what the situation called for."

Ms. Lockhoof clarified that if a test was initially negative, meaning no blood was present, she stopped the testing process, but if the presumptive test was positive for blood, she would then have to confirm if it was human blood.

She used a test called Ouchterlony to determine if the sample was indeed human. Utilizing a plastic petri dish, she filled it with a gel that is very similar to Jell-O, but slightly more solid. She then cut a hole in the congealed substance and put in the questioned stain. In a second hole she added a liquid chemical mixture called antihuman. If the questioned stain was human blood, then these two areas diffused toward each other; the result being somewhat like a paper towel lying over a wet area and absorbing the liquid.

If the two areas did join, then a white line would form between the two areas; that is called a precipitin band. All the scientist had to do was look for that white line; if there, then it was positive for human blood.

In some cases Ms. Lockhoof then tested the blood stains using another technique called absorption/elution to determine what type of blood was present. This was done by manipulating the DNA and checking with a microscope how it clumped. In the McGinn case she then made blood cards in the laboratory and mailed them to others who were scheduled to do further DNA analysis.

Ms. Lockhoof told the jury that in addition to the blood examination, she had also tested some items to determine if semen was present.

That test, called an AP test, or acid phosphatase, was another color indicator. The presence of semen was indicated by a positive color change after certain chemicals were sprayed on the sample. The AP test was then followed with additional checks to look for semen-specific constituents, such as actually seeding spermatozoa or protein that is found specifically in semen.

Articles that Ms. Lockhoof had been given to test that didn't respond for presumptive blood included a pair of socks, a mesh tank top, a bikini swimsuit top, and a pair of eyeglasses.

When Haney asked Lockhoof to explain what she had done with the socks, she paused momentarily to pull on a pair of latex gloves before handling the exhibit.

"I get nervous when I carry all this stuff around and everybody else puts on these gloves," Haney explained. He smiled, but his remark had a slightly serious timbre.

Holding the sock, the lab tech showed how she had cut out an area of the garment thought to be positive for blood and tested it. She stated she had thought the sock might be positive because of a dark spot, explaining that over time blood can turn to a darkish brown. However, it was determined that the spot was soil.

Ms. Lockhoof told the jury she had also run tests on suspicious spots found on tennis shoes submitted for analysis. The stains proved positive for blood and on further examination it was determined it was type A blood.

Haney produced medical records from the Galveston, Texas, hospital were Stephanie Flanary had been born indicating that she had type A blood.

Soft mumbles could be heard throughout the audience. It appeared Haney was finally beginning to present physical evidence that could link the victim and defendant.

Next Ms. Lockhoof testified that she tested a number of stained areas in the car. All proved to be type A human blood. Again, the same as the victim's.

The blood expert stated that after first spraying McGinn's blue jeans with Luminol to see if there was blood undetectable by the human eye, which produced negative results, she tested a number of visible spots. Only one stain, on the right back leg of the pants, proved to be blood. Type A blood.

The underwear submitted proved positive for blood, but Lockhoof did not test for type.

The ax was also scrutinized for blood, which was found to be type A. The ax had then been forwarded to other agencies for DNA analysis. Other items that had shown positive in the Austin lab were sent to the FBI laboratory for further inspection, along with known blood and DNA standards from Ricky McGinn and Stephanie Flanary.

In addition to the car, ax, and clothing, Lockhoof had scrutinized a paper towel found in the console of the Ford Escort. It, too, contained blood smears, but of the type O blood group.

"Did you examine the sample of blood of the defendant, Mr. McGinn?" Haney asked.

"Yes, I did," Lockhoof said, adding that it was determined to be type O.

Ms. Lockhoof explained that she had studied vaginal slides from the victim microscopically and was able to observe spermatozoa. In other words, the vaginal slide was positive for the presence of semen. Both the anal and oral slides were negative for semen.

"Are there other tests that can be conducted with semen to identify more closely the possible contributor?" Haney wanted to know.

"Yes," Lockhoof said. "The test that I employed was to look for a blood type of the possible semen donor. In a body fluid you can secrete your blood type. In this instance I looked for the blood group substances that were present, and I detected the A and the H blood group substance."

When Haney asked if she could determine who had contributed the semen, the expert witness stated that she had no information as to the blood group of the semen donor, but claimed she could not exclude the suspect.

"Is there anyone you could exclude?" Haney asked.

"You could exclude a person who is a B secretor," she answered.

From a chart prepared by the witness, she stated that the combination of all the blood profile factors reflected 90 percent of the Caucasian population.

"Did you analyze blood samples from Steve Sirois?" Haney asked.

"Yes, I did. Mr. Sirois was determined to be blood group A. He could not be eliminated as a semen donor of the stain on the victim's shorts," Ms. Lockhoof stated.

Supporters of McGinn's could be heard whispering among themselves concerning Steve Sirois's nonexclusion as a possible semen donor. When the judge announced a fifteen-minute recess, supporters from both sides eagerly gave their own interpretations of the testimony regarding the implications to both McGinn and Sirois. The McGinns were encouraged that their suspicions regarding Sirois had been reinforced by his inclusion as a possible semen donor. The Talleys disregarded the idea as preposterous.

Once the jury was escorted from the courtroom, Judge Cadenhead addressed the gallery.

"Members of the audience, we're having problems with you folks. There is a lot of talking going on out in the hall and as you come into the hall. It makes it difficult to hear in here. So I would ask that you be very quiet in the hall, and absolutely out in the main hall and as you come past the glass door. That would sure help us. We appreciate it very much."

As the judge politely admonished the crowd, McGinn made notes:

This woman has been before juries before. She is up showing them what she believes to be blood on a bumper guard. Blue jean pants, says it had one spot of what she says was blood. Says it's consistent of A typing. Analyzed a paper towel—blood group O, says it's my type. Analyzed ax—blood group A type. This woman is hurting me bad. Says everything she tested and then shows it exactly to the jury. I believe she was also probably coached before her testimony.

As the crowd entered the courtroom more quietly, Ben Sudderth remained seated as he prepared to cross-examine Ms. Lockhoof.

He introduced himself, his client, and Sky Sudderth, the blood expert whom he brought in to listen in on Ms. Lockhoof's testimony. Sky just happened to be Ben Sudderth's son.

"Based upon your knowledge, what percentage of the population belongs to blood group A?" Sudderth asked the witness.

"The percentage of the population with blood group A that are Caucasian is 35.8 percent," Lockhoof replied, adding that testing to determine racial background was unavailable.

Sudderth asked if Janet Talley, Denise Flanary, or Steve Flanary's blood types had been determined. When Ms. Lockhoof responded no, Sudderth repeatedly asked why not.

"It wouldn't be significant to you that there was someone else in that household, maybe two other people that were getting in and out of that car and riding in that car and all over the house that had blood group A? That wouldn't have been significant to you?" Sudderth asked sternly.

Ms. Lockhoof defended herself by explaining that those particular typings had not been requested by investigating officers.

"Do you feel like you have a duty to carefully and impartially consider all the evidence that is presented to you?" Sudderth asked.

"Yes, I do."

"But you didn't check to see if Janet McGinn belonged to blood group A, did you?" Sudderth questioned.

"I did not consider testing those blood tubes," Lockhoof replied.

Sudderth continued to drive home his point that the blood found in the Ford Escort was "consistent" with that of Stephanie Flanary but could not be conclusive, since other members of the household had not been tested. In addition, he cast a questioning shadow on the blood in the tubes provided by Grubbs and Mercer, claiming they had been represented as the blood of the victim.

It was becoming apparent that Sudderth was building a defense on a suspicion of conspiracy.

In a standard move often used to discredit a scientific finding, Sudderth asked repeatedly if scissors and other instruments used while testing various items for blood were cleaned between examinations. Ms. Lockhoof told the jury that it is standard procedure to clean each soiled implement with alcohol before beginning a new test in order to prevent crossover contamination.

Sudderth asked if Lockhoof had kept a chart indicating when disinfecting had taken place, but the witness stated that the procedure was routine and no records were kept. Sudderth attempted to implant in the minds of jurors that crossover contamination may have taken place in the laboratory, thus causing a greater number of items tainted with the victim's blood.

Lockhoof admitted that she could not say definitively that the blood stains on McGinn's clothing were type A, only that they were consistent with type A blood group. In response Sudderth asked, "There is not one single thing there that connects this man to Stephanie Flanary, is there?"

"Not with the testing I did, no, sir," Lockhoof answered.

During the short afternoon recess, McGinn jotted down his thoughts:

Couldn't get good test on Steph's blood, but are trying to convict me on blood. This woman is helping the State a lot. I do believe this woman has spent some time with Lee Haney the D.A., going over and over what she was gonna say and how he would question her and how she would answer. They say the blood in the car is inconsistent with my blood but we don't know that. So they say it is consistent of the blood type of Steph, although they couldn't type her. She keeps reading off the tags of her chart when she is explaining the sample on the bottom of her very own chart. This woman has to refer back to her books to what she has already testified to. She also tries to talk too fast to be heard good or understood by someone who is sitting to her side or back.

We are on break right now and the D.A. is running around looking like he has already won the case. There is a lot of whispering from the audience. I really don't believe this should be allowed. There sure is a lot I don't understand about how they come up with their answers.

Court is back in session with my lawyer questioning. Now this witness has a hard time answering the questions she's asked. Says they didn't test Janet or

Steve Flanary's blood for type. Now she says there is
no type O in A semen. And there was A group in
semen found on shorts. I say again, this girl sure
knows how to play up to the jury.

During redirect Lee Haney asked, "As far as this discussion about direct comparison of the blood of the victim
with the blood on the ax, you yourself performed such a
comparison, didn't you?"

"Yes, I did," Ms. Lockhoof said.

"And you found that the victim's blood, although you
couldn't determine her type from your sample, the records
indicate she had type A, and the blood on the ax at least
had this agent, or whatever that type A blood has. So is
that consistent or inconsistent?" Haney asked.

"That is consistent with what I've said," Lockhoof responded.

Relief spread over the jury and audience like a welcome
spring rain. The testimony had been long, tedious, and occasionally difficult to follow, as scientific evidence often
is.

Ricky McGinn was beginning to grow weary. Sitting in
the courtroom all day, listening intently to each witness,
and keeping a record of his own reflections was arduous.
His spirits were sinking. He hoped the State would soon
rest and his lawyer would be able to present evidence that
would sway the jury in his direction.

His mood elevated slightly when he thought of the one
thing he could do to help his own defense. McGinn looked
forward to the day when he himself would be testifying.

SEVENTEEN

Ricky McGinn's blue eyes turned dark as they narrowed and his jaw became rigid. He scowled at Steve Sirois, Stanley Sirois, and Kay Lobstein as they stood before the judge, agreeing to tell the truth. McGinn obviously doubted they would.

He huffed to himself, his shoulders rising and falling slightly. Steve had been his best friend, yet McGinn knew he was in court to testify against him, just like his father, who stood next to him at the front of the courtroom.

Steve Sirois was one of the men McGinn had told his attorney he believed capable of murdering Stephanie; in fact, he had made the allegation to his family a number of times throughout the course of his two-year incarceration while awaiting trial. McGinn only hoped Sudderth would be able to cast doubt on both Siroises' testimonies.

But it wasn't either of the Sirois men who began the day's court proceedings; rather, it was Kay Lobstein, an employee of Oleta's Liquor Store.

Ms. Lobstein told the jury that because Ricky McGinn had been coming into the store regularly for about a year prior to the murder of Stephanie Flanary, she immediately recognized him on the morning of May 22, 1993, at 11:30. Although Lobstein didn't see the face of the child with him, she did notice a curly-haired little girl seated low in the car.

"He walked down the counter, back there to the beer

cooler, got his beer out of the window and then he went over to the Coke machine. He opened up the door, like he was going to get a Coke for the little girl, and then he changed his mind," Lobstein said.

"He put his beer up on the counter; then he decided he wanted a bag of ice. So he went over there to get the ice. I gave him some candy to give to the little girl. He paid me. I gave him his change and told him thank you and out the door he went."

Haney established that it was a twenty-pack of Lone Star Light beer, then turned the witness over to the defense.

Sudderth had no questions and Ms. Lobstein was excused.

Ricky McGinn wrote:

Kay Lobstein—From Oleta Liquor Store—Knows me from Oleta's. Says I went over to where the Cokes are kept but this is not right.

McGinn's posture, which had relaxed as Lobstein testified, stiffened as Stanley Sirois approached the witness chair.

The senior Sirois told the court that on May 22, 1993, he left his house because there were a "slew" of kids there for the weekend, including Denise Flanary. He escaped to the library, then to Brownwood Automotive, and ended up spending considerable time at the Brownwood Café, where he met with friends and drank coffee.

Sirois went into a lengthy dissertation of his movements once he left the Brownwood Café, including stopping at the E-Z Mart for a piece of fried chicken.

"On the way back, as I got to Ricky and Janet's, I noticed a car out in front, and I was curious because I thought they had that little Ford Escort. They had had trouble with it getting started lots of times. It was a little diesel. I thought, 'Good Lord, they traded cars. I won't have to worry about getting the battery charger out when Janet is here and getting the car started,' " Sirois stated in a deep Texan accent.

Ricky jotted notes on his pad:

> Stanley Sirois—He never had to start our car. Says he saw a strange car and he knew who's car it was, so I'm wondering, why he really stopped. This is something he never done before. I bet this man couldn't tell the same story tomorrow. This man is a real story teller, that's for sure.

Sirois described going to the front door of the McGinn house, knocking three or four times, and not getting an answer. He then walked around to the back of the house and saw Ricky coming toward him. He noticed the red Ford had been nosed into an overgrown hedge.

The witness stated he had talked to McGinn for a few minutes, asking how his injured leg was doing. Sirois claimed McGinn said it was much better and even held it up for Sirois to see.

"Where is Stephanie?" Sirois said he had asked McGinn. "He said, 'Stephanie is pretty sick; she is in the house; she is on the bed asleep.' "

"I said, 'What did she do, eat something that wasn't good for her?' He said, 'No, God, don't tell anybody. I'll tell you what happened. She kept bugging me for a beer. She kept it up and I finally went and gave her a six-pack. She drank the first bottle and she finished the six-pack and got sick. She just had to go in and try to feel better, to lie down.' "

Sirois told the jury and audience that when he questioned Ricky as to why he had given Stephanie the beer, McGinn had given him the analogy of how when a mother catches you smoking she'll give you a whole pack of cigarettes and make you smoke them until you get real sick and don't want to smoke anymore.

Answering Haney's question as to McGinn's demeanor at the time, Sirois claimed he knew that McGinn had consumed a couple of drinks and had a buzz on. He added that McGinn was wearing cutoff blue jean shorts, a grayish green shirt, and low-cut tennis shoes.

"He is lying about what I was wearing," McGinn added to his notes.

The questioning of Stanley Sirois was completed within minutes.

McGinn glared as his former friend Steve took the stand. He was uncertain what the younger Sirois would say, or how he would portray him to the jury.

After establishing that Steve Sirois and Ricky McGinn had been friends for nearly six years, Lee Haney asked Sirois if he was aware that McGinn had suffered an on-the-job injury.

"Yes, sir, I know he had been hurt. I wasn't working with him at the time," Sirois responded. "It would come and go. There were several things that Mr. McGinn did that I would inform him he shouldn't do, and I would never think, hurt like he was, he could."

As an example, Sirois mentioned McGinn moving a large metal desk into his new residence in Owens, as well as lifting a heavy barrel of water and carrying it into the house. But later under cross-examination, Sudderth had Sirois admit he hadn't actually seen McGinn move the desk or the barrel. Sirois had merely assumed, seeing it done, that McGinn had somehow accomplished the feat.

Concerning the night of May 22, 1993, Sirois said that at about 8:30 that night he received a call from McGinn stating that Stephanie had gone for a walk and hadn't returned. Sirois told his friend that as soon as he finished cooking dinner and fed the kids he would be right over.

"He told me that he better wait there because Stephanie

might return. I said I figured they were going to Bob and Gwen's [Stephanie's grandparents]. If she is going anywhere, she is going to head that direction. I said I'd look for her on the way.

"He said, 'You better take the back roads because she would have had to go down the dirt road.' So I said I'd go that way," Sirois testified.

McGinn looked angry as his former friend told the court that McGinn had not called his wife or the sheriff by the time he arrived at his house about 9:15 P.M.

Sirois said that he first called and talked to his wife, Robin, then McGinn spoke with Janet. Sirois described McGinn as crying and emotional, saying he didn't know what he was going to do. Both Sirois and McGinn had advised their wives to stay in Arlington.

In the sequence of events recited by Sirois, McGinn then called the sheriff's office and told them that Stephanie was missing. According to Sirois, Deputy Roberts had shown up between 9:30 and 9:45 P.M.

McGinn angrily jerked up his pen and scrawled across the paper:

> Steve Sirois—He is lying about the phone calls.
> He wasn't even at the house when I called the cops.

Sirois claimed he had been at the McGinns' helping with the search most of the night, except for the times he returned to his own house to check on his father, paraplegic father-in-law, and the children who were staying there. In the morning, at the request of the REACT team, the Ford Escort had been moved from the carport, where Sirois had seen it parked earlier, to a place out by the highway. Sirois was unsure as to who had moved the vehicle.

He then watched as the search dogs worked, and he stated that he had seen one of the canines "hit" on the red car by jumping up on the back end.

Sirois admitted he left the search for a while to attend to his father-in-law who had been taken to the hospital by ambulance, but he stated he later returned to the McGinns'.

Again McGinn became agitated when Sirois sat taller in his seat and began to expound on how he had taken care of anything anybody needed at the search site.

"Cokes, food, anything that they needed. I was giving out money just to get it for the people that were out there," Sirois boasted.

What Sirois didn't tell them was that later he demanded money for a journalist's interview, stating that he had been out fifteen hundred dollars, "feeding those people."

McGinn wrote with a heavy hand:

> This man is sure wanting credit for everything. He sure wants to be important. This man really never did much. This man sure does lie. Man, these people just remember what they want to, and what the D.A. wants them to remember.

As Sirois continued, he spoke of having blood and pubic hair voluntarily taken at the emergency room. He stated that a nurse, doctor, and Deputy Mercer were in the room during the procedure and that the samples had been sealed in a box to be sent for testing.

Just after Judge Cadenhead announced a midmorning recess, Ben Sudderth asked to approach the bench. Lee Haney had filed a motion with the court to disallow the defense from introducing Sirois's past criminal history.

"This witness was convicted in Comanche County for drug dealing and it is my belief that he has been a drug dealer during the ensuing time over the years. The defense will show that he has no visible means of support. He works periodically.

"I will produce a witness who overheard him demand pay, threatening a person for not paying him. I will produce a witness who will testify that in the recent past Sirois seems to always have drugs on him. This person was working with him. And I believe I should be entitled to ask him if he does deal in drugs. We're going to offer it to show that violent conduct would be consistent with his style of life," Sudderth told the judge.

Judge Cadenhead reaffirmed the motion until Sudderth could show some sort of evidence about prior convictions that would be admissible for impeachment of the witness.

The lawyer assured the judge that he would "get it out of him" in the presence of the jury.

McGinn sat back, a slight smirk hidden by his mustache. He had confidence that Sudderth would show Steve Sirois for who he really was.

True to his word, Sudderth pounded the witness on his on-again, off-again work history. Sirois denied that he had been out of work for more than a couple of months at a stretch, and maintained that his lifestyle was unaffected because of his wife's lucrative employment. He was unable to give Sudderth a definitive answer as to how many months he worked in 1994, 1993, or 1992, merely stating he had worked most of each year in question.

Sirois denied having a drinking problem but admitted that it had been Ricky McGinn who had gotten him to church, attending with the McGinns in Rising Star, where McGinn's father had been the pastor.

"Do you recall out at the McGinn house late Saturday evening when a man came up and reported an old tan-looking pickup had been going up and down the road, passing his house very slowly, saying and shouting obscenities to little girls that were out in the yard?" Sudderth asked.

"No, sir," Sirois said.

"Do you recall that the information that had been received was written down so it could be delivered to the police?" Sudderth inquired, pressing the witness on the issue.

"No, sir," Sirois said flatly.

Sudderth was operating on information conveyed to him by Francis McGinn concerning the man, the note, and asking Sirois to give it to investigators. Francis had even mentioned that she had witnessed Sirois handing the note over and the deputy shoving it deep into his front pocket. Sudderth knew that Francis McGinn would never lie to him about the incident; he could, however, believe Sirois wasn't telling the truth. But why? Sudderth thought he knew.

"Mr. Sirois," Sudderth continued, "do you know Lisa McGinn?"

"Yes, sir."

"Do you recall about two weeks after May 22, 1993, that you were at a place out on one eighty-three called the E-Z Mart, when you saw Lisa McGinn?" Sudderth asked.

"I can't recall exactly, where or when," Sirois responded.

"Do you recall you were standing there in the store with a man with reddish blond hair?" Sudderth asked.

"No, sir."

"Do you recall telling the man, 'I want my money and I want it now'?" Sudderth continued.

"No, sir. That's ridiculous, absolutely absurd," Sirois stated with more denial than necessary to answer the question.

"Do you recall the man telling you he didn't have the money then, but that he would get it next week and pay you?" Sudderth pressed.

"No, sir."

"Do you recall being very angry and threatening the man?" Sudderth snapped.

"No, sir. Another lie."

"Most of those have been told by you in this courtroom today, haven't they, Mr. Sirois?" Sudderth said with contempt.

The crafty defense attorney wasn't about to let it go.

He continued questioning by asking if Sirois recalled driving his car in front of Lisa McGinn's as she left the E-Z Mart, with the unnamed man pulling in behind her, successfully boxing her in.

"You don't recall trying to frighten her in some way?" Sudderth asked.

"No, sir. I've never frightened anybody in my life," Sirois claimed.

Approaching the subject of his departure from the search site, Sudderth asked Sirois how many times he left and how long he had been absent each time. Sirois was unsure, gave a guesstimate of departing three or four times, with the longest duration of an hour and a half.

Before Judge Cadenhead allowed Ben Sudderth to present evidence and question Sirois on his past criminal history, he excused the jury for lunch and heard the testimony outside their presence.

Sudderth read from a criminal history originated by the Department of Public Safety: Possession of marijuana, February 8, 1978. Driving while intoxicated, no disposition date. Possession of marijuana over four ounces, Comanche County, disposition September 8, 1982, four years' probation. Driving while intoxicated, Fort Worth, Texas, 1982, two years' probation.

"Mr. Sirois," Sudderth began, "the court has read from a document that was furnished regarding what's commonly called a rap sheet. It indicated that in 1982 you were convicted of the offense of possession of in excess of four ounces of marijuana and placed on probation for four years. Were you not?"

"Yes, sir."

Lee Haney stood and approached the bench. "Mr. Sudderth was this man's lawyer," Haney announced. "If he is going to talk about any privileged communications, we will object to that."

Sudderth assured the court he would not delve into any

attorney-client discussions he had had with Sirois at the time he represented him and continued his questioning.

Sirois admitted he had been arrested with marijuana in a school zone but denied that he had intended to sell to the teenagers who frequented the convenience store where he was apprehended. He admitted that in his younger years he had used drugs but contended he now avoided drugs and had nothing more to do with them.

Concerning his work history, Sudderth asked if his employment over the last ten years was consistent with that of a person who makes his living dealing drugs, but Sirois said no, it was more consistent with a downturn in the construction industry.

The questioning was complete, with Sudderth announcing that he intended to bring up the E-Z Mart incident in front of the jury by introducing a defense witness who would testify to it. Judge Cadenhead agreed but reminded the attorney that his ruling on the introduction of Sirois's criminal history remained the same—the defense couldn't bring it up. Sudderth would have to be very careful in his questioning and accusations.

Following the noon recess, Joe Bob Talley, Janet's brother and McGinn's former friend, took the stand.

Talley stated he had been on duty as a San Saba, Texas, police officer when a dispatcher had read the teletype of a missing girl in Brown County. He recognized the description as that of his niece Stephanie, and then the dispatcher had read her name over the airwaves.

Talley had rushed back to the office and immediately called Rick McGinn. It was 4:00 A.M. and McGinn had told Talley that there was plenty of help searching for Stephanie; he needn't rush over. The frightened uncle did hurry back home, changed from his uniform into civilian clothes, and asked a friend to drive him to Brownwood. They arrived just before 6:00 A.M.

Talley claimed the red Ford Escort was parked in the

carport when he arrived, but a short time later McGinn said he needed to get away for a little while and left the area in the red car, returning a short time later.

"I believe he was wearing a pair of blue jeans and a T-shirt," Talley said.

"Did you hear anything that the defendant said at that point?" Haney asked.

"He said, 'That damn sheriff's investigator don't need to be out here,' " Talley stated.

In a huff McGinn wrote:

> Joe Bob Talley—Says he saw me drive the car and said I told him that Mercer didn't need to be there. Can't really identify the clothes I had on.

Talley hadn't been actively involved in the search for his niece on Sunday and hadn't gone to the McGinn property at all on Monday following her disappearance. But on Tuesday he had received a call about 11:30 A.M. stating that a body had been found. Talley drove to the site where officials had told him the body was located to identify his niece.

"I didn't want my mom or dad or sister to have to see her," Talley said, his throat tightening with emotion.

McGinn wrote:

> He's sitting there now trying to build up to a cry for when they show him a picture of Steph. I can see it written all over his face. Now he wants to play up to the jury. When in fact this is the way he does all the time.

"Did you identify the body?" Haney asked.

"Yes, sir, I did. It was Stephanie's," Talley said, appearing close to tears.

When Haney showed Talley an autopsy photo of the

girl, his sadness bubbled to the surface. Tears rimmed his eyes.

As Haney passed the witness to the defense, Talley took a few deep breaths, his chest expanding with each inhalation as he struggled to regain composure.

McGinn added:

Now that he is crying, the D.A. passes the witness. Wants to put the burden on my lawyer to make us look bad if we get too rough with him.

McGinn sat back and listened.

Sudderth took no pity on the victim's uncle, establishing that at thirty-five years old Talley had been married and divorced four times, had been unemployed for two years, and was living with his mother and father. Talley's work record over the past few years showed a man who bounced from job to job, staying a mere week at one, the longest duration, nine months.

Sudderth implied that Talley's less than admirable work record was due in part to his addiction to drugs. Talley denied the allegation, but then he admitted that it could have been a contributing factor in his many discharges.

In an attempt to establish Talley as an abusive person, Sudderth asked if it were true that his sister, Janet, feared him. Talley didn't take the bait, denying any frightful feelings from his sister.

"Do you know a young lady named Brandy Craig that's about the same age as Stephanie was?" Sudderth asked.

"No, sir, sure don't," Talley said, sounding even more Texan.

"Did you ever lock Brandy Craig in a closet?" Sudderth asked.

"No, sir, not that I recall," Talley said evasively.

"Did you ever beat Brandy Craig?" Sudderth persisted.

"No, sir."

The McGinn family had informed Sudderth that Brandy had talked with a close friend named Nicki, confessing to her the incidents with Joe Bob Talley. According to them, Talley had locked the girl in a closet while he molested Stephanie. Brandy had reportedly described the cries of her young friend and the horror of being in a closet unable to help Stephanie while she prayed that he wouldn't come after her as well.

Sudderth was unable to get Talley to admit to any history of abusive behavior, effectively closing the door to any implication that he, not Ricky McGinn, had raped and murdered Stephanie Flanary. He passed the witness.

When Haney announced he had no further questions, Judge Cadenhead excused the jury for another out-of-presence questioning.

Talley admitted under oath to Sudderth that in 1979 he had been ordered by the court to receive psychiatric treatment in a case of aggravated assault. Talley had struck a sixteen-year-old boy in the head with a handgun, then been ordered to the Austin State Hospital for evaluation and six months of outpatient counseling. The boy had been a friend of Janet's and his battery was what had caused her to fear her brother.

At the conclusion of his questioning, Sudderth informed the judge that he believed he should be allowed to go into the matters regarding Talley's violent background before the jury. Judge Cadenhead disagreed, overruling the request.

Sudderth was discouraged, as was his client.

"The judge won't let us go into background of this man. I sure wonder why," McGinn wrote.

Sudderth needed to show the jury the explosive, violent side of Joe Bob Talley in an effort to represent him as a viable suspect in the case.

Sudderth had a number of suspicious persons he believed could have killed Stephanie, including Talley, yet he had been ineffective in convincing the court to allow the introduction of imperative testimony on any of them.

At 2:45 P.M. Judge Cadenhead announced that the court was dismissing early. McGinn was glad. It had been a difficult day. A day filled with negative emotions. Anger. Resentment. Betrayal.

EIGHTEEN

On day seven of his trial, McGinn walked into the courtroom as though a heavy burden were strapped to his back. His stoop was more pronounced, his limp overtly obvious.

Verilyn sat on the wooden bench behind the defense table. Her eyes reflected the sadness she felt for her brother. Her belief in his innocence had never faltered. As difficult as it was to sit and listen to the accusations fired at her younger sibling, she knew it was even more difficult for her mother to sit downstairs, unaware of what was happening in the courtroom, unable to defend her baby boy, as she often called Ricky, against the barrage of denunciations being waged against him.

Meanwhile, Janet Talley sat comfortably in Lee Haney's office on the third floor of the old courthouse. The six days of testimony had taken a toll on her as well. She yearned to be in the courtroom, to hear the evidence against her former husband firsthand, to have the many gaps in her understanding of the events filled. Instead, she sat quietly and waited, just as Francis McGinn waited on the floor below her.

In the courtroom the first order of business was to hear a motion filed by Ben Doyle Sudderth. He had asked the court to rule on his motion to disallow DNA evidence if the odds against a random match were less than 95 percent. The judge agreed and so ruled.

The day's testimony began with Dr. David Bing, Ph.D., Director of Clinical Testing at the CBR Laboratories in Boston, Massachusetts. The laboratory is a diagnostic testing lab that does forensic testing and is a totally owned subsidiary of Harvard Medical School.

Dr. Bing interpreted forensic testing as a type of diagnostic testing that is performed on biological material that is collected at scenes where alleged crimes have occurred. That scientific testing produces results that are then usually presented in a court of law because the test results relate to the alleged criminal acts.

As to DNA, the doctor said it is considered the blueprint for life. DNA is found in every cell in the body, and found in that DNA is all the information that is necessary for making life exist.

Half of a human comes from the mother and half from the father. Humans are, therefore, made up of two individuals.

No two people are really the same. Everybody is very different, with the possible exception of identical twins. That's because the cells actually split so that those two individuals get identical copies.

People can share things that look the same, such as a genetic property that distinguishes males from females. The genetic code in the DNA is located in a package of information called the chromosome.

There are other kinds of traits that humans have in common as well. For example, they have two eyes, two arms a heart. These are all encoded in the DNA. These are things that are shared between humans, but variations do exist. Some people have different-colored hair or eyes. Some are shorter than others. Some have larger feet than others. Those variations are encoded in the DNA.

DNA has codes, similar to letters strung together to make words. DNA's codes are composed of just four letters: A, T, G, and C. Three of those letters represent amino acid. Amino acid is what makes up proteins, and proteins are what go together to make living cells.

DNA, as applied in the court setting, is genetic testing, and genetic testing is a method to look for the variability in the DNA.

Every cell in the body has a complete copy of the DNA. You can compare blood cells that have a nucleus to cells from saliva, to a hair root, to spermatoza in semen, to urine, or to cells isolated from bone, teeth, or tissue. If hair is used, the root is needed because that is where the cells are found.

No matter where the DNA comes from in the body, it's going to be the same.

Dr. Bing told the court that in the McGinn case he tested for six different markers in the DNA.

He had received a package from Michelle Lockhoof at the Texas Department of Safety in Austin, Texas, via Airborne Express. He stated that the package was sealed, and after opening it, he identified several items found inside: an item labeled ax scrapings, stained strings from ax, blood crust from metal frame, blood from Ricky McGinn, blood stain from Stephanie Flanary, stain on victim's shorts, piece of material from shorts, piece of shirt, piece of the victim's shirt with stain, and pubic hair.

After numbering each item with his own system, Dr. Bing actually extracted DNA from each of the items. The DNA was purified and then the amount of DNA in the sample was actually measured, then the DNA of each item was copied.

To demonstrate his findings, Lee Haney set up a chart prepared by Dr. Bing. It contained all the numbers that he assigned to the tested items.

A distinctive female voice interrupted the proceedings. Everyone turned to look toward the jury box.

"Can we display this in a little better manner?" a female juror asked. "I'm having a hard time seeing it."

Haney moved the exhibit so that all the jury could see it clearly. The juror smiled and nodded slightly, indicating her ability to see the chart and her appreciation.

The scientist deciphered each of the columns of his chart in language that seemed foreign at times. McGinn was as confused as the jury appeared to be, expressions of concentration on their faces.

McGinn recorded the moment:

Dr. David Bing—CPR Boston Lab—This guy talks to the jury in long length to make himself look all that. I don't believe this jury understands a word he says but they will think he is really something by all the talk and big words he uses. He says he was on leave from his job from 1983–1986. I wonder why he was on leave.

Finishing the puzzling terminology of the columns, Dr. Bing moved on to the rows shown on his diagram. The first row showed that whoever was the donor of the DNA for the ax scrapings had A alleles, paired genes determining characteristics. The second, the stained strings from the ax, was the same as the scrapings, as was the blood crust from the metal frame. The fourth, a blood stain from Ricky McGinn, indicated a different DNA type than was found on the ax and on the metal frame.

"So already we know that sample is from a different person, that Mr. McGinn is not the donor of the DNA taken off the previous items," Dr. Bing stated.

The fifth row, a blood stain from Stephanie Flanary, was marked with "NS," standing for none seen. Dr. Bing indicated that the stain was very light and difficult to work with. He was unable to obtain a DNA type. That could have been because there was not enough blood to examine the stain or because the DNA had degraded, as DNA will do outside the body.

The sixth row represented the victim's shorts. Dr. Bing prefaced his findings by saying that in sexual-assault cases where a stain is left behind, it contains semen as a result of the sexual assault. That stain will, in most cases, be a mixture of two individuals. It will be a mixture of the person who was assaulted and it will be a mixture of spermatazoa from the assailant. It is possible, however, to separate those two kinds of cells through DNA technology, separating nonsperm cells from sperm cells.

But with all the technology at their disposal, Dr. Bing and his staff were unable to obtain a result. He indicated that, more likely than not, there just wasn't any DNA there to really test. Likewise, he was unable to test any DNA on the victim's-shorts control, or small sample of the fabric. He had the same results with the victim's-shirt control. He found the same DNA type on the blood stain of the shirt as he had found on the ax and metal frame. Meaning, the blood stains belonged to Stephanie Flanary.

Dr. Bing finally came to the results of his testing done on the pubic hair, the one piece of evidence most interesting to those in the audience.

"The hair that we got, when I examined it under the microscope, there was a little root material on the bottom of it. So I proceeded to try to isolate DNA from that root.

"As a control we cut a piece from the shaft of the hair. The shaft of the hair has no cellular material on it that contains nuclear DNA. So that is run as a control.

Dr. Bing explained that the hair could possibly have other cellular material on it, such as blood. That blood could possibly be typed.

"That would be consistent with that hair not coming from the individual who might be typed at the root. It might come from another source. So I run that control," Dr. Bing said in a lengthy explanation.

Despite all of his testing, Dr. Bing was unable to give

a reportable genetic type. In other words, the pubic hair test was inconclusive.

Referring to a second package received from Michelle Lockhoof, Dr. Bing identified it as Steve Sirois's blood stain. Sirois was excluded as the donor of all other blood stains analyzed.

Haney, having finally gotten through the detailed scientific material, passed the witness to Sudderth.

Sudderth, rather than further muddying the waters with more explicit jargon, decided to summarize Dr. Bing's findings for the benefit of the jury.

"The blood found on the ax, the metal frame, and on the victim's shirt appears to be the same blood. Doesn't it?" Sudderth said, going straight to the point.

"Yes, it does," Dr. Bing said.

"But it's not the blood of Ricky McGinn, is it?" Sudderth asked.

"No, it is not."

"Now, then, the blood from the same three items don't match Steve Sirois, do they?" Sudderth inquired.

"No, they do not."

"The pubic hair doesn't match Steve Sirois, does it?" Sudderth asked artfully.

"I can't come to any conclusion about that," Dr. Bing stated.

"You cannot come to a conclusion as to whether or not it matches Steve Sirois or not. Is that correct?" Sudderth said, emphasizing his point to the jury.

"No."

Sudderth stated that Dr. Bing had been testifying for over an hour, but it all boiled down to the summary he made in less than fifteen minutes.

"If we had been able to test pubic hair roots and his blood, that possibly could have exonerated Ricky McGinn, couldn't it?" Sudderth asked, simplifying the doctor's former lengthy explanation.

"That's correct," Dr. Bing said.

"But you couldn't make that test. And it would certainly be a grave mistake to start making assumptions based upon those tests that you couldn't make. Is that correct, Dr. Bing?" Sudderth asked.

Dr. Bing said that a more positive way to state it was that in forensic testing a positive result is the only thing that can be interpreted Ultimately he admitted he could not make a positive interpretation.

Sudderth then returned to his familiar attack, asking the doctor if he had run tests on blood or pubic hair donated by Steve Flanary or by Joe Bob Talley. Dr. Bing admitted he had not, only testing the items sent to him by the Department of Public Safety in Austin.

Sudderth thanked Dr. Bing and passed the witness. The attorney was clearly hoping the jurors would grasp the implication that authorities had again focused on McGinn without pursuing the possibility of other suspects.

Haney had no further questions and Dr. Bing was excused at 10:40 A.M.

The state's next scheduled witnesses were not present in the courtroom and weren't expected until the next day. To the gratification of the jury, their heads swimming with DNA facts, the judge announced a welcome early release.

As the jury moved out of the courtroom and the audience waited for their departure before taking their own leave, Ricky McGinn turned to his sister Verilyn. They exchanged smiles and quick words of encouragement. McGinn was escorted from the hall of justice, back to the county jail, where he would eat a sandwich, change into his county-issued jail uniform, and wait for the eighth day of his trial to begin.

The next morning the jury, McGinn, and the audience looked refreshed from the extended recess. However, the two attorneys, who had worked on their respective cases throughout the night, appeared haggard and starved for sleep.

"State ready to proceed?" Judge Cadenhead asked.

With Haney responding that he was, and Sudderth responding in like manner, Sudderth began his cross-examination of Steve Robertson, the person who had examined the hair submitted to the DPS lab in Austin.

Robertson began by answering the defense's question concerning the difference between identification evidence and association evidence.

He stated that identification evidence is like a fingerprint, something uniquely coming from a certain source and no other. While association evidence would be like having a black-and-white dog at home, then finding black-and-white dog hair in your car and saying that black-and-white dog hair came from your dog or from any other black-and-white dog. That's an association, not an identification.

Sudderth's questioning became tiresome as he attempted to have the witness admit that the hair he tested in the McGinn case "could be" that of McGinn but that his testing hadn't ruled out the possibility of other donors.

Under the heading of "Steve Robertson—DPS Lab Austin—Cross-examine," McGinn wrote:

> Doesn't want to answer Ben's questions. I believe because if he answers Ben's questions it would make him to be wrong about his earlier statement on the stand. He sure is hesitant about answering questions. He won't answer questions straight out.

Robertson explained that he had looked at all the characteristics of the hair when conducting his tests, including the length, diameter, color, individual pigment granule size, shape, the distribution of the hair, the presence of the medulla and its shape, thickness and color and variation in the thickness in the cuticle. He added that characteristics are generally shared to some extent by all persons of the Caucasian race.

"Would you say there is in general more variation among Caucasian scalp hairs than among Caucasian pubic hairs?" Sudderth asked.

"Yes, sir."

"So isn't it true that the probability that two persons would share pubic hair characteristics is greater than two persons would share scalp hair characteristics?" Sudderth continued.

"Yes, sir."

Robertson stated he had examined five pubic hairs from McGinn and found that they had similar microscopic characteristics to the one found in the vagina of Stephanie Flanary.

"Were any of the hairs identical to the hair found in the vagina of Stephanie Flanary?" Sudderth asked.

"If you consider identical to the minutest detail, no," Robertson answered.

"Is it your testimony today that the hair found in the vagina of Stephanie Flanary originated from the pubic hair of Ricky McGinn?" Sudderth asked.

"It could have, yes, sir."

Robertson stated further that he had no doubt that the hair matched McGinn's pubic hair, leading to a conclusion that it could be his or someone else's with hair like his, and conceding finally that the hair could have come from someone else.

As Sudderth concluded, Haney prepared his redirect questions.

"Is it your job to decide whether this hair is Mr. McGinn's beyond a reasonable doubt?" Haney asked.

"It's my job to come here and tell you in my opinion it could be his or somebody with hair just like his. My

understanding is, it is the jury that's giving the weight to
that testimony," Robertson answered.

McGinn observed in his journal:

> Now the D.A. will ask the same questions and get
> the answers he wants the jury to hear. D.A. is leading
> him to answers. I don't believe he really answered the
> questions asked truthfully. He gave different answers
> to same questions by Ben and the D.A.

Sudderth had a few questions yet to be answered by
Robertson. Had he examined the hair of Steve Flanary or
a person who was represented to have been seen driving
up and down the roads in a tan van? Robertson answered
by stating he had examined only the hairs given to him,
those of Steve Sirois, Stanley Sirois, Joe Bob Talley, Ricky
McGinn, and Stephanie Flanary.

Kenneth Crawford, a questioned document examiner for
the Texas Department of Public Safety Crime Laboratory,
approached the stand and took his seat.

Lee Haney handed Crawford a note that had been found
by one of the SAR dog teams about one hundred yards
beyond the tank, on the fence line of the McGinn property.

Crawford had been given a sample of the handwriting
of Ricky McGinn to make a comparison with the note
found in the field. The handwriting analyst had concluded
that the handwriting on the note was the same as Ricky
McGinn's.

As Crawford testified, McGinn wrote, in the same handwriting that was being questioned:

> Kenneth Crawford—DPS Crime Lab Handwriting
> expert. This is the guy who says it was my handwrit-
> ing on the note. This is really stupid and a waste of
> money. I have already said it was mine. The D.A., I
> believe, is just wanting to seem important and try to

make this note seem like a real piece of evidence in the case. I believe this guy is nutso or maybe on drugs. Probably had to get up too early to get here.

Crawford stated he had compared every detail of both the note and the defendant's sample writing—the letters, numerals, and other marks that had been made. He stated that every person, through years of practice, develops individualities in details that become recognizable as their own.

On cross-examination Sudderth answered the unasked question of almost everyone present in the courtroom: what did the note say?

"It says, 'Follow Fence To Dirt Road.' Is that correct?" Sudderth asked Crawford.

"Yes, sir."

The defense counsel asked the witness if as a child he had ever played the game treasure hunting. He described a game where notes would be left at various places, such as note number one, "Follow Creek," or note number two, "Follow the Tree Line," or go so many steps in a certain direction. McGinn had told his attorney, as well as investigators, that he had indeed written the note found in the field. However, he had contended all along that it had been penned as part of a game he had played with the girls.

Before noon Judge Cadenhead called for a three-day recess in order that jurors could observe the Memorial Day holiday.

NINETEEN

There were looks of dismay from the audience on the eighth day of trial as Linda Harrison identified herself as yet another expert in the area of serology and forensic DNA analysis. Would they have to endure another day of scientific mumbo jumbo? Fortunately, Harrison actually defined DNA in layman terms understandable by everyone in the courtroom.

On the notepad McGinn jotted down a couple of quick observations:

> Linda Harrison—F.B.I. I guess this will be another witness for the semen supposedly found in Steph's shorts. You can tell she has been on the stand more than once. She knows how to play the jury. She is sure making the jury believe she is really smart. I do believe she has gone over with Lee Haney the D.A. on what and how to ask her questions. D.A. made sure to let her explain to the jury that this test is used by a lot of places.

Harrison explained DNA stands for deoxyribonucleic acid, a chemical substance found in all living organisms— humans, animals, plants, and bacteria.

"It's actually the DNA that is responsible for the transmission of information from one generation to the next," Harrison said.

As had Dr. Bing before her, Harrison spoke extensively, using graphs and projections from an overhead device to explain the process of DNA analysis in explicit terms.

Finally, after considerable testimony, Mr. Haney addressed evidence submitted to the FBI lab for testing in regard to the McGinn case.

Again, as Dr. Bing had previously stated in his findings, Ms. Harrison was also unable to develop any profiles from the semen sample from Stephanie's shorts. She couldn't reach any conclusion. Results were also inconclusive for the source of semen on the vaginal swabs, the blood stain on McGinn's gray shorts, or any DNA profiles for the known blood sample from Stephanie Flanary. She was able to determine the stains on McGinn's tennis shoes and blue jeans did not originate from him, but she was unable to compare it with Stephanie Flanary's due to the degraded state of her DNA.

McGinn added to his notes:

She showed diagrams that I didn't get to see. I really don't think this woman should be able to stand there and tell the jury all the stuff about how to come to conclusions. I'm afraid they might try to come to conclusions on their own and we know they are not qualified to do so. I really believe she is just wasting the court's time trying to show the jury she is smart. I can't see why she can't just get down to the work she done in this case. She sure made it clear, stating twice that the blood didn't match mine from the tennis shoe. On the jeans she was able to say the blood not mine. I really think the D.A. is wasting time here. She is just telling what has already been said here in court. I really believe this is just a trick of the state to try to overwhelm the jury to keep their minds swayed to the state and keep them believing that I am guilty before I even put on my testimony or witnesses. I'm afraid already it will take a miracle to convince this jury to find me not guilty.

After an hour of testimony, Ben Sudderth began his cross-examination, and as he had done with Dr. Bing, he summarized Ms. Harrison's statements in a few short minutes.

"If the test had not been inconclusive, you might have identified the donor or excluded a donor, couldn't you?" Sudderth asked.

"I could have included him or absolutely excluded him, yes," Ms. Harrison stated.

Having made his point—that there was no way his client could be directly implicated by DNA—Sudderth relinquished the witness.

The lack of conclusive DNA hadn't stopped the district attorney from building his case against McGinn. He had explored every possibility in hoping to connect the blood found on McGinn's clothing to the victim. Dr. Arthur Eisenberg, an associate professor in the Department of Pathology at the University of North Texas Health Science Center in Fort Worth, was called on to take the testing one step further.

Dr. Eisenberg arrived in Brownwood the morning he was scheduled to testify. Utilizing a slide presentation, the doctor demonstrated how DNA can be isolated, then cut in fragments to identify an individual. What makes people different, what distinguishes one person from another, is the length of the piece of DNA that you inherit from your parents. Typically, most people will have two different-sized pieces. The chance of your mother and your father giving you the same-sized piece is rare.

The testing procedure described by Dr. Eisenberg is often used in paternity testing. Since half of the DNA comes from each parent, only two possible results can occur. One piece of the child has to match the mother; one piece of the child has to match the father.

Irritated by yet another expert witness evaluating the blood and semen samples, McGinn wrote:

> Dr. Arthur Eisenberg—Fort Worth lab—Another one to brag about how smart he is to impress the jury. This guy is showing slides to the jury on how he can match a child to the mother and father. And now I guess I won't get to see the pictures. I really believe I should be able to. I guess he will go through showing pieces that show the same thing. I believe this is another ordeal of the District Attorney Lee Haney to over prove a point he has already established. This just plants more stuff in the mind of the jury.

In relation to the McGinn case, Dr. Eisenberg's lab received blood stains from Janet Talley and one from Steve Flanary, as well as one from Denise Flanary. In addition, he received scrapings from an ax.

"What we were asked to do by the DPS lab was to determine in a reverse paternity analysis if the blood from the ax could have originated from the offspring of Janet Talley and Steve Flanary," Dr. Eisenberg stated.

The results of the reverse paternity tests indicated that the probability that Janet Talley and Steve Flanary were the biological parents of the individual whose blood was recovered from the ax was 99.9999999 percent.

Furthermore, Dr. Eisenberg had determined through his tests that the blood stain of Denise Flanary and the sample from the ax couldn't be excluded as coming from Janet Talley and Steve Flanary, but clearly the sample on the ax was not that of Denise Flanary.

In Dr. Eisenberg's final analysis, it was his opinion that the blood stain on the ax was that of Stephanie Flanary.

He stated that the blood on the blue jeans couldn't be excluded as originating from Stephanie Flanary.

McGinn added to his notes:

There is nothing there to include me in this although the blood in the car and the blood on the ax and the ax being found in the pickup at my house. It is going to be hard for the jury to not place me in the picture. I also believe this man is having a way big impact on the jury.

When Haney passed the witness, Sudderth, as before, summarized the doctor's findings. He asked few questions before passing the witness back to the prosecution.

McGinn recorded:

When Ben was questioning him he wanted to get smart and give smart-aleck answers. The way this guy put up his papers tells me more that he gave the D.A. questions to ask. You can tell the guy is here for nothing but to help the D.A. get a verdict of guilty, not whether or not I'm innocent. He didn't look at the jury when answering Ben's questions like he did with the D.A., instead he looked at the D.A. This guy has really been an impact on the jury. What this does is really put the burden on me or my lawyer to prove me innocent. I hope and pray this jury has not made up their mind yet. You can tell that this guy gave the D.A. the questions for him to ask. I believe this gave the state the edge on my lawyer.

Lee Haney stood, resting his fingertips on the tabletop, and announced, "The state rests."

As the jury was excused for the day, and the audience began milling around the courtroom discussing the state's case and anticipating what evidence the defense would present, McGinn watched Haney carefully.

Finally he picked up his pen and jotted down a few quick lines before being taken back to the jail: "Now the D.A. is running around like the big rooster of the yard. The D.A. feels now he has won this case."

McGinn had been waiting for more than a week for the opportunity to have his case presented to the jury. May 31, 1995 he arrived at court both nervous and scared.

Ben Doyle Sudderth stood before the court and announced that his first witness would be his client, Ricky McGinn. He asked the court to instruct the district attorney not to bring to the jury or let it be known that McGinn had been arrested for any other offense other than the one for which he'd been convicted, kidnapping.

Judge Cadenhead granted the motion.

McGinn wrote:

Ben to give his opening statement first, then I will take the stand. Right now I am nervous or scared or something. I guess I will just have to wait to see how things come out with me on the stand. The Lord knows I need help this morning while I'm on that stand so I will just wait and hope.

McGinn took a long deep breath as his attorney approached the jury to present his opening statements. The butterflies in McGinn's stomach were fluttering at the speed of hummingbird wings. He said a prayer for Ben and for himself.

"Now, in the old Perry Mason and Ben Matlock TV stories, about halfway through our testimony and evidence, someone should be expected to jump off of the witness stand and confess that they are the one that committed the offense," Sudderth said with a slight smile. "I don't expect that to happen in this case."

Sudderth reminded the jurors that it's not the responsibility of the defendant to solve a crime. He told them that his client didn't have the ability, the resources, or the obligation to explain the circumstances of the crime.

"The purpose of the opening statement is to sort of draw a road map for you, to let you know where we're going and how we're going to get there," Sudderth said.

That said, Sudderth outlined his intent in presenting McGinn's defense.

When the defense counselor had finished outlining his plan, he said, "We think that this testimony and evidence will be testimony and evidence that will show you and demonstrate to you that there were several other persons who had more opportunity and who, apparently, have not been totally candid and open with this jury.

"We ask you to listen very closely. We will try to move as fast as we can. And we appreciate your attention in advance. Thank you very much."

In a strong voice Sudderth announced, "Ricky McGinn."

McGinn stood, buttoned his blue jacket, and limped toward the bench, where he was sworn in by Judge Cadenhead.

Whispers circulated around the courtroom in anticipation of the defendant's testimony.

Verilyn smiled at her brother, and as their eyes locked, she gave a slight head nod of encouragement.

The defense began with McGinn telling how he had met Janet Talley.

"I was real impressed," McGinn said of his former wife.

He twisted in his seat as though trying to get comfortable. He later admitted he was trying to calm his nerves. He knew all too well that this was the one chance he had to tell his story, to convince the jury of his innocence.

Sudderth then focused on McGinn's employment at the time of his injury.

"We were carrying Sheetrock upstairs. I was backing up the stairs when my feet slipped. I fell down on the stairs with the Sheetrock. I went down a couple of steps on my backside. I knew I was hurt, but I went ahead and finished out that day and half of the next day," McGinn stated.

McGinn had hurt his leg, hip, and lower back in the accident. He had sought treatment from his family doctor, Dr. Billy Carpenter of Rising Star, and then with Dr. Walter Loyola, a neurologist in Abilene. McGinn stated he had been instructed not to do any stooping, bending, or lifting. He had been essentially put out of work.

The defendant concurred with prior testimony that there was no running water at the residence in Owens where he, Janet, and the girls had moved three weeks prior to Stephanie's death. He told the court that they hauled water from town or from Janet's parents' house in several water jugs: five gallons, ten gallons, and thirty gallons.

Sudderth established that if water weighs roughly eight pounds a gallon, then thirty gallons would weigh 240 pounds.

McGinn admitted he had tried to move the large water container but was unable to get it into the house alone. Most often, he said, they would have to dip water out of one container into another before it could be taken out of the car. Explaining that the water they carried in was the only water available to them, he said he would occasionally fill the bathtub to bathe or would take a bath in the tank.

"When I was growing up, I had to take a bath in a creek. Wasn't no different to me," McGinn said.

On the morning of May 23, 1993, three of the water jugs were in the car and the thirty-gallon container was behind the house, McGinn said.

He told jurors that he bowled until the time he got hurt, but he denied going to clubs at night.

When Sudderth asked if Janet frequented the clubs,

McGinn said she would occasionally go to the pub with her mother and some of her friends while he kept the kids at home.

In chronological order McGinn began to relate the events that occurred May 22, 1993, beginning with the departure of Janet for the bowling tournament. He said Steve Sirois was still there with a number of kids. Denise liked playing with them, so she'd asked if she could go to Steve's house. Sirois agreed; so when he left, he took Denise with him.

According to McGinn, he began to work on his pickup while Stephanie went swimming in the tank. He explained that the transmission had messed up and the torque converter had torn up the flywheel.

While he was working on the truck, he said his brother Randy came by to pick up a kitten for his daughter's birthday. Then he and Stephanie left to go into town and get some beer at Oleta's store.

McGinn said he had planned to drive around on the back roads and let Stephanie drive a little, then go back home and work on the pickup. McGinn stated he wasn't aware of the time.

When he returned, he'd focused his attention on the pickup, and Stephanie had gone swimming again. After a time McGinn had decided to go down to the tank where Stephanie was swimming and fish for a while.

He asserted Stephanie had driven the car down to the tank, backed it up, and parked it by the dam. He admitted that they had always thrown back any fish caught there before, but he decided to try to cook and eat them that day.

Stating that they had nothing to put the fish in, he had directed Stephanie just to throw them in the back of the car. They caught about ten of the pollywogs, also known as mud cats because of their taste.

He indicated they had cooked the fish over a fifty-five-gallon barrel, cut in half, with a grill rack on top. He had used mesquite wood for the fire and discarded the remains in a shed near the house where a number of cats had made their home.

"I think we probably need to back up." McGinn interrupted the testimony. "While I was working on the pickup, Stephanie was drinking my beer with me."

"Why were you allowing this twelve-year-old to drink beer?" Sudderth asked.

"Well, I would rather my kids know that they could do it at home, so they didn't have to run around somewhere else and do it," McGinn said.

McGinn answered yes when Sudderth asked him if he didn't think twelve was too young to experiment, but he stated that when he met Janet, four years earlier, the girls were already allowed to drink. He added that the only time Stephanie drank was when she would take a drink from their cans.

McGinn told the court that Stephanie had gotten sick to her stomach on the afternoon of May 22, and he told her to go in the house and lie down.

"I didn't feel sorry for her," McGinn stated. "I was hoping maybe that would learn her a lesson. If she got sick enough, maybe she wouldn't want to drink no more."

He indicated that Stephanie woke up from her drink-induced nap and asked to go to her grandparents' to go swimming.

"I told her it would be just a few more minutes and I would be ready to go," McGinn said.

He indicated she'd told him she was going for a walk. She'd headed off toward the tank, and that was the last time he saw her.

About an hour after McGinn said his stepdaughter went for her walk, he began looking for her. He called his friend Steve Sirois and told him Stephanie was missing and asked him to help look for her. When Sirois arrived, McGinn asked him to go through the pasture and look because he was tired and hurting, and he didn't know if he could walk through the pasture again.

"It was about to get dark, and Steve said he didn't know if he could see. I had flashlights, but he said he didn't know the pasture, but that he would drive around some more. I said, 'Go back the way that you didn't come over here. I will try to look in the pasture some more,' " McGinn continued.

McGinn claimed he went back to the search, then decided to call the police to get some help. While he waited for them to arrive, he continued looking for Stephanie.

"I called my mother and she said, don't worry about it, she would call everybody else," McGinn said.

Deputy Roberts arrived, the REACT team began coming in, and his relatives and friends began searching as McGinn stayed at the house. He claimed he never suggested that the search should not extend across Highway 183.

He said the search was temporarily suspended when a hard rain came in but resumed later.

Explaining the cap and note found in the field by one of the REACT team members, McGinn said, "Stephanie liked to play detectives, like a little treasure hunt. Her and her friend had been out there hiding notes. Finally they talked me into doing it with them. So we sat down there at the kitchen table, and I wrote out a bunch of notes. I walked through the pasture, putting those notes along the fence line and in trees. The cap was one of the clues that was put on the fence, with a note. They had to look under the cap to find the note."

McGinn indicated that the game he described had occurred about two weeks before Stephanie's disappearance.

Continuing his chronological account, McGinn said that at about 6:00 A.M. he decided to drive up to the end of the dirt road, approximately four miles round-trip, because it hadn't been searched during daylight. He claimed he drove at no more than twenty-five miles an hour and never stopped his car along the way. McGinn insisted he noticed no blood in the car as he drove along the unimproved roadway.

"When you got back, what did you do?" Sudderth asked.

"David Mercer called me over to his car; he said he needed to talk to me. He said, 'What did you do?' Right there, to me, he was blaming me for Stephanie's disappearance."

McGinn admitted that after the accusatory way in which Mercer had talked to him, he had indeed told Joe Bob Talley that Mercer didn't need to be there.

Next, McGinn said, he had given Grubbs and Smith permission to search the car and the house. McGinn raised the hatchback of the car for investigators and moved the water jugs around so that they could inspect it. He stated he was unaware of what they were searching for, but he had been told that the search dogs had hit on the car. He didn't take the jugs out of the car because at that point Glen Smith had asked him to step back.

Then Glen Smith asked McGinn where Stephanie was.

"I told him I didn't know where Stephanie was, that is why I called all of these people," McGinn said.

Next McGinn had shown Smith where he had thrown the leftovers of the fish and the grill where he had cooked them.

"You went in on Sunday afternoon to the sheriff's office. At whose request?" Sudderth asked.

"Glen Smith."

"Did he make any representations to you as to what would happen after he got through talking to you?" Sudderth asked.

"He told my mother and them that was there in the

house when we left that I would be back in a little while," McGinn answered.

"And has that little while now extended into two years?" Sudderth asked.

"Over."

"Did you have anything to do with Stephanie's disappearance except to consent to her going walking that afternoon?" Sudderth asked his client.

"No, sir," McGinn answered definitively.

"Do you know anything about how she met her death?" Sudderth asked.

"No, sir."

Following a brief morning recess, court reconvened with Sudderth continuing to question his client.

Appearing a bit more relaxed than prior to the short intermission of his morning testimony, McGinn stated that he didn't know why Stanley Sirois stopped by his house. He was sure he'd known that the car parked in his yard belonged to Tracey Shulze, one of the women who had gone to the bowling tournament with Janet and Robin.

In reference to his phone call to Janet on the night of Stephanie's disappearance, he told the jury that he didn't know how to get hold of Janet until Steve came over and telephoned Robin. At that time he told Janet that Stephanie was missing and that he was unable to find her. He admitted telling Janet to wait until the next morning to come home, just as Sirois had advised his own wife.

Knowing that the prosecution would bring up McGinn's prior conviction for kidnapping, Sudderth decided to take the offensive approach and broach the subject with his client before the district attorney had a chance.

"There was a friend of mine that had gotten some stuff stolen out of his vehicle. He had gone to the cops several times and told them where it was and everything, but they wouldn't do nothing.

"He wanted me to go to this guy's house and get him

and bring him out in the country to meet him, where he could talk to him and see if he could get his stuff back," McGinn explained.

He detailed how the man had attempted to run and was caught and brought back to the location a couple of times before his friend began to beat the man.

McGinn admitted that he'd pleaded guilty to kidnapping and received a probated sentence.

Sudderth had asked his client all the questions he believed pertinent in explaining the events of May 22, 1993. In passing the witness to the prosecution, Sudderth could only hope that the jury had listened carefully to McGinn's version of the circumstances and had believed his explanations.

Lee Haney stood and walked toward the man he was certain was responsible for the murder of Stephanie Flanary. He looked forward to the showdown.

The prosecutor began in a slow tempo, with observers expecting him to lead up to a crescendo of accusations.

McGinn swallowed hard. The fear he'd felt prior to taking the stand, which had subsided as his attorney had questioned him about the events of the night Stephanie disappeared, returned as Haney approached him.

Holding McGinn's underwear, shorts, tennis shoes, and shirt up for identification, Haney asked when the defendant remembered last wearing the garments.

"May 22, 1993," McGinn responded.

Then Haney presented McGinn's blue jeans and boots, repeating his question.

"May 23, 1993," McGinn said.

The accused stated that when the rain began to fall in the early-morning hours of May 23, he had gotten cool and went into his house and changed from shorts into jeans and slipped out of his tennis shoes into boots. He had also changed shirts.

Haney handed McGinn the note that was found on the fence of his property line, "Follow Fence To Dirt Road."

McGinn admitted writing the note, just as he had when his own attorney had asked him about the scrap of paper.

"Now, is there anything on that note that indicates when it was written?" Haney asked.

McGinn acknowledged there was not.

Addressing the injury to his back, Haney attempted to have McGinn admit that after being instructed not to bend, stoop, or lift, he had still bowled in his regular weekly league. McGinn, however, stated that he had attempted to bowl with his wife and in-laws, but that it was too strenuous and he had not completed the three-game series. On subsequent nights the team had carried him blind, meaning they had merely used his average rather than him physically participating in the games.

Continuing in an attempt to show the jury that McGinn's injury would not have made it impossible for him to carry a ninety to one-hundred-pound girl down an embankment to the culvert, Haney approached the subject of toting water to McGinn's rural residence.

"Y'all didn't have water turned on at that location. Is that correct?" Haney asked.

"That's correct," McGinn stated.

"It would have cost three hundred dollars to have that done?" Haney questioned.

"Somewhere thereabouts. I'm not sure exactly now how much it was. Between two and three," McGinn said.

"Didn't think you had enough money to do that?" Haney asked, setting up for his next question.

"No, sir, we didn't."

"Had enough money to buy beer and cigarettes, but not enough to turn on the water?" Haney asked smartly.

McGinn repeated that it would have taken $200 or $300 to have the water turned on at the house. Then he concurred with the prosecutor that he had carried a five-gallon container of water into the house, but he insisted he had had assistance in carrying the ten-gallon container, as well as the thirty-gallon barrel that was generally only three-quarters full before it was hauled into the house.

After Haney had a long question-and-answer session with McGinn concerning his past employment and places he and Janet had lived, he asked about drinking beer on the day of Stephanie's disappearance.

"Was Stephanie drinking out of your can, or she had her own beer?" Haney asked.

"No, sir. She was drinking out of mine," McGinn said.

"How many did you drink?" the prosecutor asked.

"Maybe four or five," McGinn said, not counting the two or three he had consumed on the way home from Oleta's.

McGinn finally affirmed that he had probably consumed twelve to fourteen beers throughout the day, but he stood firm at four or five as the number Stephanie had helped him drink. He claimed he had stopped drinking when he began searching for his stepdaughter.

"The story about the fish blood; that is your story and you're sticking to it. Right?" Haney asked with an air of sarcasm.

"I never said nothing about no fish blood. They asked me if I would open the car. I said, 'Yeah, sure, I'll open it, but it may smell like fish.' I never told them it was fish blood," McGinn argued.

McGinn insisted he didn't know how the blood got in the car and that he had only told investigators about going fishing because that's what he had done that day.

"Now, there have been people come in and testify about what you told them, correct?" Haney asked.

"Well, I believe they said some of the things that I didn't say," McGinn offered.

"What part of, say, Don Roberts's testimony about what

you told him do you disagree with or quarrel with?"
Haney asked.

When McGinn was unable to give a specific answer,
Haney began going down a list of statements Roberts testified McGinn had made to him on the night of the reported disappearance.

Following several statements made by Roberts and confirmed by McGinn, Haney stated, "She left, going west,
past the north end of the tank, toward the back of the lot,
which she did frequently, and then returned to the house
by way of County Road four-seventeen, though she did
not."

"I believe I told him that sometimes she would come
back on the dirt road, and sometimes she would circle
around the pasture and come back on the other side,"
McGinn corrected.

"You also said you could not locate her and called the
sheriff's office at approximately nine-forty P.M.," Haney
said.

"I never told him no time. No, sir," McGinn insisted.

Haney covered McGinn's conversation with Deputy
Mercer and his consent to give samples for the rape kit.

Sudderth asked for an early lunch recess, telling the
judge that he needed to discuss the scheduling of additional witnesses with his secretary. As the judge granted
the request, McGinn released a deep sigh. He was doing
fine, answering all the questions Haney had thrown at him,
but he knew better than to think the formidable prosecutor
had already waged his full attack.

Verilyn McGinn Harbin walked downstairs to the first
floor where her mother awaited word of her son's trial
appearance. Verilyn escorted her mother outside and to a
nearby park, where they sat and talked in private.

Francis couldn't eat during the hour and fifteen minutes
the court was on break. She was too upset, too tense know-

ing her son was being questioned by Lee Haney. She wanted to know every detail.

Having been swept away to the county jail for a quick sandwich, McGinn reentered the courtroom ready to face his accuser.

"Now, Mr. McGinn," Haney asked, beginning the afternoon session, "at what point did you first tell any of the law enforcement officers this business about going fishing the day before?"

"When they first started questioning me, that morning," McGinn replied.

The defendant explained that he had told investigators that the fish had swallowed the hooks, bled a lot, and they had been thrown in the back of the car. He had given the information the day he was asked what he had done with the fish he said he caught.

"What was the purpose of your going out there and looking for her?" Haney asked, concerning the search he claimed to have made.

"To see if I could find her," McGinn said.

"And if she was injured, you would have picked her up if you could have, wouldn't you?" Haney inquired.

"Yes, sir, if I could have, I sure would have," McGinn said.

"And you would have put her in the back of the car and taken her to the hospital if that's what was necessary, wouldn't you?" Haney asked in support of his contention that McGinn may well have been able to lift the ninety-pound girl and put her body in the car.

"No, sir. I would have put her in the front seat of the car." McGinn spoke so softly that jurors had difficulty hearing.

Switching gears, Haney questioned the defendant about the felony kidnapping he had been convicted of six years before. Again McGinn's responses were so low that jurors had to ask that he speak up.

"What was the man's reaction when he saw your friend?" Haney asked, referring to the kidnap victim.

"Acted like he was pretty scared," McGinn admitted.

As he had with his own attorney, McGinn recapped the events that led to his arrest and conviction for kidnapping including that he had driven the man back to town and left him at his house.

Haney's questioning ended with inquiries about telephone bills and what McGinn had to eat the night of Stephanie's disappearance as well as the following day. Then, with surprise registered on the faces of several in the audience, Haney passed the witness. He hadn't hammered McGinn as expected, hadn't produced any surprises.

Sudderth had a few more questions for his client.

"Have you ever seen that ax before, till you saw it here in the courtroom?" Sudderth asked.

"No, sir," McGinn said.

"Has the man that you assisted in tying up or participated in it in some way, back in 1987, has he written you a letter just this week, wishing you well in this matter?" Sudderth asked.

"Yes, sir."

The gallery registered surprise, many asking themselves why McGinn's kidnap victim would wish him well.

Haney rose again to address McGinn.

"Do you deny having sexual intercourse with Stephanie Flanary?" Haney fired at the witness.

"Yes, sir, I sure do," McGinn said with conviction.

"On Saturday [May 22, 1993] or any occasion?" Haney pressed.

"On any occasion," McGinn stated.

"Do you deny that Stephanie was killed?" Haney asked.

"I don't deny it, no," McGinn said.

"Well, we've had some people that have identified this body as being hers, and I will ask you to identify it if you have any doubt in your mind," Haney stated.

"I thought that is why I was on trial," McGinn said.

Haney handed him a photo of the body of Stephanie Flanary and watched for McGinn's reaction. McGinn looked at the photo, then to Haney, sadness and sorrow in his eyes.

"Can you identify it?" Haney asked.

"Yes, sir. It is Stephanie," McGinn said softly, his head bowed.

"Thank you. Do you need to take a break?" Haney offered.

McGinn shook his head no.

Haney was almost through. He had only one additional point to make.

Looking at a map showing the McGinn property and the surrounding area and pointing to a portion of the map, Haney asked, "Your testimony was that in the early-morning hours of Sunday, you went in your Ford Escort and traveled down this road, in this direction."

"Yes, sir, over to this highway," McGinn said, indicating on the map.

"You could have taken a right on County Road three sixty-six from that road, could you not?" Haney inquired.

"I guess you could, yes."

"And had you taken County Road three sixty-six, it would take you back to U.S. Highway one eighty-three, would it not?" Haney proceeded.

"Yes, sir."

"And then, if you crossed U.S. Highway one eighty-three, it would take you down Farm-to-Market Road fourteen sixty-seven, would it not?" Haney asked.

"Yes, sir."

Haney was prepared to ask his final question.

"And four-tenths of a mile from U.S. one eighty-three, on Farm-to-Market Road fourteen sixty-seven, has been identified as the place where the body was found in the culvert. Is that correct?"

"Yes, sir," McGinn said. "Can I have some water, please?"

Sudderth responded to the request, handing his client the glass of water. McGinn drank, swallowing hard. He mentally prepared to answer more of the district attorney's questions, but, to his surprise, Haney passed him on to Sudderth. Sudderth had no further questions.

At 1:30 P.M. McGinn returned to his seat. He had done all he could to enhance his case; it was now up to Ben Sudderth and the remaining defense witnesses to help prove him not guilty.

A tall young man timidly walked into the courtroom; his eyes shifted anxiously from the jury to the judge to the defendant. Sudderth hoped the teen's testimony would at least create reasonable doubt.

TWENTY

John Dustin Bilbrey was a seventeen-year-old who had graduated from Rising Star High School. In May 1993 he was a high school sophomore and a personal friend of the McGinn family.

Like many in the Rising Star community, "Dusty," as he was known to his friends, had volunteered to look for Stephanie Flanary.

Through Sudderth's questioning Dusty relayed to the court a drive he and the lawyer had taken the week prior to his testifying in court. The two had been driving down Highway one eighty-three when Sudderth punched his odometer to reset the mileage meter. Sudderth had instructed the teen to tell him to stop whenever there was something he wanted the defense attorney to see.

The duo proceeded east on Highway 1467 until Dusty Bilbrey hollered, "Stop." When Sudderth's car came to a rest, it was perched atop a culvert, four-tenths of a mile from the McGinn house.

"Why did you tell me to stop?" Sudderth asked his witness.

"Because it was one of the culverts that we checked. It was Sunday when they had all the helicopters and everything out there. Sunday, May twenty-third," Dusty said nervously.

Dusty Bilbrey described heat-sensitive helicopters flying

overhead as he bent down, thoroughly inspecting the inside of the culvert. He'd seen nothing but slow-running water.

"You're quite sure you checked the culvert that is four-tenths of a mile from Highway one eighty-three going east on fourteen sixty-seven?" Sudderth asked.

"Yes, sir."

"And are you quite sure that when you checked that culvert in the evening of May 23, 1993, on a Sunday, that there was no body in that culvert?" Sudderth asked to make certain jurors understood the implication.

"Yes, sir," Dusty replied.

There was a buzz among the courtroom gossips as everyone began to ponder the implication of Bilbrey's statements. If Ricky McGinn had been taken to the Brown County Sheriff's Office around noon on Sunday and arrested later that night, and if Stephanie Flanary's body wasn't in the culvert on Sunday evening, as Bilbrey said, then who had put it there sometime before Tuesday when the corpse was discovered?

Bilbrey's testimony could have devastating implications for the prosecution. Haney immediately took action to neutralize the young man's words.

"When was the first time that you reported checking this culvert to any law enforcement agency?" Haney asked.

Bilbrey twisted nervously. He was certain of what he had told the court, but his lack of sophistication made him apprehensive. His words came out softly as he asked Haney to repeat the question. He then admitted that he had never reported to authorities the results of his search.

About two weeks before the beginning of McGinn's trial, Dusty Bilbrey had visited Francis McGinn's home. As a friend of the family, he had gone there to pick up a graduation present from Francis's granddaughter. Bilbrey related to the McGinns the incident of inspecting the culvert and finding nothing. At the insistence of Francis, the young man had contacted Sudderth and ultimately taken him to the culvert in question.

"Did you ever tell anybody before two weeks ago when you were at the McGinn residence?" Haney asked.

"No, sir," Bilbrey admitted.

Neither Haney nor Sudderth had any further questions and Bilbrey was excused. Only time would tell if the jury believed the teen's story or if it had added any significance to the guilt or innocence of McGinn.

Betty Laird, a counselor at the Girl Scout Camp at Lake Brownwood, was next on the defense witness list. She told the court that being a friend of the McGinn family's, she had joined the search for Stephanie a little after midnight on Sunday morning. One of the places she had looked for the missing girl was in a Dodge pickup truck parked on the McGinn property.

"Did you open the door at a level where you could see underneath the seat and see the area of the vehicle?" Sudderth asked, setting up his next question.

"Yes, sir."

"Did you see any kind of ax or weapon there?" Sudderth prodded.

"No, sir."

Laird described trash and other "stuff" she observed in the pickup cab, but she denied seeing any type of weapon. Likewise, she had found neither Stephanie nor anything of significance at the outbuildings she had searched along with Mike McGinn.

Laird had observed Ricky McGinn during the search and she agreed with the defense counsel that he appeared both genuinely concerned and worried for the missing child. Laird had, however, never spoken to Ricky McGinn personally.

As Lee Haney began his cross-examination, Laird clarified that she had not actually opened the doors to the

Dodge truck but that they were already open when she arrived.

"Which door did you look in?" Haney asked.

"I glanced around both doors, really," Laird said.

"Okay. What did you see in the pickup?" Haney wanted to know.

"Nothing special," Laird stated, adding that she had not seen anything at all under the seat.

Laird was released as Brittney Anderson entered.

Anderson had been a friend of the McGinns' for years and was Lisa McGinn's onetime roommate. She had helped McGinn pack, take down the water bed, and load some of the heavier things when he moved his family to the Owens Community. She believed McGinn was in pain and told the court that, due to his injury, he had been unable to lift much.

Like Bilbrey and Laird, Anderson had joined in the efforts to find Stephanie on Saturday night, May 22. She had helped form a human chain that involved more than fifteen people crossing the back pasture while holding flashlights in hopes of finding the girl.

In an effort to eliminate possible hiding places, Anderson had peered through the windows of the empty Dodge pickup, but she hadn't opened the doors or looked under the seat. She had also searched an old building close by the property.

The elusive tan truck once again arose as Sudderth questioned Anderson about efforts she had made in attempting to locate both the vehicle and the driver.

"Were you ever able to locate the tan truck and the man with the reddish blond hair?" Sudderth asked.

"No, I have never seen it," Anderson admitted.

Haney's cross-examination focused on Anderson's relationship with the McGinn family more than on any information she might have for the court. After asking only a dozen questions, Haney excused the witness.

McGinn had little to write about following every of the defense witnesses. He sat listening intently as every person talked about their role in the search for Stephanie and their knowledge of McGinn and his family. He watched the jurors' faces but had no indication of how they were responding to the testimony.

McGinn's thoughts were interrupted by the announcement of Vondell Stewart, the next person called in his defense.

A close friend of Francis McGinn's for twenty-two years, Mrs. Stewart had been called the night of Stephanie Flanary's disappearance to pray for the child. Not only had Mrs. Stewart prayed, she had also gone to Owens to be with Francis during the crisis.

"Were you there when a man reported a person in a truck with reddish blond hair driving up and down that road?" Sudderth asked.

"Yes," Mrs. Stewart said. "He said that there was a man down the street a little ways hollering obscene language to little kids out in the yard playing, telling them they need to get their underclothes on, and that he had reddish blond–looking hair and was driving a tan-colored pickup.

"I gave Sister McGinn a pen and paper and she wrote all of this down and gave it to Steve Sirois. He took it to the law officers and handed it to them."

"And did the law officers appear to have any interest in this report at all, Mrs. Stewart?" Sudderth asked.

"I couldn't hear what they were saying from where I was, but he said they told him they were checking out other leads at the time," Mrs. Stewart said.

Sudderth switched his attention from the mystery man to Janet Talley.

Responding to Sudderth's questions, Mrs. Stewart told the court that Janet had arrived home around 4:00 on Sunday afternoon from the bowling tournament in Arlington.

In Mrs. Stewart's opinion, Janet was intoxicated, barely able to stand.

"Did she appear to exhibit any concern over Stephanie?" Sudderth asked.

"Not at first, she did not," Mrs. Stewart replied.

Lee Haney made only two points during his brief cross-examination. First, Mrs. Stewart never saw the mysterious man alluded to by others, and second, she didn't approve of drinking by anyone, including a twelve-year-old girl or a twenty-five-year-old man.

McGinn sat back in his chair and waited for the jury to retire to the jury room for a brief recess. He was concerned about the next witness on Sudderth's list.

Lisa McGinn had been an ardent supporter and she was determined to help clear her brother's name. Aiding in the search for Stephanie, Lisa had even put herself at risk in an effort to learn about the mysterious man seen cruising the roads prior to Stephanie's disappearance. Now she was about to take the stand in her brother's defense. McGinn hoped his baby sister would be able to withstand the pressure.

With the jury back in place, Lisa McGinn took her place in the witness chair and locked eyes with her brother.

The twenty-nine-year-old, with long, wavy hair that was cut short on the sides and top but hung down her back, explained that she was in Abilene, Texas, with friends when her brother first called their mother on the evening of May 22, 1993. As soon as she received word that Stephanie was gone, she'd hurried back to Rising Star, picked up her mother, and headed out to the home of Ricky and Janet McGinn.

Lisa McGinn had immediately joined in the search, looking all around the property and going to an old motorcycle shop in Owens. While at the shop Lisa had seen a man in a tan-colored pickup truck. At about five feet eight inches, the man was close to Lisa's own height. He had reddish hair and a mustache.

"He acted kind of off-the-wall, I guess you'd say," Lisa said, describing the man's behavior to the jury.

"Did you see anything that was covered up on the floorboard?" Sudderth asked, referring to the strange man's pickup.

"Yes, sir. Looked like a hump of something with a blanket just threw over it," Lisa McGinn said.

"Did you ever see that man again?" Sudderth asked.

"Yes," Lisa said. "A couple of weeks later, I saw him at E-Z Mart, used to be called Bubba's, out toward Rising Star. I seen him and Steve Sirois in there talking. And I walked up and overheard a conversation."

"What did you hear said?" Sudderth asked, attempting to introduce testimony that would impeach Sirois as a witness for the prosecution.

"Steve Sirois told the man that he had two weeks to get him his money, or else. Steve sounded mad. And then I walked up closer, and they saw me. And that was it. That's all that was said. When I left, they left behind me. Steve Sirois was in front, and the other guy was behind. They had me boxed in [my car]," Lisa McGinn explained.

She told the court that she had made an effort to get out of the situation by speeding up and slowing down or pulling over, but the two men would respond in like manner. Lisa had finally escaped the encounter when additional traffic approached. She was positive the man in the pickup she saw at the old shop on the night of Stephanie's disappearance was the same man who'd helped Sirois box her in.

McGinn shook his head, disturbed by the testimony his sister had given. He pulled his notepad closer and wrote a couple of impressions: "Lisa McGinn—involved with all of this mess. Had encounter with Steve after I was in jail."

Lisa McGinn, her slim body trembling slightly as she

spoke, related another encounter with Sirois the day before Stephanie's body was found. She stated that Sirois had claimed to know that Ricky was guilty of the crime and that he had sources of information to confirm it.

Sudderth redirected his questioning, asking questions relating to Stephanie's drinking habits.

Lisa told the jury that on more than one occasion she had seen Stephanie go to the refrigerator in her home, get a beer, open it, and drink the entire can in the presence of her mother. Stephanie had only been eight or nine years old when Lisa first observed the behavior. Francis McGinn, a minister who was opposed to drinking, had voiced her concerns over the practice, but Janet had merely shrugged it off.

After telling the court that, in her observations, Ricky could not have lifted a ninety-pound weight due to his back and leg injury, Sudderth said, "Let me ask you this. Did you go to the culvert there, four-tenths of a mile east on Highway one eighty-three, and observe the location of where the body of Stephanie Flanary had been located?"

Lisa McGinn replied yes, she had been at the site the day after Stephanie was found. She had noticed the steepness of the embankment leading down to the opening of the culvert and the rocky terrain. In her opinion Ricky would never have been able to navigate the incline, much less carry a ninety-pound or one-hundred-pound body down into the ravine and place it in the narrow opening.

Additionally, Lisa stated that while she was at the site, inspecting the interior of the tin horn, she had plainly seen sticky, undried blood and a handprint smaller than Stephanie's and not large enough to be Ricky's on the interior wall. Her brother Randy had videotaped the print.

As had the witness before her, Lisa commented on Janet's condition when she arrived home from the Arlington bowling trip.

"She was very intoxicated," Lisa testified.

"Did she seem to be concerned or have any interest in the fact that this little girl was missing?" Sudderth asked.

"In my opinion she was too drunk to know the difference," Lisa McGinn said, a bit of bitterness in her voice.

"All right, now, what kind of car did Ricky and Janet normally drive?" Sudderth asked.

"An '87 Ford Escort."

"Did you have occasion to be in that car on the night of May 22, 1993?" the attorney asked.

Lisa had been in the car, having been asked to move it so that the REACT team could get through the gate of the property. Lisa hadn't noticed any blood or smears, hadn't smelled anything unusual or abnormal.

Sudderth had covered the subjects he intended to pursue with Lisa McGinn. He passed the witness.

McGinn jotted down a couple of additional thoughts:

> I really don't believe Stephanie ever drank as much as people say. I wonder just how drunk Janet was when she got home.

Both McGinns, the defendant and the witness, took deep breaths and prepared for Lee Haney's expected grilling.

Haney began refuting Lisa McGinn's testimony instantly by getting her to admit that she hadn't arrived at her brother's house until nearly 11:00 P.M., clearly indicating that it was dark outside, not just beginning to get dark as she had earlier testified.

Lisa was surprised to hear that both Betsy Laird and Brittney Anderson had testified under oath that they had never seen a man or a tan truck at the old motorcycle shop, as Lisa claimed. She told Haney that the license number had been written down and she believed it had been passed on to the police.

As soon as Lisa McGinn stated that the man had been sitting in his pickup, Haney retorted with, "So you were able to describe this man as being five feet eight inches tall, based on him sitting in his pickup. Is that correct?"

"He got out of the pickup one time," Lisa explained.

"When was that?" Haney asked.

"Somewhere during the course of our conversation. But he wasn't out but for just a minute. But it was long enough for me to see what he looked like," Lisa answered.

"Why did he get out?" Haney asked.

"Because he wanted to. I don't know," Lisa said, somewhat flustered.

Haney continued the interrogation, asking about the make and model of the truck, if the location was well lit, and how long her conversation had lasted.

McGinn watched the questioning with concern for his sister. He wrote in his journal: "The D.A. is sure tearing Lisa up. I hope she can hold up ok."

Moving to the subject of her encounter with Sirois and the other man, she stated that she didn't report the incident but had gone straight to her mother's house.

Asked about the videotape of the culvert, Lisa McGinn stated that the handprint was on the right side of the interior of the tin horn.

"How do you tell the sex of a handprint?" Haney asked, a bit of sarcasm in his voice.

"It just didn't look like any woman's hand I ever saw," Lisa replied.

Concerning the subject of Stephanie's drinking, Lisa insisted she had never seen Ricky give the girl any beer, but she admitted that Stephanie drank every time her mom would let her.

"So I guess she would drink if Rick let her, too, wouldn't she?" Haney asked.

"I guess she would," Lisa said.

Lisa McGinn admitted that any conversation her mother had with her brother about Stephanie's drinking hadn't stopped him from letting her indulge. She added that she had heard Ricky object a number of times to Stephanie's consumption of beer.

Haney passed the witness.

Both brother and sister were relieved when Lisa was released from the stand.

Sudderth broke the tense mood of the courtroom when he asked his next witness, Betty Floyd, "Mrs. Floyd, where do you live?"

"Rising Star, Texas."

"Is there anybody left in Rising Star today?" Sudderth asked lightheartedly, referring to the small population of the community and the number of witnesses from the tiny town.

Mrs. Floyd told a story of picking up a man, about five feet eight inches, fairly stocky, wearing Western clothes and a cowboy hat, beside a tan pickup parked by the side of the road. His truck had broken down, and Mrs. Floyd had taken him to Rising Star and dropped him at what the man indicated was a friend's house.

Mrs. Floyd knew the friend's house well. It belonged to Louie Wyatt, the Rising Star chief of police. When she later questioned Wyatt about the man, asking his name, Mrs. Floyd stated, "He said, 'I don't want to talk about it.' "

Sudderth passed the witness and Haney had no question. Mrs. Floyd stepped down.

Sudderth had just added another building block to their defense of conspiracy.

Mike McGinn glanced toward his brother, then to his sister Verilyn as he settled into the witness chair at the front of the courtroom.

He related much the same story as his sister regarding the mysterious man seen at the old motorcycle shop the night of Stephanie's disappearance, but he stated he did not recall the man getting out of the pickup.

In addition, Mike McGinn said he had seen the man

before, in the flower shop where Mike worked in Brownwood. He believed the man's last name to be Jackson. Then he recalled seeing him at his brother's house the night Stephanie was reported missing.

"I just saw him walking around, through the crowd of people. As far as I know, he wasn't talking to anybody, just walking around, looking, I guess," Mike said.

Like Lisa, Mike had noticed the man's truck floorboard on the night they encountered him at the old shop.

"I saw just the right-hand floorboard was full of stuff. And it was covered with clothes or something. I don't know what was in there or what it was, but it was just covered up with clothes," Mike said.

Mike McGinn testified that he had seen his brother limping a lot and that his leg would "kind of go out" as he walked, impeding his mobility. Mike had helped him move from Brownwood to Owens because, he stated, his brother was unable to do it himself. His ability to lift was impeded.

As Mike was excused and Sudderth and Haney approached the bench to discuss the possibility of recessing for the day, McGinn wrote: "Mike McGinn—Was involved in all of this mess. Not a very good witness though."

The defense had called it a day, indicating that they had only a few witnesses left before they would rest their case.

McGinn returned to the jail for another night of restless sleep—miles away, in Rising Star, his mother lay awake most of the night, praying.

TWENTY-ONE

It was June 1, 1995, day eleven of the McGinn murder trial. Everyone involved—the McGinn family, the Talleys, Janet, the attorneys, the jury, and those who had been attending each day—was weary. Ben Sudderth knew something no one else expected, this was the day he intended to rest his case.

Judge Cadenhead's homespun humor added a bit of levity to the otherwise stoic atmosphere. "Before we begin today, we told you last week that we were not going to work on Friday, the second of June. Now, matters have developed where we could. But I'm going to leave it up to you folks," the judge said, addressing the jury.

"Let's do it," a juror blurted out, tired of the grind of the trial and ready to return to his normal routine as soon as possible.

Another concurred, "Let's do it."

"Well, has anybody purchased weekend tickets to Bongo Bongo or anything like that?" the judge asked, smiling.

"Unanimous," spoke up a juror.

One hand was raised among the fourteen jurors and alternates.

"You can't win," a man told his fellow juror.

Judge Cadenhead ordered a three-minute break for the jury to discuss the options of working or taking Friday off.

Within minutes the panelists were back in their seats.

"I believe you folks have decided to work from 8:30 in the morning until noon," Cadenhead announced. Cadenhead then swore in Sudderth's first two witnesses.

As the second witness left the courtroom to await his turn on the bench in the hall, Dr. Billy Carpenter took the stand.

Prior to Dr. Carpenter's retirement in November 1994, he had been in private medical practice in Rising Star since 1967. In March 1993 he had seen Ricky McGinn for an injury that McGinn said had occurred five days earlier.

While taking McGinn's medical history, Dr. Carpenter was told that McGinn had fallen, hitting his butt or hips. He was experiencing pain in that area. Dr. Carpenter had taken X rays, which didn't indicate a fracture, and he prescribed an anti-inflammatory drug.

Two days later, when McGinn returned complaining of pain when he had a bowel movement, Dr. Carpenter referred him to a neurologist.

Sudderth had no further questions and Haney had no questions at all.

The second of the two doctors entered and prepared to answer questions from both attorneys. Dr. Walter Loyola, a native of Puerto Rico, had been a neurosurgeon in Abilene, Texas, for eight years.

McGinn added to his notes:

Dr. Loyola—From Abilene—specialist in neurology. I guess will testify to my injury. Hope he can remember. Prescribed shots that I couldn't really afford so didn't go back.

The doctor described his medical specialty as one that deals with problems of the brain, with the spinal cord, or the nerves in the arms, legs, or face. He performed surgery on patients who had back, brain, or neck problems.

When Dr. Loyola examined Ricky McGinn on March 19, 1993, he learned that the patient had never had any back problems until March 12, when he fell backward while carrying a piece of Sheetrock.

"The first time that I saw him, I concluded that he basically was having what we call a sciatica. That is an injury to the sciatic nerve. That is a nerve that goes from the back all the way down to the right leg.

"I wasn't sure of what was causing the sciatica. By the history it seems that it was related to an injury that he had in his back. He also had some evidence of some injury to the ligaments in the leg, too," Dr. Loyola stated.

As the doctor described the injuries as normally painful and disabling, a couple of jurors glanced over at McGinn, their eyes drifting to his injured leg.

As treatment Dr. Loyola added a pain medication to the anti-inflammatory Dr. Carpenter had already prescribed. He saw McGinn on two additional visits, then advised him, because he wasn't any better, to have an injection of cortisone in his spine. An MRI, a computer picture of his spine, hadn't shone any specific compression to the nerve. Believing that McGinn probably had a stress injury to the nerve, Dr. Loyola believed the cortisone inside the canal of the spine could relieve his pain. McGinn had not returned for the injection.

"If the patient is denied medical treatment, and two years later he is still walking with a decided limp, what conclusion would you reach from that, Doctor?" Sudderth asked.

Dr. Loyola agreed with the defense counsel that some patients will get better without treatment but that some continue to experience pain and in some cases even atrophy, where the muscles get smaller. In that case physical therapy would be advised to keep that muscle tone in better shape.

While under examination by Lee Haney, Dr. Loyola stated he determined if a patient was having discomfort if the patient provided that information.

"The MRI showed no evidence of ruptured disk or pinched nerve. Is that correct?" Haney asked.

"Yes, sir," the doctor responded.

From the doctor's notes he indicated that the procedure of injecting a steroid into McGinn's spine was set for April 20, 1993, but that it would have to have been done at the hospital by an anesthesiologist. He admitted he didn't know if McGinn had ever had the procedure performed.

Haney passed the witness.

On redirect Sudderth brought to the attention of the court that McGinn was a "self-pay" patient, meaning he was personally paying for treatments and had no insurance to cover the costs. For that reason McGinn had not had the recommended treatment.

On recross Haney presented the topic of adrenaline and the effect it can have on a person's ability to do things they ordinarily wouldn't be able to accomplish.

Dr. Loyola used himself as an example in describing the effects of adrenaline on individuals.

"I can relate that to myself because I do a lot of brain surgeries and some of my brain surgeries will last eleven or twelve hours. Most of the surgeries are done under a microscope. And I spend those eleven or twelve hours without eating, without drinking, and without going to the bathroom. That has to do with endorphins and adrenaline."

The neurosurgeon stated that adrenaline levels can be increased by pain, anger, anxiety, stress, and fear.

"Is alcohol a pain medication in a sense?" Haney asked.

"Well, I think that anything that makes you less alert will decrease your level of pain a little bit," Dr. Loyola said.

McGinn added to his notes:

Now the D.A. is questioning about adrenaline. I guess he wants to say my adrenaline was up. The D.A. sure wants to confuse this jury.

As Dr. Loyola left, a third sibling of McGinn's took his seat in the yellow chair at the front.

Thirty-seven-year-old Randy McGinn was the tallest and most trim of the McGinn brothers. As he ran his fingers through his short brown hair and waited for his brother's attorney to ask the first question, Ricky McGinn wrote:

> Randy McGinn—took video of culvert. Was involved in searching. Will show and prove up part of the video of the culvert to this jury. Will try to show the jury the hand print in the culvert.

On Tuesday night, several hours after the discovery of Stephanie's body in the culvert, Randy, along with his wife, sister Verilyn, and brother-in-law Sammy, climbed down into the ditch leading to the opening of the tin horn. Randy had seen a handprint on the interior wall from outside the culvert. He had filmed it with his handheld camcorder, which had an attached light.

Sudderth asked the judge to air the tape outside the presence of the jury while Randy identified it as the tape he had a part in shooting at the crime scene.

McGinn had been watching the television screen with keen interest, but he couldn't seem to make out what Randy was talking about. He wrote:

> To me it didn't look very plain but maybe it will be plain enough to the jury. Maybe he can make them know he did see the handprint that he is trying to show.

After the jury returned, Sudderth asked Randy if he would like to amend his testimony as to when he shot the video after seeing the date illuminated on tape.

"May 26, Wednesday night," Randy corrected.

As the tape rolled for the jury, Randy commented that it wasn't as clear as he had thought it was, but that the handprint was there. A few moments later he said in a strong voice, "Right there."

The video was stopped.

The image on the screen was fuzzy, but Randy insisted that it was clearly visible with the human eye the night he saw it in the culvert.

"How do you know it was a handprint?" Sudderth asked.

"Just by the shape of the way it was. You could just tell it was a handprint," Randy responded.

Haney was back on his feet.

"You don't know whether or not other people, drawn by curiosity or whatever other motive, may have gone to that culvert between the time the law enforcement officers left Tuesday and the time you arrived Wednesday night, do you?" Haney asked.

"I guess they could have, yes, sir," Randy said.

"Was there anything at the scene when you arrived to keep people from going there?" Haney questioned.

"No, sir," Randy said, later acknowledging that he didn't know how the print had gotten there.

The second half of the tape would be presented through testimony of Lisa McGinn. Ricky McGinn's apprehension returned as his sister was recalled to the stand. Apparently, he was worried that his sister's testimony might do more harm than good:

> Lisa McGinn—To identify and try to show what part of the culvert she taped. I'm afraid Lisa is really too nervous to do this. I'm afraid Lisa will be torn up and won't be much good. She is really too nervous to be on the stand. I'm afraid of what the D.A. might be able to do to her. She gets mixed up really easy seems to me.

Lisa said she had taped the recording on Wednesday, May 26, during the daylight hours. As her brother before her, Lisa watched the video along with the jury and instructed that the tape be paused at one point.

She identified for the court a handprint. "Because of the way it was smeared, along the side, on the day when we were there, you could see the different fingerprints," Lisa McGinn said.

There were no additional questions from Sudderth. He seemed content to have admitted into evidence the handprint through both Randy's and Lisa's testimonies.

Haney set the record straight by pointing out to Lisa that the date on the video indicated that the tape she took was actually shot on Thursday, May 27, rather than Wednesday, May 26, as she had said. And after the video Randy had made, not before.

"Were there any police or other law enforcement agencies still there at the scene? Anything to keep anybody who wanted to from driving by and going down and looking in that culvert?" Haney asked.

"No, sir," Lisa said.

"D.A. is still trying to confuse her. He is really working hard to mix Lisa up," McGinn added to his notes.

Sudderth then asked two additional questions: First, was the blood dry? Second, would the handprint have to have been made while the blood was still wet?

Lisa McGinn stated the color of the print was still real red and she thought it would have had to be wet to make it appear in that manner.

As before, McGinn was relieved when Lisa was excused.

Sudderth was beginning to move at a fast pace. He called his fourth witness of the morning. Diane West, the daughter of Vondell Stewart, had been present when her mother and Francis McGinn were told about the man in the tannish pickup hollering at little girls who were playing in their yards.

West repeated the information her mother had given, confirming the words the man had allegedly used while yelling at the little girls—that they should get on their panties and bras. She also stated that Francis McGinn had written down the information, then given it to Steve Sirois to deliver to Deputy Glen Smith.

Haney's cross-examination point was that West hadn't heard the man who, someone else said, was making remarks to the children, nor had she seen him.

Within a matter of minutes West was excused.

Witness number five was Jesse Dale Bilbrey, also known as "Trey." The brother of Dusty Bilbrey, the first defense witness, Jesse had also joined in the search for Stephanie Flanary on May 22.

Trey had searched two old pickups parked at the McGinn residence. One, a white Dodge, the other a brown Dodge. He stated he had opened the doors to the pickups and looked inside.

"And were you situated so that you could see if there was anything under the seat or in the backseat?" Sudderth asked.

"Yeah," Trey Bilbrey said. "We had a flashlight so we could look under there. We looked behind the seat, too. We were looking for flashlights."

"Did you find an ax?" Sudderth asked.

"No, sir."

"If there had been an ax under the seat of the Dodge pickup, were you in a position to where you could have seen it?" Sudderth asked.

"Yes, sir."

Sudderth passed the witness.

"Tell me what you remember seeing in the brown pickup," Haney said, beginning his cross-examination.

"It was an old truck. It didn't look like it had been run for a while. It was old papers, old rusty tools, little bitty, like drill bits, probably," Trey Bilbrey answered.

"Do you remember seeing a speaker box in either of the pickups?" Haney asked.

"No, sir."

"Do you remember what was in the back of either of the pickups, the bed?" Haney asked.

"No, sir."

Trey Bilbrey was excused.

As Burl Chambers, the defense's next witness, began his testimony, courtroom observers wondered what a licensed mortician from Cisco, Texas, was going to tell the court. It wasn't long before their questions were answered.

"Based upon your experience and your educational background, about how long does it take blood to dry, assuming it's not raining and that it is normal weather?" Sudderth asked.

"That depends upon what I will call different factors. Basically, the amount of humidity in the air, whether the blood is on a nonporous surface, or if it's on a porous surface, if it's on clothing or something of this nature.

"Blood primarily, fifty to fifty-five percent of blood is plasma, which is predominately water. So water will evaporate fairly fast in a dry, nonhumid environment. If it's around concrete, anything that is cool and moist, it will take a longer period of time.

"I'll say about eighteen to twenty-four hours if it is not in a large diameter of blood," Chambers responded.

Sudderth wanted the mortician to be a bit more specific to McGinn's case. He asked, if the blood were found in a metal culvert in Brown County, how long would it take to dry?

"Twenty-four to thirty-six hours it should be tacky. Usually within forty-eight hours blood will be almost dry," Chambers said.

The defense was trying to make the point that if Stephanie's body had been put in the culvert on Saturday, May 22, any blood found in the culvert on Wednesday or Thursday would have been completely dried, not sticky or tacky.

McGinn wrote on his pad: "Burl Chambers—Cisco, Texas—Mortician testifies to how long it would take blood to dry or be sticky."

Under cross-examination Chambers gave an analogy to demonstrate in layman's terms the process of blood drying.

"It's like making Jell-O," Chambers said. "Usually you use hot water with a granular box mixture. The hot water dissolves the granules. Then most people will normally put in ice cubes or put it in the refrigerator.

"Blood is at body temperature, which is ninety-eight degrees. So as it cools, like Jell-O, it starts getting tacky. It starts congealing.

"And it is the same principle. But lying there in the natural state, it is going to take it longer to congeal. Usually eighteen to twenty-four hours you're going to wind up with the top surface tacky. And if it is of any depth, there is still going to be a liquid."

Chambers added, prompted by Haney's questioning, that if water came in contact with the blood it could reliquefy.

Then Haney waged an assault on Chambers's qualifications as a blood expert.

The mortician admitted that his state license qualified him to prepare human remains for preparation of embalming and for conducting funerals. He also admitted that he had never testified in a court of law as an expert witness in the field of serology or pathology, adding that a forensic serologist or forensic pathologist would be better qualified to express an expert opinion.

McGinn added to his notes:

D.A. wanted to prove he wasn't qualified or didn't know what he was doing. This was his first time to testify.

Leaving the jury with doubt concerning Chambers's testimony, Haney had no further questions.

Sudderth asked for a fifteen-minute recess to allow him time to telephone possible witnesses he anticipated presenting later in the day. When court reconvened, Francis McGinn, walking slowly and with difficulty, was seated in the witness chair.

Francis looked at her son; a smile crossed her lips, but pain ran deep in her eyes. She knew in her heart there was no way her baby boy could have killed Stephanie, the girl he had been raising as his own. She hoped she could make the jury believe in her son. She ran a hand through her gray hair, adjusted her eyeglasses, and prepared to be questioned by Ben Doyle Sudderth.

Francis proudly told the jury that she was the mother of Ricky McGinn, as well as five other boys and three girls.

The mother of nine would do anything to help her children, including assisting Ricky and Janet move into the house in Owens. At her age and with her physical limitations, Francis hadn't been able to lift any heavy objects, but she had done what she could to pitch in.

She didn't dwell on her own health problems, but she explained to the court that Ricky had difficulty walking, often dragging his leg along as he made his way around the property.

Francis McGinn related the story of being told about the man with the reddish blond hair, writing it all down, and having Steve Sirois give the note to authorities. To her knowledge, the lead had never been acted on.

The soft-spoken mother told of her daughter-in-law Janet arriving home, drunk, in her opinion, and the number of volunteer searchers that scattered across the McGinn property looking for Stephanie.

Ricky McGinn feared Lee Haney would mistreat his mother on the stand. He was afraid that his mother's heart couldn't take an intense drilling by Haney, but Haney was kind, almost gentle with Francis.

Francis had answered an earlier question by Sudderth, saying Ricky called her about 8:30 on the night Stephanie disappeared. Haney, however, told her telephone records actually revealed that he had called her at 9:53 P.M.

Francis McGinn was certain it had been earlier, but she admitted she couldn't be positive.

Haney had a few other questions before excusing the defendant's mother.

As Francis exited the courtroom, she linked eyes with her son. In a soft whisper Francis said, "I love you."

After his mother had left the courtroom and his attorney was at the bench asking for a lunch recess so that his next witness would have time to travel from Fort Worth, McGinn wrote:

> Francis McGinn—my Mama—Just testified to the fact that leads were given to the cops but the cops didn't follow up on the leads. She wanted to tell more but was stopped. The D.A. didn't try to do much. I think he might have been afraid to try an attack because he knows it wasn't investigated very well at all. He also knows they threw me in jail too early and therefore they have to prove it was me. Although, I really believe it has been up to Ben to prove I was not guilty.

As the jury and people who had been seated in the audience scurried away to eat lunch, Verilyn Harbin again took her mother to the serenity of the park. They talked about Francis's testimony and how the trial appeared to be going.

As his mother and sister contemplated the impact that defense witnesses might have had on the jury, McGinn sat in the Brown County Jail, eating his sandwich and doing his own reflecting.

The afternoon session began with Byron Max Courtney,

a criminalist from Fort Worth, Texas. His duties included examining physical evidence in mostly criminal cases, although he had some experience in civil cases as well.

The fifty-year-old expert witness had been sent a copy of the trial transcript containing the testimony of Steve Robertson, the DPS lab expert called by the prosecution, as well as exhibits presented during Robertson's testimony.

Courtney, who had twenty-five years of hair analysis under his belt, had been asked by Sudderth to examine the pubic hair found in Stephanie Flanary's vagina and compare it to the sample taken from Ricky McGinn.

Courtney acknowledged that he knew Steve Robertson well, respected his work, and, in fact, considered him a good friend.

The scientist explained how in his laboratory hair analysis was basically conducted as microscopic examinations.

The hairs were wet-mounted on a slide, becoming transparent so that the technicians were actually able to see through the hair.

Then, using a polarized-light microscope to look at single hairs and study those side by side, the lab workers actually compared them simultaneously.

In addition, in order to help him remember what a particular segment of hair looked like, a digital image, actually a videograph, was taken. Courtney was then able to print those images on a video printer.

Prefacing his comparison results, Courtney stated that no two hairs are just alike, although they may have many similar characteristics.

"Don't pubic hairs show less variation than scalp hairs?" Sudderth asked.

"Yes," Courtney stated.

Courtney had examined five pubic hairs from McGinn, the same ones selected and tested by Steve Robertson.

"Were any of these hairs identical to hair found in the vagina of Stephanie Flanary?" Sudderth asked.

"No," Courtney said.

Verilyn Harbin nodded her head, affirming her belief that Ricky had not raped Stephanie.

Courtney stated that when he said they were not identical, he meant that the hairs had at least some differences.

Sudderth set up a chart in front of the jury to aid in demonstrating the procedures he used to test the hair samples.

"The differences I see are that there tends to be a difference in the relative darkness of the hairs, between the known hair of Ricky McGinn and the questioned hair.

"And there is a difference, without saying yet the significance of the difference, in the medulla of all of the hairs, between the known and the questioned," Courtney stated.

"Now, what opinions or conclusions did you reach as a result of the comparisons, examinations, that were carried out in your laboratory?" Sudderth asked.

Courtney looked directly at Sudderth as he addressed the defense counsel. "My first opinion was that the questioned hair from the vagina of Miss Flanary, in fact, does show all the characteristics of being a Caucasian pubic hair."

At the top of his legal pad, McGinn wrote:

Day #11 trial—6–1–95
Max Courtney—Fort Worth—Criminalist—
I believe this guy is the hair expert. He looked at the same hair as Steve Robertson. He says no two hairs are the same. Says some hair from different people may over lap. I hope his opinion is that it is not my hair to match that of the hair that came from Steph's vagina. So I wish he would get on with the answer and let me know what he thinks will be his answers.

"In my opinion Stephanie Flanary is excluded as being the source of that hair. The known hairs from her are significantly different from the questioned pubic hair.

"In comparison with the known hairs of Ricky McGinn, I can neither exclude or associate that hair as coming from Ricky McGinn. I think it is inconclusive.

"It may very well have come from him. A lot of it looks like his hair. But I see differences that would stop me from saying that there is an association," Courtney stated.

Courtney had asked for a second opinion from Frank Shiller, Courtney's former boss, who had retired after forty-three years of service to the Fort Worth Police Department Crime Lab. Shiller, who now worked for Courtney's private consulting firm, had reviewed the hair slides and concurred with Courtney's findings.

Haney's questioning of the witness revealed that Courtney had not tested anyone's hair other than McGinn's, having been asked to conduct the analysis only the week prior to the start of the McGinn trial. And Haney wanted Courtney to tell the jury again that though he could not conclusively say the hair belonged to McGinn, he couldn't exclude McGinn as the hair donor, either.

As his witness left the courtroom, Sudderth asked to approach the bench. He had subpoenaed a Dallas television station for news footage containing an interview with Trooper Capuchino. The defense alleged that the Texas State trooper had made statements, on camera, that he had discovered the body of Stephanie Flanary in his rearview mirror while cruising the back roads of Brown County.

Sudderth explained to Judge Cadenhead that the people to whom the subpoena was directed had been out of the city and were not scheduled to return until the next morning. He announced that he would rest if the prosecution and the court agreed that if the film were found, viewed, and determined to be of evidentiary use, the defense could at that point present it to the jury.

As Sudderth stood before the bench asking for the inclusion of the news footage, if acquired, McGinn added to his notes for the day:

> I don't believe Courtney helped one bit. He may be trying to protect his friend Steve Robertson. How can you tell between hair? He offered the stuff about the pubic hair from Steph not matching without even being asked. I really wish he hadn't done that but no one objected so I hope it will be ok. I believe this guy is hurting us more than anything. I don't believe these are the same answers Ben acknowledged over the phone. I believe he has done severe damage to my case. The D.A. is already celebrating as if he has won.
>
> Defense Rests

TWENTY-TWO

As the courtroom regulars filed into the Brown County District courtroom on June 2, they expected to hear closing arguments from both the state and defense. There was surprise and a bit of disappointment that the guilt/innocent phase of the trial would be prolonged by the state's rebuttal witnesses.

First on the agenda was B. J. Fowler, a resident who lived just within sight of the culvert where Stephanie Flanary's body was found.

Fowler testified that his wife had been released from a Dallas hospital only days before the Flanary murder and he had been staying close to the house, taking care of her. He hadn't noticed any activity on the Farm-to-Market Road until the highway patrol showed up on May 25.

After the body was discovered, Fowler said that four men came to his house to question him regarding anything he might have seen in the area. He remembered Mike McCoy and Valton Posey were two of the four men, and he had told them exactly what he had just related to the prosecutor.

Sudderth couldn't believe his ears. Fowler's testimony was in direct contradiction to the prosecution's prior witnesses.

"Do you know why those officers would appear in this court and testify that they didn't interview any of the people in the area?" Sudderth asked.

"No, sir. I don't have any idea," Fowler said.

"When were you contacted to testify in this case?" Sudderth asked.

"Well, last week sometime," Fowler said.

Sudderth's contained anger was beginning to boil. He wanted to know who had contacted Fowler about testifying and if anyone had talked to him prior to his appearance in court. Fowler said Bob Grubbs had talked to him about two weeks ago while the trial was in progress.

The next witness slated to appear was Mrs. Fowler, but before Haney could call her, Sudderth objected to her appearance. He also asked that testimony of her husband be struck from the record as well.

"Mr. Grubbs was under the court rule at the time that he went and talked to these witnesses. He was under instruction not to talk about this case to any person, except these attorneys. In direct violation he has been out pumping up witnesses for the state, and we object to the testimony that they are eliciting in violation of the rule," Sudderth argued.

Judge Cadenhead overruled the objection and Mrs. Fowler was escorted to the stand.

McGinn, unhappy with the judge's ruling, wrote on his pad:

> Mrs. Fowler—Ben objected to these witnesses because Bobby Grubbs, Texas Ranger, went and talked to them after he had already been sworn to the rule and the trial was already started. But the judge overruled the objection. So that means to me, the cops can break the rules but no one else is supposed to.

Under oath Mrs. Fowler said that she remembered the police blocking off both ends of that particular part of the road. As she watched, she had wondered what was happening and had thought back to what was going on in the neighborhood around that time.

She added that after law enforcement personnel had cleared both ends of the roadway, they went straight to the Fowlers' house and questioned her husband.

Under Sudderth's questioning Mrs. Fowler confirmed her husband's story of Bob Grubbs coming to their house within the previous two weeks and asking if anyone had spoken to them about what they may have seen prior to the discovery of the Flanary girl's body.

McGinn commented on paper:

At the time of this stuff this woman's husband said he brought her home from the hospital on Friday. She testifies that the cops talked to her and her husband after the trial was already started. Ben done went and made the D.A. mad.

Hugh Conn, the next witness, a twenty-seven-year-old grocery store employee, claimed to have been a friend of Ricky McGinn's when they worked together at Clean-All Chemical. He had participated in backyard barbecues, bowling, riding around together, and he had helped a little with the McGinns' move to Owens.

Conn claimed that he had been aware of McGinn's injury and had observed him having difficulty walking, limping badly on some days, but at other times the injury was barely noticeable.

He stated he had seen McGinn lifting and loading a number of items during the move to Owens. He also testified that he had seen McGinn bowl, although he hadn't performed as well as he had prior to his injury.

In response to Haney's question concerning McGinn's relationship with both Stephanie and Denise, Conn stated, "Seemed like he was always good with the kids. He would wrestle around with them and do things with them a normal father would do with their kids. Play around, tickling, wrestling-around-type stuff."

Pressed by the D.A. to recall a conversation Conn had with McGinn concerning any comments he may have made about Stephanie and their tickling and playing around, Conn said, "He made the comment to me about how she was filling out as a lady and how he had to watch himself, or something like that."

The prosecutor was quick to ask if Conn was suggesting that there was anything improper, and he responded, "No."

The only questions Sudderth asked referred not to his client but to Conn's personal life. Conn had been living with a female Brownwood police officer for about two years.

The implication was subtle, but Sudderth managed to get in yet another suggestion that law enforcement in Brown County was out to get Ricky McGinn.

The words written on McGinn's paper read:

> Hugh Conn, Jr.—This man is really trying to help the D.A. He never saw me bowl after I got hurt. I believe all he helped move was boxes. I don't believe he should ever be able to testify because of living with this lady cop of Brownwood.

The state had only one rebuttal witness left to call. Dennis Dorris.

As the owner of MEDIVAC E.M.S., Dorris had first become acquainted with Ricky McGinn as an employee of his company. McGinn had moved on and Dorris hadn't seen him until about a week before Stephanie was reported missing.

Dorris said McGinn had come by his office and asked about a job. He hadn't been specific about what kind of job he was looking for, but to Dorris, McGinn hadn't appeared to be injured, hadn't appeared any different from when he was previously employed by him.

Again Sudderth, as he had with past witnesses, asked about Dorris's relationship with county and city officials in regard to his ambulance business.

"As long as the city and county here favors you with this bid, you don't have to worry about competition, do you?" Sudderth asked.

"I worry about competition every day," Dorris stated.

McGinn was disappointed in his former friend's testimony:

> Dennis Dorris—He is lying. He knows I had gotten hurt. I really didn't think he would lie so much. I should have known this by the way he acted when he was touring the jail. I guess ya just never know people who you think are your friends.

After a weekend filled with anticipation and preparations for their closing arguments, both Lee Haney and Ben Sudderth were ready to wrap up the case and send it to the jury for deliberation.

Judge Cadenhead dismissed the two alternates, one man and one woman, thanking them for their service and diligence. He then directed his attention to the twelve men and women remaining in the jury box, who would deliberate the fate of Ricky McGinn.

The judge read the charge to the jurors, telling them the principles of law they were to apply in reaching a decision.

Mr. Haney would begin the closing arguments; then Mr. Sudderth would present the defense's closing. Mr. Haney would have a final presentation, since the burden of proof still remained with the prosecution.

Just as Judge Cadenhead was about to give the floor to Haney, Sudderth asked if he could go to the bathroom.

"Right now?" Judge Cadenhead asked.

"Yes, now," Sudderth said, his nerves overtaking his body.

Within minutes Lee Haney stood before the jury, ready to convince them that Ricky McGinn was guilty of capital murder.

"We've heard about fifty-three witnesses, give or take, and looked at over two hundred exhibits. And, now, you've heard all the evidence that there is in this particular case," Haney began.

"I am charged with prosecuting someone who has been charged with a terrible offense. We're all here because a young lady was brutally raped and murdered."

Tears pooled in the eyes of Janet Talley. She and other witnesses had been allowed in the courtroom for the closing arguments. Now she sat in the stark courtroom and listened as the prosecutor spoke of her dead child and the man she was certain had killed her.

Across the aisle Francis McGinn's hands twisted in her lap. If her son was found guilty, as Lee Haney was asking jurors to do, then, like Stephanie, he would be gone from her forever.

"We're about to lay that burden down, and we're going to lay it down squarely on your shoulders. And that is what y'all get the big bucks for," Haney said tongue in cheek, referring to the $6 per day the jurors received for their service.

"Seems to me, back during the Second World War, all those young men and women that served their county in that war got twenty-one dollars a month as their starting pay. And that is a pretty good analogy because, like those young men and women, you're called upon to perform a function that requires courage."

Haney covered the definition of reasonable doubt and told the jury that the ruler they used to measure the evidence was up to them.

He cautioned them about the "rabbit trails," or "red herrings," presented by the defense in an effort to distract their attention from the evidence in the case. Citing some of these distractions, Haney listed the following defense's contentions: McGinn was unable to drag the body down into the culvert, Janet Talley was a bad mother, the defendant's injury was debilitating, maybe the biological father did it, blaming Steve Sirois, Joe Bob Talley as a potential suspect, the bloody handprint in the culvert, and the red-headed man.

"So" Haney said, "after talking about the things that the defense wanted to talk about, instead of the evidence, let's talk about what the evidence in the case really is."

Haney began to run down a list of some thirty pieces of evidence from a number of sources. He cited: opportunity to commit the crime; a delay in notifying people of her disappearance; getting the twelve-year-old drunk; always asking the two girls to go swimming with their tops on until they moved to Owens—meaning he thought of his stepdaughter in an inappropriate way; telling investigators that Stephanie never went east of Highway 183; driving the Ford Escort away Sunday morning and being gone ten or fifteen minutes—implying that he went to the culvert to make sure the body hadn't washed out or to push it up farther into the tin horn; McGinn's comment that David Mercer didn't need to be there, when he should have wanted the investigator to figure out what had happened to Stephanie; the preposterous story of the fish blood and the cats that cleaned up the fish remains; the cap and the note that McGinn said were in the field because of a game that had been played two weeks before the murder.

"Maybe you believe that that cap hung on that fence post for two weeks. And maybe you believe that that little note laid there on the ground without getting blown away for two weeks. But it's consistent, not only with playing a game two weeks before, but also consistent with maybe playing a game that day, a game that ended in tragedy," Haney said.

Haney talked about the fire that someone saw around dusk on the night of Stephanie's disappearance and McGinn's inability to remember if he had burned that day or not. The D.A. painted a picture of Stephanie being killed near the Ford Escort, the fire started to cover the blood stains, the body put in the back of the car, and blood draining down into the wheel well and out onto the bumper.

"The car was full of blood," Haney said dramatically. "And whose blood was it? It was Stephanie's blood."

The district attorney mentioned the cadaver dogs alerting on the car, and he summed up the hours of scientific testimony that eventually showed how the blood in the vehicle, confirmed as type A human blood, and that of Stephanie's blood had the same enzymes.

Likewise, the hair in the car was determined to be Stephanie's, and it was concluded that the blood on the ax belonged to a child of Janet and Steve Flanary.

Lee Haney asked, "Where is the ax found?" Then he reminded the jury that it was hidden in McGinn's pickup truck, parked on his property.

He emphasized that type A blood, Stephanie's type, was found on McGinn's clothing. Haney, though, saved the most damning evidence for last.

"The pubic hair in the vagina matches McGinn's," Haney said, omitting that DNA experts had actually testified that it may or may not have been McGinn's, that results were actually inconclusive.

"If that is his pubic hair in her vagina, then he raped her. And if he raped her, he killed her," Haney said with passion.

"What the evidence, taken as a whole, tells us is, beyond any doubt, on or about the twenty-second day of May, 1993, that there was indeed an aggravated sexual assault of Stephanie Flanary, and, indeed, she was intentionally killed. Because you can't accidentally hit someone in the head three or four times with an ax," Haney said in conclusion.

"That's what the evidence shows, and that is the verdict I ask you to tender."

The courtroom was silent. The words of Lee Haney hung over the people like a net of despair, trapping them beneath the darkness of an evil deed.

Judge Cadenhead broke the silence with a strong rap of his gavel. Court would be in recess for ten minutes, giving everyone an opportunity to prepare for the next onslaught of partisan evidentiary representation.

Ben Sudderth began by thanking the jury, then moved quickly to a point of law that he hoped he had been able to instill in the minds of the jury throughout the trial.

"The court says a reasonable doubt is a doubt based on reason and common sense after a careful and impartial consideration of all of the evidence in the case. It's the kind of doubt that would make a reasonable person hesitate to act in the most important of his affairs. Proof beyond a reasonable doubt, therefore, must be proof of such a convincing character that you would be willing to rely and act upon it without hesitation in the most important of your own affairs," Sudderth told the jury.

He then reminded them that if they had a reasonable doubt, then they must acquit the defendant and say by their verdict, not guilty.

Sudderth began to go over the evidence of the trial, beginning with the statement Haney had made that the pubic hair found from the vagina matched Ricky McGinn's.

"That's not true. That's simply not true," Sudderth said, reminding the jury that Steve Robertson, Haney's own witness, said it *could* have been McGinn's.

"That's a far cry from matched," Sudderth said.

He also reminded jurors that the pubic hair of the Caucasian race is very similar.

The defense attorney began to go over some of the things that he felt were consistent in Ricky McGinn's testimony. First he said that Janet Talley left about 9:00 A.M. to go bowling in Arlington. That was not disputed. He said that Denise went to stay with some friends. That was not disputed. He said Stephanie went walking. Sudderth contended that if that were not a normal practice of the child, then her mother would have disputed that in court.

McGinn was described as a good father and that statement was supported by more than one witness during the trial. No evidence had been presented that the two had anything but a normal, good relationship.

McGinn said he cooked fish from the pond for the first time. Sudderth stated that, although Janet Talley had never done that, she wasn't there that day to know if it had been done or not.

The defendant described the number of cats that were on the property. If that weren't true, Sudderth believed Janet would have disputed that on the stand.

There had been an abundance of testimony that Stephanie drank beer, and some evidence that she had been drinking since she was eight years old. Sudderth said if the jury was to jump on Ricky McGinn because he allowed her to drink some beer out of two or three or four or five or six of his cans, that would be ridiculous.

Sudderth reviewed McGinn's actions on the evening of May 22, 1993, beginning with walking the seven-acre pasture himself looking for Stephanie when she failed to return home in a reasonable time from her walk. Then he had called Steve Sirois, who came over but refused to walk out in the pasture to search.

Next McGinn had called the sheriff's office and they came out.

Sudderth backtracked and talked about Stanley Sirois

suggesting that Ricky had changed clothes between when he saw him and later in the day, and the inference by the prosecution that he could have burned them, along with blood evidence. But, Sudderth told the jury, the problem with that is they had scooped up some of the burned area and taken it to a lab and found nothing.

The defense attorney stated that the prosecution wanted to convict on a combination of factors.

- Opportunity: Sudderth told the jury that the worst crime McGinn committed was last seeing Stephanie alive.
- Delay in notifying: How do they know? McGinn first looked all over the seven acres.
- Gave beer to Stephanie: Sudderth suggested Janet needed to be on trial for that one.
- Informed investigators that Stephanie never went east of Highway 183.
- Ricky McGinn drove the Ford Escort away on Sunday morning.
- McGinn stated, "That damn investigator doesn't need to be here" because David Mercer wasn't interested in finding Stephanie; he was interested in trying to make a case against Ricky McGinn.

Then Sudderth pointed out that the state's own witness, the doctor who performed the autopsy, put the time of death at two to three days. Sudderth calculated that that was between seven o'clock Sunday morning and seven o'clock Monday morning.

"Stephanie McGinn may very well have been alive at that time," Sudderth said.

And then Sudderth accused the district attorney and investigators of taking editorial license with the fish blood story, assuming it was preposterous to think anyone would throw fish in the back of a hatchback and that they would bleed from hooks they had swallowed.

"Then the cap and note, to criticize him and fall all

over him because he has enough interest in this little girl to play an innocent game, just about causes me to fall off the loft," Sudderth said in a folksy manner.

Sudderth admitted there was blood in the Escort, but he contended that he didn't know, the prosecution didn't know, and the jury didn't know how it got there. And he stated they knew it was type A blood, but they didn't know whose type A blood.

Yes, hair in the car matched Stephanie's, but to Sudderth that didn't matter. It was common to find hair in a family car a victim often rode in.

As to the blood on the ax, Sudderth concluded that the blood on the ax may have been Stephanie's, but that evidence alone couldn't convict McGinn, not when two witnesses had searched the pickup on Saturday night and there was no weapon in the vehicle.

As to the hair on the ax matching Stephanie's, Sudderth argued that the ax wasn't McGinn's, that he had never seen it before.

He next addressed how the ax had been found hidden. "Now that's sinister," Sudderth said. "The pickup had been searched twice and the ax wasn't found until Wednesday, and McGinn had been in jail since Sunday."

Sudderth began tallying the evidence again.

- Underwear, human blood: You're going to have some blood on underwear now and then.
- McGinn's shorts with the type A blood: The defense wanted to know where they had been after the police took them as evidence. What had they been in contact with?
- McGinn's blue jeans with a speck of blood: The stain on the back of his jeans was not much larger than the head of a pin. Nobody knew how it got there.
- The pubic hair: One expert said McGinn couldn't be ex-

cluded; the other expert said it could be the defendant's. No one knew for sure.

- The semen on Stephanie's shorts: Sudderth argued that they didn't know whose it was. They didn't know what blood matched it. There hadn't even been enough sample to test.

"Ladies and gentlemen, we have blank pages, and there hasn't been a thing that has connected this man right here," Sudderth said, pointing to his client, "to any criminal offense. That's their case."

Again Sudderth brought up the reddish blond man and Steve Flanary as possible suspects. He told the jury that two people might be able to carry that body without getting blood on them. They might have been able to carry it down a steep hill and put it in the culvert. But, Sudderth insisted, Ricky McGinn could not have.

In the last ten minutes of Sudderth's closing arguments, he recapped the testimony of each witness. When he came to Janet Talley, Sudderth said that she wanted to blame Ricky for her not coming in earlier from Arlington. Then when she did get home, she was "as drunk as Cooter Brown." Regardless, she always said Ricky had spent a lot of time with the girls, teaching Stephanie to drive, playing games, going fishing.

"Now, it's not my job to solve the crime for the state. And it's not your job. But if you feel like the state hasn't proved by competent evidence beyond a reasonable doubt that Ricky McGinn, and not someone else, committed this offense, then it is your duty to vote not guilty," Sudderth closed.

Because the law places the burden of proof squarely on the prosecution, Mr. Haney was allowed to have the final argument before the jury.

The district attorney stood before the jury. If McGinn was found not guilty, Haney told them, he was facing them for the last time. If McGinn was found guilty, then Haney would be back asking for punishment. But for that moment, Lee Haney told the jury, he could only think of Stephanie Flanary, the twelve-year-old victim.

"What a terrible thing it is to kill a young girl," Haney said. "And not only did this defendant, based on the evidence here before you, kill this girl; before he killed her, he took away all that she had, and it wasn't much.

"He took away her innocence by raping her, and he killed her.

"He made her last hours or minutes on this earth filled with terror. Because, you know, she saw that ax coming for her skull. And she stuck up her little hand to try to stop it, and you see what happened when she did that.

"He took her away from her friends, who thought the world of her, her family that loved her, her mother, her sister, her grandparents. He took that all away from her.

"He took away from her the joy of swimming or going for a walk in the pasture. He took away from her graduating from high school, maybe being a cheerleader.

"He took away from her the junior, senior prom, falling in love with someone, getting married, having children.

"All that she ever was going to have, he took it away from her. And he did it cruelly and heartlessly, and turned a pretty little girl into this," Haney said, holding up a picture of the victim for jurors to see.

The tears that had pooled in Janet Talley's eyes spilled down her cheeks. Haney was right. She believed, as the prosecution did, that Ricky McGinn had taken all that away from Stephanie and had taken Stephanie away from her. She hoped the jury would take little time in finding him guilty.

Across the aisle Francis McGinn's eyes blazed hot with anger. Lee Haney was accusing her son of the most heinous crime she could ever imagine. She believed it was a lie. She believed in her son.

"I have to ask you to look at all of the evidence in the

case," Haney said, "and use your reason and your common sense, and tell this man that he is guilty of capital murder. Thank you."

Judge Cadenhead recessed the court at noon. Then they all began the wait for the jury's verdict.

TWENTY-THREE

As courtgoers broke for lunch, the jury began their deliberations.

At 12:45 P.M., only forty-five minutes after being excused to the jury room, the first note was received from the jury foreman.

Judge Cadenhead called the court to order with Sudderth, McGinn, and Haney all present to hear the jurors' two requests.

First, they wanted all the physical evidence, photographs, and written testimony about the hair. They also asked for a supply of surgical gloves.

Second, the jury wanted access to the chart Mr. Haney had presented during his closing arguments listing the elements of his case, along with the easel that held it in the courtroom.

The second request was denied, since it had not been tendered into evidence.

The jury returned to their task until 2:35 P.M., at which time excerpts from witness testimonies were called for. Specifically, what time McGinn was spotted burning something in his yard and what time he drove his car off the property Sunday morning. They also wanted to compare Robertson's and Courtney's testimonies concerning the hair. Only the first of their requests was granted.

At 6:20 P.M. Judge Cadenhead announced from the

bench, "The bailiff has informed me that the jury has a verdict in this case."

People scrambled into the courtroom, eagerly taking their places to hear the long-awaited verdict.

"Now, you folks in the audience, you've been very well behaved to this point. I would ask that no matter what the verdict is, that we have no outbursts or remarks or anything from any member of this audience. Is that understood?"

Several members of the gallery nodded their heads to indicate compliance, while others sat braced against their seats for the jury's decision.

No one knew from the stoic faces of the men and women who had become familiar fixtures in the courtroom for more than two weeks what their verdict was or how they had reached their decisions.

Francis McGinn clung to Verilyn's arm and muttered prayers to her beloved Jesus.

Janet Talley took in deep breaths, hoping the jury had the courage to make what she believed to be the right decision and announce that Ricky McGinn was guilty of capital murder.

Both mothers sat trembling in their seats, their hearts pounding rapidly. Each scared. Each hopeful. Each suffering their own loss.

Judge Cadenhead looked to the jury foreman and asked if their verdict was unanimous.

"Yes, it is," the foreman answered.

The judge read from the paper handed to him by the bailiff.

"We, the jury, find the defendant guilty of the offense of capital murder, as charged in the indictment."

Ricky McGinn stood before the court, unwavering. His mother wept tears of pain and sadness, rocking back and forth in the arms of her daughter. Janet Talley smiled broadly, happy with the jury's decision, pleased her daughter's death had been avenged.

Less than an hour after being found guilty, Ricky McGinn sat in the dimness of his jail cell and wrote in his journal:

> Haney done his first arguments and then Ben done his thing. Haney got up and lied about things. Anyway, to make a long story short, the jury deliberated a little over six hours and then came back with a verdict of guilty of capital murder. Now Mr. Haney is catting around like the cock of the walk. Well, his day will come. But right now I must concentrate on the rest of the trial.

Ricky McGinn laid his pen on his tablet and laid his head on his bunk. Tomorrow was another day. He would no longer be fighting to prove his innocence—he would be fighting for his life.

The day following the announcement of guilt, all parties were back in court to begin the penalty phase of the trial.

Ben Sudderth approached the bench, presenting an oral motion for consideration.

McGinn remained seated at the defense table. He looked tired and worn from the days of trial proceedings culminating in the announcement of his guilt. He wrote on his pad:

> Ben is making a motion on 6–6–95 for none of my record or accused statements about me to be brought up, but I don't believe it will do any good.

Then, moments later, McGinn added:

> As I figured, the judge overruled the motion.
>
> Well, most of the crooked cops are here by now. I'm sure they want to look good in front of the crowd. Especially David Mercer and Mike McCoy, and

Bobby Grubbs. I believe these are the main three cops that need to be checked out in this county.

Well, they have made most of my family leave the courtroom. I really don't know why, except they were witnesses in the trial. But they won't be now, so I don't know why.

As in the guilt/innocence portion of the trial, Lee Haney, representing the state of Texas, began with his opening statement.

"At the punishment phase of the trial, when the jury has to determine what the appropriate punishment is in any case, then the background and character and the things he has done in the past are very relevant.

"You already know, because the defendant testified about the kidnapping case in which the defendant was previously convicted. We expect to bring other evidence that will show other acts of misconduct that the defendant has committed in the past," Haney said.

Sudderth, as before, wished to reserve his opening remarks until he began his client's defense. Haney called his first witness, Pamela Kay Adams.

Ms. Adams told the court that she had met Ricky Nolen McGinn in August 1986 at the K Bar Club in Rising Star. McGinn had come over to the table where Adams and her friends were sitting; then he had asked her to dance.

When the group decided to go out to the local twenty-four-hour truck stop for a late-night meal, McGinn asked if he could ride along. After eating, he asked Adams to take him back to the club to pick up his car; then once that car was delivered to his house, he asked her to give him a lift out to the farm located in Carbon to pick up yet another vehicle.

"What, if anything, happened after you arrived at the farm near Carbon?" Haney asked Adams.

"He pulled a knife on me, and he raped me," Adams said.

Surprised looks were exchanged by members of the audience, but the jurors' faces remained placid.

"First he put the knife to my cheek and told me to take my clothes off. I told him, no. So he put it to my side and told me if I cooperated, I wouldn't be hurt. That's when he took me inside the farmhouse and he made me get undressed. Then he made me undress him. He made me have oral sex. Then he sat down in a chair and he made me sit on him and have vaginal sex. Then he pushed me down on the floor and he had vaginal sex again.

"He stopped to smoke a cigarette. And while he did that, he put his toe inside me and then he made me suck his toe.

"Then he made me have vaginal sex in the chair again. And he made me masturbate him with some kind of hair conditioner.

"And then he made me have oral sex again, and anal sex, and vaginal sex again. And he just alternated, back and forth until he was ready to climax. And then he made me have oral sex again, and he made me swallow it.

"He had me put my clothes back on, and he took me back to town.

"But the whole time he was telling me if I didn't do what he said, he would kill me. So I did," Adams said, her soft voice trailing off so that she could hardly be heard.

Courtroom observers had been spellbound by the story Adams told, most sitting in shocked muteness. But the story of the sexual abuse hadn't stunned them as much as when Adams told the jury that when she got out of the car, McGinn had said politely, "Thank you."

Adams had reported the incident to the local constable, had gone to the hospital, and had given a statement to the police. Charges had been filed against McGinn, but he was never taken to trial.

"He told me it wouldn't do any good, that they would never get him; they would never do anything to him," Adams said.

Sudderth's cross-examination questions inferred that Ms. Adams had approached McGinn at the bar, that she had sat in his lap, and that she was the one who suggested they go do something. Ms. Adams adamantly denied each of the allegations.

She also rejected the idea that her ex-husband had forced her to file the rape charge against McGinn or lose custody of their kids.

As soon as the prosecutor called Sonya Mash Vaughn as their next witness, Sudderth was before the bench again, arguing that her testimony not be allowed.

While his attorney fought to keep out more prejudicial testimony, McGinn wrote:

> Pamela Kay Adams—Seems to me she can't re- member what happened on the night she met me. She is really getting wild with her story. I sure must be a bad man that even the cops are afraid of me. This woman can sure lie good. She sure put on a good act for the D.A. and jury. Sure makes me look bad. Even when she knows the case was kicked out because her ex-husband went around bragging that he told her to file rape or he would take the kids away from her. So the case was dropped and I never heard anything.

McGinn looked up from his paper momentarily to listen to Sudderth argue against Sonya's testimony. Then he wrote:

> Sonya Mash (Vaughan) [*sic*]—Ben is objecting to this witness because of her story and it has been over ten years ago. And naturally the judge overruled the objection.

Vaughn, a sophomore at Abilene Christian University in 1985, had been leaving the local mall when McGinn blocked her exit and approached her car.

The brown-haired stranger asked Vaughn if there was a club nearby and she told him about Cowboys, a popular nightspot for the country-and-western set. She agreed to go with him to the dance hall, but first he followed her to her campus dorm where she changed clothes.

McGinn drove them to Rising Star, telling Vaughn he had to take some car parts back to his house before going dancing. Outside the house Vaughn had spotted a horse and, loving to ride, asked if they could take the horse out before going on to Cowboys.

Vaughn told the jury that after riding they returned to McGinn's house.

"That's when it all started," Vaughn said. "We started out kissing; then he wanted to go further. That's when I wanted to go home, but he wouldn't let me."

"How did he keep you from going home?" Haney asked.

"He just had me pinned down on the bed. He tried to have sex with me. He wanted me to lick his penis. Also, he started doing me, and he started to enter me. I pushed him off," Vaughn said.

"Did you say anything while this was going on?" Haney prompted.

"I kept telling him, 'Don't, I want to go.' He just kept forcing himself on me. So I literally pushed him off the bed, kicking him. That's when he got up, walked around the bed, and gave me quite a few punches with his fists," Vaughn continued.

"What happened next?" Haney asked.

"I said, 'Stop.' 'I'm sorry.' But he just kept going, wanted to have sex with me. Finally I said, 'For God's sake, let me go, please.' Finally it kind of dawned on him and he let me go," Vaughn recalled.

The now-married mother of two then told the court that she and McGinn put on their clothes and got in his car. They ran out of gas, went back to the house, and she rode the horse to a neighbor's and called her dorm mother to pick her up at the truck stop.

Vaughn admitted she didn't call the police for a couple of days because she was scared and a bit shaken up over the ordeal.

"At anytime while you were out there at that farmhouse, did y'all have sexual intercourse?" Haney asked.

"Yes," Adams said softly.

While Sudderth prepared to cross-examine the witness, McGinn wrote in his journal:

I believe she is having a hard time remembering. I can't remember her very well. I remember riding horses but I really can't recognize her. I do remember running out of gas and the woman taking the horse. Says I raped her but really I never raped her. We did have sex but I would bet she enjoyed it more than I did. For I don't even remember it that well. I believe I would have remembered her if it was good. I still don't recognize her.

Following the course of his original objection to Vaughn's testimony, Sudderth had the witness admit that the incident had occurred ten years prior to her appearance at McGinn's trial. Then he pressed Vaughn by repeatedly asking a question followed by, "This person you have never met before," suggesting that if she hadn't gone with someone she hadn't known, the event wouldn't have happened.

Vaughn told the jury that it had been a constable who picked her up at the McGinns' neighbor's house and taken her to the truck stop to meet her dorm mother. She claimed she was too scared and upset to tell the officer about the rape and just wanted to go back to school as soon as possible.

"And did you ever file charges against Mr. McGinn?" Sudderth asked.

"I probably did. I don't remember," Vaughn said, relying on her ten-year memory. "I reported it to the sheriff's department a couple of days after it happened."

Francis McGinn cringed as she saw Latasha McGinn enter the outside doors of the courthouse. She knew why her twelve-year-old granddaughter was there. To testify against her father. *To lie,* Francis thought.

After promising to tell the truth and identifying the defendant as her father, the young girl sat back in her chair and waited to be questioned.

"Latasha, I'm going to ask you about something that happened around Halloween, when you were three or four years old," Haney began.

McGinn and his sister Verilyn knew Latasha had been fine when she made the accusations, but remained silent.

"We will object," Sudderth interrupted. "This is too remote to call on a child twelve years old, to remember something that happened back when they were three years old. The remoteness makes it inadmissible.

"Also, the prejudicial effect far outweighs any ends that it might serve toward justice."

"Overruled, Counselor," Cadenhead said, nodding toward the prosecutor to move on.

Latasha said that the incident had occurred when she and her father were sitting on the living-room sofa watching TV.

"What happened next?" Haney asked.

"He laid me down on the couch, and pulled my panties down and stuck his middle finger in my vagina. He moved it around a little, and then took it out and put my panties back up," Latasha said.

"And then what happened next?" Haney prompted.

"We went to bed," Latasha said.

The girl told the court that her father had threatened to kill her and her mother if she ever told anyone about the incident. She said she didn't tell until later, when she shared her experience with a family friend.

"And did you ever go to a doctor about that?" Haney asked.

"Yes, sir, because I was bleeding whenever I went to the bathroom," Latasha said, adding that she had been sent to the emergency room and given a catheter to aid in urinating.

Once Haney passed the witness, Sudderth immediately began trying to discredit the girl's damning testimony.

Latasha denied the defense counsel's accusations that her mother had told her what to say when she took the witness stand against her father. She admitted that she had told her aunt Verilyn that the incident hadn't really happened and that the reason she told the story was because at the time she was angry at her father. But, Latasha stated, she had actually lied to Verilyn, not to the court.

"Why would you not tell Verilyn the truth?" Sudderth wanted her to explain.

"Because they told me that I could not see my father, and that he would die if I—" Latasha's answer faltered.

"Who told you that?" Sudderth wanted to know.

"Verilyn."

Sudderth then entered into evidence a letter Latasha had recently written her father.

" 'Dear Daddy,' " Sudderth read. " 'How are you? I really hope you're doing fine. Dad, I really, really love you a lot. No matter what happens, I will always love you. No matter what anyone says about you or me, there will always be a place in my heart for you. Daddy, please write me back soon. Love you always, Latasha McGinn. P.S. I will always love you. Also, tell granny that no matter how she feels about me, I will always love her, too. Love always.' "

Try as he might, Sudderth couldn't get Latasha to admit that she had been angry with her father when she was five years old and had lied in court about the molestation in an effort to get even with him. Latasha held firm, insisting that she had not lied, but had told the truth about the sexual abuse that had happened nine years earlier.

Frustrated with his inability to get the girl to recant her statement, Sudderth sat down.

On redirect Haney concentrated on one incident when Latasha was about five years old and her father had come to visit.

"What was going on at that time?" Haney asked.

"He came over for visitation, after I told my mom about what he had done to me. She said that the only way he could see me is for her and one of my aunts or uncles to be there," Latasha explained. "And he said, no. He had a stick. So he threatened to beat her to death, and beat the door down."

Latasha had called her uncle for help and he had come to the house to help.

The twelve-year-old was excused and the court recessed for lunch.

Beside Latasha McGinn's name, her father wrote:

This little girl is just like her mother about making up stories. Someone has really gotten this child mixed up. She has sure gotten a vivid imagination. This little girl has sure learned to lie. Like I said, she is just like her mother. I just don't know where she could come up with this stuff without her mama's help.

When Francis McGinn was told of her granddaughter's statements in court, she was enraged. The matriarch of the McGinn family decided right then and there that she no longer had a granddaughter named Latasha. She disowned the girl, and rebutted her lies.

Francis wasn't any happier when she learned that the state's last witness would be Imogene Bible, Latasha's mother.

Imogene and Ricky McGinn had been married on May 23, 1980, and were divorced on January 27, 1984. It had been nearly four years of a turbulent relationship, which produced an only child.

Haney asked Bible to think back to Halloween 1987 and describe any unusual behavior she may have noticed from her daughter.

"She went into the bathroom and she was bleeding," Bible said. Then she added that she had asked Latasha if anyone had messed with her. At the time the child had said no.

During an examination at the hospital emergency room, the doctor suggested that the child may have been molested.

"I just couldn't believe it," Imogene Bible said. But, she added, Ricky hadn't really had much to say when he heard the news.

After the examination and the pediatrician telling her mother that Latasha had been molested, she was admitted to the hospital for treatment. Medical care included insertion of a catheter for kidney dysfunction. Five days later she was released.

Bible stated that Latasha eventually told her of the incident with her father and she had informed him that he was not to see their daughter unless she or one of her family members was present. She claimed he became violent, threatening to beat her to death.

As a result of the incident that both Imogene and her daughter had described for the court, terroristic-threat charges had been filed against McGinn, but the case had not been pursued.

In her final remarks to the jury, Imogene Bible reiterated her daughter's statements about their conversation with Verilyn, and she insisted she had instructed her daughter to tell the truth in court.

Under questioning by Ben Sudderth, Bible stated that the conversation with Verilyn Harbin had taken place at the county jail where she had taken Latasha to see her father. Sudderth scrutinized their motive for trying to see McGinn, but Imogene insisted that it was because Latasha loved her daddy and wanted to see him. She was not, however, on her father's visitors' list and couldn't go in without one of the McGinns accompanying her.

In order to persuade the McGinns to take Latasha to see her father, Imogene had agreed to sign a statement attesting to the fact that the molestation had not happened, that it was a lie.

"How many times has your daughter told you that the statements that had been made relating to her father molesting her were not true?" Sudderth wanted to know.

"Just that one time," Imogene stated.

With the dismissal of Imogene Bible from the witness stand, Lee Haney rose and addressed the court.

"As to the punishment phase of the trial, Your Honor, the state rests."

Only four witnesses had been called in an effort to help the state prove that Ricky Nolen McGinn was a danger to the community and needed to be punished to the fullest extent of the law. Lee Haney wanted Ricky McGinn put to death.

Ben Doyle Sudderth rose and faced the jury—he needed to take advantage of his right to make an opening statement; he wanted to let the jury know what he intended to present in support of his request that they spare his client's life.

The ardent defense counsel outlined the upcoming testimonies of three witnesses. He didn't mention that he planned to recall his client to the stand, in support of his own cause. He did inform the court, much to the relief of audience and jury alike, that he planned to present his defense in the penalty phase all in that one afternoon.

McGinn's eyes followed Gaynelle Calloway as she approached the stand. He hoped her testimony would negate any damage Pamela Kay Adams had done to his case.

Ms. Calloway had lived in Rising Star, her bedroom facing the trailer where the McGinns and Ricky resided. In addition, Ms. Calloway claimed to know who Pamela Adams was and could recognize her voice.

Sudderth wanted to know if Ms. Calloway remembered the night Pamela Adams had referred to in connection with her encounter with McGinn. Ms. Calloway said she did.

The elderly woman told the court that at first the lights of the car McGinn was driving woke her up when the beams hit her bedroom window. She could hear Ricky McGinn and a woman who was with him laughing. They seemed to be having a good time. Ms. Calloway said she recalled she had wished they would quiet down so she could go back to sleep, but the laughter had continued awhile longer.

"I do believe it was Pam and Ricky," Ms. Calloway said, although the darkness kept her from seeing the two people outside her window.

Three or four days later, Ms. Calloway learned that Adams had claimed that McGinn had raped her.

"Did you find it very odd to have somebody outside of your window giggling and laughing at that time of the morning, and [then] claiming they were being raped?" Sudderth asked.

"Yes, sir."

Ms. Calloway had communicated her observations to investigators at the time.

Then, about six months later, Ms. Calloway was with

friends, including McGinn, eating at the local truck stop when Pam Adams came in with two other people.

"She began to taunt him," Ms. Calloway said. "She would say, 'Honey, do you know where I live? Honey, do you know the way to my house? Honey, do you know my phone number?' I thought it was so strange. I found it strange that a woman who had claimed that Ricky raped her would want to be right there were we where and would taunt him like that."

Calloway claimed Ricky had just sat quietly, taking the taunts, his fists tightly clenched on the tabletop.

Everyone in the group had signed sworn depositions to the facts and Calloway believed that had aided in the decision not to prosecute Ricky for rape.

As Lee Haney asked his questions of the witness, he produced a copy of a motion for dismissal in *State of Texas* v. *Ricky Nolen McGinn*. He read it for Ms. Calloway, indicating that the case was dismissed not because of any depositions she and her friends may have signed, but because the state failed to afford him a speedy trial.

As Ms. Calloway was excused and Verilyn Harbin called to testify, Ricky McGinn jotted three quick lines on his pad:

Gaynelle Calloway—I haven't seen this woman in years. But did do work for her. She used to cut my hair. A good witness.

The moment Ben Sudderth announced Verilyn Harbin's name, Lee Haney approached the bench.

"I'm not going to object to this witness testifying, even though she has been in the courtroom during portions of the trial," Haney said. However, he wanted Verilyn Harbin to be instructed not to discuss her testimony with any potential witnesses or with the press. Haney had seen McGinn's older sister interviewed on TV concerning the trial and he knew she had spoken to Dusty Bilbrey during jury selection. He simply wanted it understood that she was to follow the court's rule.

Verilyn Harbin discussed the events that occurred with Latasha and Imogene Bible at the Brown County Jail, stating that she had told her niece that the only way she could get in to see her father was if one of the McGinns took her in.

"We asked her why should we let her in, after the things she had said about her daddy. And she said she didn't say them. I asked her if she had told her mother that she didn't, and she said no," Harbin explained.

Sudderth asked if she had pursued the topic with the girl's mother.

"I sure did," Verilyn Harbin said emphatically.

With tears in her eyes, Verilyn Harbin stated that Latasha told her mother the molestation hadn't happened. Imogene had responded with a directive that the girl would have to tell the D.A., welfare, and the doctor.

According to Verilyn, Imogene had agreed to meet her and the defense investigator to discuss her upcoming testimony, promising not to speak out against Ricky, but Imogene had failed to appear at the scheduled meeting.

Harbin's posture and attitude changed visibly as Lee Haney approached. She didn't like Haney and believed he was unjustly prosecuting an innocent man—her brother.

Haney made a point about Latasha's statement concerning her father's innocence in her molestation claim coming directly after she was told the only way she could see her father was if a McGinn took her in.

Verilyn Harbin stated that she had only spoken to Dusty Bilbrey during the jury selection, not the trial itself, and only because he had come to her mother's house and related the story of searching the culvert.

When Haney commented on her television appearances,

Harbin snapped, "You've seen me *twice*," with emphasis on the last word.

As his sister left the stand, Ricky and Verilyn exchanged smiles, his of thanks, hers of hope.

McGinn wrote:

> Verilyn Harbin—testified to what Latasha stated to her and mama and what Imogene Bible said. The D.A. brought up stuff that had nothing to do with this portion of the trial.

Then McGinn laid down his pen and limped toward the stand.

He recalled for the court the night he met Pamela Adams, stating that she was coming on "real heavy," sitting on his lap, kissing him all over.

"I'm just a man," McGinn said, a slight smile nearly invisible under his mustache.

He told of taking Adams to the farmhouse in Carbon and having sexual intercourse the rest of the night. Not only did he state that the sex was consensual, he said that she wasn't ready to go home but that he "couldn't go no longer." They had gone to his parents' trailer in Rising Star, sitting in the car laughing and talking; then he'd gone inside and she'd gone home. The next night he learned from friends that Pam had accused him of rape.

McGinn indicated that he had been told that Adams's change of heart toward him had something to do with a jealous husband.

In reference to Sonya Vaughn, McGinn stated he wasn't surprised that she had agreed to go out with him after just meeting, stating, "It's happened to me a lot. I've never had a problem picking up women."

As with Adams, McGinn denied abusing Vaughn or forcing her to stay. He claimed she was only upset because she had to call someone to come from Abilene to get her.

The defendant disagreed with Imogene Bible's statements that he had threatened her with a stick, stating he had only gone to her house to tell her to have the cops stop following him. He claimed he was being harassed by the authorities, constantly being stopped and asked whose vehicle he was driving.

"Everything I got, she thought that she should get it," McGinn explained.

As adamantly as he denied the rape charges and the terroristic threat against Bible, he discounted the allegations of molesting his daughter.

To Lee Haney's questions he merely stated that each person who had spoken out against him was lying.

McGinn walked back to his seat at the defense table. The jury took note of his irregular gait as Ben Sudderth asked for a recess to allow his next witness time to arrive in Brownwood from Austin. Court was recessed.

Dr. Richard Coons, an M.D. whose specialty was forensic psychiatry, also held a law degree from the University of Texas. He had originally been contacted by Bob Spence, McGinn's first attorney, who'd been killed just prior to the previously scheduled trial. Spence had asked Coons to evaluate McGinn as to whether he was sane or insane at the time of the offense and about his future dangerousness.

The doctor had spent two hours of personal one-on-one interview time with the defendant and read the reports that Spence had forwarded to him for his review.

Stating his opinion, Coons said, "I cannot say that there is a probability that he would commit criminal acts of violence in the future."

Coons based his opinion on three things. First, McGinn's basic history of violence was against females and if sentenced to the penitentiary, he would be in contact almost exclusively with males. Second, McGinn wasn't a large man and he had a back problem. That would leave him much less likely to be attacking someone, and more likely to be a victim himself. Third, someone convicted of the kind of crime McGinn was accused of and sent to prison was likely to be picked on, rather than picking on someone else.

Haney's first question was "You could not say that there was a probability, but can you say there is not a probability of future violence?"

Coons restated his position, saying that the probability was well under 50 percent that McGinn was likely to reoffend.

Under scrutiny by Haney on the details of each of the offenses McGinn had been accused of committing, the doctor said he had all the information at his access, either through reports or from McGinn himself. He contended that the events did not represent an escalation of violence, but rather an on-again, off-again pattern; he held firm to his opinion that Ricky McGinn posed no future threat.

In an effort to reinforce his plea for confinement rather than death, Sudderth presented information that if sentenced to life based on 1993 sentencing guidelines, McGinn would not be eligible for parole for thirty-five years. The defendant would be seventy-three years old and the likelihood of him living that long in prison was minimal.

McGinn observed:

Dr. Richard Coons—This is the psychiatrist I went to see in Austin. He testified to the fact that I wouldn't be a threat to society. The D.A. is sure trying to turn him around. I sure would like to know who has been teaching Haney what questions and how to ask them. They sure made the D.A. mad. Which is really pretty often. When he doesn't get his way he gets mad and acts like he would like to throw a temper tantrum like a little baby would. This stupid D.A. doesn't realize it would be harder to do thirty-five years in prison rather than being on death row. He has his head set on giving someone the death penalty that he can't even think anymore about who or when. He just wants to give someone the death penalty.

At least one of the jurors might have had some insight into McGinn's chance of success in prison. A counselor at a rehab for juvenile offenders, he had some knowledge of the system.

Sudderth called Joseph Wade Hardeman. The name was familiar, but most in the courtroom couldn't place where they had heard it.

Hardeman, a guest of the state at Gatesville Prison for aggravated robbery, was the victim McGinn had kidnapped years earlier. He explained the circumstances of his kidnapping and his brutal beating while tied to a tree.

Sudderth had called Hardeman in connection with a letter he had written McGinn the previous week.

"You wished him luck and told him to keep his head up and you was for him and all those things. Didn't you?" Sudderth asked.

"Yeah. I don't have no hard feelings," Hardeman said.

"I believe you told me that you feel like Ben Freeman had talked Ricky into this, and he was less culpable. Is that correct?"

"Yes."

Hardeman stirred uneasily as Lee Haney approached. He knew the prosecutor well. Haney had been the one to represent the state in his own case and had won a conviction and Hardeman's incarceration.

Haney brought out the fact that during Hardeman's own trial, he had stated that the reason he had gotten into trouble was because of the beating he suffered from McGinn and Freeman.

Hardeman stated that Freeman had beaten him with a post oak stick and a mesquite switch.

"Did McGinn participate at all in that?" Haney asked.

"Not that much, no," the witness said.

But Haney emphasized that McGinn had helped Freeman catch Hardeman when he tried to run away and had taken him back to the tree for further punishment. For their actions Hardeman had received a $250,000 judgment against both Freeman and McGinn, but had he only collected a portion of the money.

The defense witnesses had all been called; Sudderth was ready to present his closing statements and turn the case over to the jury to deliberate punishment.

"WE REST," McGinn wrote on his pad in large letters.

But the state wasn't finished. They had one rebuttal witness to call, requesting a recess until the following morning.

McGinn was livid. "Now the D.A. wants to call some more witnesses. I really think this shouldn't be allowed," he wrote.

The next morning court was resumed as usual. Everyone in attendance was wondering, *How much longer?*

At the top of his paper, McGinn wrote:

Day #15 Trial 6–7–95

We rested yesterday so now today we will see if this stupid D.A. will want to call more witnesses, or if he will go ahead with the closing arguments. Well, the D.A. says he will call a rebuttal witness. He just never stops.

Dr. Harold Scott was sworn in and took his seat at the front of the courtroom.

Scott, a psychiatrist in private practice in Brownwood, had never met McGinn or examined any of the records concerning allegations against him.

Haney asked for Dr. Scott's opinion on a hypothetical scenario of a man accused of several crimes.

The prosecutor then went into explicit details of each rape, the kidnapping, the alleged molestation of a five-year-old girl, and the murder of a twelve-year-old female.

"If you will assume that all of those things are true, do you have an opinion as to whether or not the defendant is more likely than not to commit criminal acts of violence that would constitute a continuing threat to society?" Haney asked.

"My opinion would be that there would be considerable risk of continued acts of violence, based on the history," Dr. Scott answered.

He told the court that his opinion was based on a number of variables, predictors of future behavior. Disordered thinking or feelings of powerlessness would be an indicator. Generally the most reliable predictor of future acts would be any history of violence or recurrent acts of violence.

The psychiatric term used for those who repeat acts of violence is antisocial personality disorder, or sociopathic personality disorder. The term describes one who basically lacks conscience, lacks internal restraint, disregards others' rights and feelings, fails to learn from experience, and has trouble conforming behavior to societal standards, unless society is very clear about the consequences. The individual must rely on external restraint, in the presence of a lack of internal restraint.

When Sudderth was given his chance to cross-examine the witness, he attacked the doctor on his credentials and experience versus his own expert witness, Dr. Coons. Dr. Scott acknowledged he hadn't interviewed thousands of prison inmates and hadn't testified in hundreds of criminal trials, as Coons had done. He verified that he had not been afforded an opportunity to interview McGinn personally or read any of the reports relating to his case or other reported accusations. He did, however, continue to stand by his opinion that, based on the history, there was a probability of continued behavior, unless there is an external restraint. He added that he was uncertain if prison confinement would be sufficient impediment.

Sudderth continued to pick at the witness, challenging the words he used, his lack of firsthand research with prison populations, and his failure to waiver on his determination of the defendant's propensity for future violent acts.

In a last desperate attempt to discredit the witness, Sudderth challenged him on the fact that he had only been approached the day before to testify as an expert witness and that he had known the prosecuting attorney for several years. The witness remained calm, reporting that he and the district attorney were not friends but had merely been associated through court dealings in the past. Not being able to shake the doctor, Sudderth had no additional questions.

McGinn put his thoughts to paper:

D.A.'s rebuttal witness—Harold Scott

Boy the D.A. just never stops. He just keeps on lying. This doctor is sure squirrely. He can't answer questions straight out. He keeps wanting to get help from the D.A. The doctor will say anything to please the D.A.

Both sides rest, now will give final arguments and of course, the D.A. will go first and last. I still don't know how they ever found me guilty, but now we wait and see what they will come up with on the punishment phase of this trial.

McGinn sat back and waited to see what Haney would say about him during his closing. The end was near. He hoped, as he had throughout the trial, that the jury had listened closely to his witnesses—and believed them.

TWENTY-FOUR

Lee Haney spoke first. He drew on his experience and emotion as he addressed the jury in his final arguments.

He first wanted them to consider the probability that Ricky McGinn would again commit a criminal act of violence and constitute a continuing threat to society. The prosecutor agreed little with what Dr. Coons had said in his testimony, other than the most reliable predictor in indicating a future danger was past behavior.

"What do we know about Ricky Nolen McGinn's past behavior?" Haney asked as he pointed toward the defendant. "We know that he raped and killed Stephanie Flanary."

Haney moved from his position in front of the jury to stand in front of the prosecution table.

"At what point on that day did he make a conscious decision to get this ax?" he asked, picking up the instrument. "You have to make a conscious decision to go get an ax and kill someone. You have to make a conscious decision to bring it back and strike, not two times, not three times. Four times," Haney said as he made a chopping motion with the weapon.

"If you look at the wounds, and even if you look at her face, the terror on it, as she brings up that one little hand in a futile, instinctive, pitiful attempt at self-defense."

Somber silence cloaked the courtroom. Only Haney's voice penetrated the utter stillness. Faces grimaced and mouths tightened as Haney painted a picture of horror and human destruction.

The prosecutor listed six criminal acts of violence committed by Ricky McGinn that he had introduced into evidence.

"You know that the kind of man that can do these things is a danger to society as long as there is a breath in his body. And as long as we as a society are going to have a death penalty, this is the conduct and this is the person that it is designed for. Thank you."

Lee Haney took his seat beside the assistant district attorney and waited with the others in the courtroom for the defense's closing argument.

The McGinns seated in the courtroom glared at Haney. They later admitted feeling a hatred they'd never known as they looked at him. They believed this man and this county were willing to sacrifice an innocent man for their own perverse reasons.

Ben Sudderth rose and faced the jury.

"Probably, by now, you have thought that this proceeding is like a Dickens novel; that is, it just goes on, and on, and on. I must confess that I'm tired," Sudderth said, reflecting on the five and a half weeks he had been in Brownwood from the first day of jury selection until that moment.

As did his counterpart before him, Sudderth recapped the evidence presented in court, conveying to the jury the doubt he had concerning the truthfulness of some of the state's witnesses. In the final analysis, Sudderth said, it didn't really matter how much credence they gave to the evidence. It was punishment they were there debating.

"So really, if you got down to it, to the bottom line, if punishment is the motive, the purpose of finding someone guilty and assessing a term or coming up with some kind of decision, if that is the purpose, if you want to punish him, thirty-five years, probably more, of being knocked around in a prison environment, I can't conceive of a greater amount of punishment that a person could be given.

"He will have the opportunity to spend the next thirty-five years, and the rest of his life, in a structured society in which he can spend that time, seeking divine forgiveness for any offense that he has ever committed."

Sudderth was running out of time, not just the thirty minutes allotted by the court for his closing remarks, and not time for himself—but time for Ricky McGinn.

"Yours is an awesome responsibility," Sudderth told the jury. "Very, very few people will ever during their lifetime be called upon to decide the issue of: does this man live or does he die? This is what is squarely on your shoulders here today. I trust that you will take the responsibility seriously.

"Now, I've done the best that I can. My responsibility, when I sit down, is concluded."

With that, Ben Sudderth returned to sit next to his client.

By law the state had the right to the last words heard by the jury. The burden of proof lay at the feet of Lee Haney—to prove Ricky McGinn was a threat to society, that he might commit additional acts of violence, that he may take another life.

Again Haney touched on evidence that had been presented in the punishment phase of the trial, in particular the testimonies of Pamela Kay Adams and Sonya Mash Vaughn.

"You'd think they raped him instead of the other way around. It's their fault that they were the victims of this act of violence. He still won't accept responsibility for all the things that he has done," Haney said. "And I haven't heard anything that leads me to believe he is going to ask for divine forgiveness."

Francis McGinn stared across the room at Haney. *What has Ricky done that he needs to ask forgiveness for?* she thought. *He hasn't done anything. You, Lee Haney, need to ask for forgiveness.*

"I've never told you that it was going to be easy. It's been a tough week for me, asking people to do things that aren't easy.

"To look a killer in the eye and tell him he is guilty is not easy.

"To ask Pamela Adams and Latasha McGinn and Sonya Vaughn to come in this court and relive the most horrible experiences of their life, that's not easy.

"But I have confidence that you will in fact do your duty."

Haney thanked the jury for their time and patience; then he sat down. All had been done that could be done. All had been said that could be said. It was in the hands of the jury.

At 11:10 A.M. the jury was escorted to the deliberation room to consider its verdict for punishment. Everyone stayed close by, not knowing how long it would take for the twelve men and women to reach one of the toughest decisions of their lives.

People mulled around in the corridors discussing their predictions of the outcome. Would a quick verdict mean the prosecution had convinced them resoundingly, or would a long deliberation mean success for the defense? It was all speculation.

Ricky McGinn wrote his final thoughts on a page of his journal:

So I will wait now and see how things come out. Haney can point at me and holler but he can't look at me in the eyes while he is doing all of his fit throwing.

At noon Judge Cadenhead announced the jury had reached a verdict. As he had two days earlier, Cadenhead warned the audience against any outburst.

The jury filed in as before, expressionless. The foreman handed the verdict to the bailiff, who in turn passed it to the judge.

As to issue number one, reasonable doubt that the defendant would commit criminal acts of violence and would constitute a continuing threat to society, the jury's answer was yes.

As to issue number two, if there was sufficient mitigating circumstances that a sentence of life imprisonment rather than a death sentence be imposed, the jury's answer was no.

Janet Talley expressed agreement with the jury's decision by uttering a soft-spoken "Yes" and grabbing the hands of friends and family.

Across the aisle the McGinn family sat stunned. Francis wept, uttering, "Sweet Jesus, sweet Jesus" for strength and comfort. Verilyn shot angry looks at Lee Haney and expressions of sadness to her brother.

Ben Sudderth asked that the jury be individually polled, with each juror affirming their death penalty decision.

Ricky Nolen McGinn stood before Judge Cadenhead and listened as he pronounced sentence: death by lethal injection. Only the fourth person in the twentieth century to be sentenced to death from Brown County. McGinn said nothing.

Within minutes, as Ricky McGinn was sped back to the Brown County Jail where he would await transport to Huntsville, and Texas's death row, Verilyn was proclaiming her brother's innocence to the press. She vowed that the family would continue to do everything in their power to prove Ricky innocent.

Three days after being found guilty and sentenced to death, Ricky McGinn was whisked from Brown County to Huntsville. The rapid transfer was unexpected. Such matters usually took several days to a couple of weeks for all the paperwork to be completed.

"It is kind of rare for it to move that quickly," Larry Fitzgerald, TDC Public Information Officer, said.

The McGinns thought the quick transfer was just one more example of how Brown County wanted to get rid of Ricky McGinn. Not only did the family expect to free Ricky, they planned to expose Brown County and the conspiracy they were certain existed in framing him.

Thus began the long, frustrating process of finding someone who believed in McGinn and who was willing to help in their campaign to clear his name and free him from his destiny with death.

In the meantime the wheels of justice continued to roll, not at NASCAR-paced speed, more like a Model T clip.

The appeals process is a complicated one that begins at the time a person is sentenced to die. In 1995 the average time spent on death row in Texas was about thirteen years, but the laws were changing and inmates were being rushed through the system at greater speeds than ever before. During that time the cases traveled through the state and federal courts as defense lawyers argued grounds to overturn the death sentence and prosecutors argued the opposite.

McGinn's appeal cited seven points, six dealing with the punishment phase of the trial, and the seventh concerning the court's failure to grant the defense a change of venue to a larger city, where crime would have been more common.

But two years after McGinn was convicted of rape and murder of his stepdaughter, Stephanie Flanary, constituting capital murder, his initial appeal was declined.

Lee Haney was pleased with the decision. However, he had empathy for Janet Talley and the Court of Criminal Appeals' timing.

"I'm a little sorry about the timing, just because the victim's maternal grandfather passed away before learning of the decision, which would have been some comfort to him in his final illness."

But Texas's high court didn't have the final word, as the case would be further scrutinized by federal courts. McGinn also had the right to file a habeas corpus writ, a procedure for obtaining a judicial determination of the legality of an individual's custody, and in federal court, to test the constitutionality of a state criminal conviction.

Richard Alley of Fort Worth had been appointed by the court to serve as McGinn's appellate attorney. He would be responsible for filing the writ with the state and federal courts. The McGinns weren't satisfied with Alley's performance and sought other legal counsel.

Since his initial incarceration in the Brown County Jail in 1993, Ricky McGinn had maintained that he was not guilty of killing his stepdaughter. His mother and Verilyn, along with other members of the family, had no doubt that he was telling the truth. It was up to them to find someone to help prove it.

TWENTY-FIVE

Tina Church sat in her home just outside South Bend, Indiana. Stacks of letters with Texas postmarks tottered on the brink of toppling from her desk as she chose one from the top of the stack and began reading.

The letter, postmarked that month, January 2000, was from Paul Colella, a Texas death row inmate who had been corresponding with Church for some time. Church had reviewed the convicted killer's file, along with dozens of others. By the time Colella had contacted Church, using his one phone call in ninety days, his state habeas corpus appeal had been denied and he was facing an imminent date on the death gurney. Church stepped in, and with her many contacts in the legal field, she had somehow gotten Colella a stay of execution.

The private investigator's pro bono work on behalf of death row inmates had become famous among the condemned. She had laughingly said, "My name must be written on every bathroom wall in prison."

Church had rapidly developed the reputation as a champion of defendants' rights and ardent opponent of the death penalty. Church's mailbox, stuffed with bills, store circulars, and notes from friends, was routinely sprinkled with letters from Texas death row inmates asking, often begging, for her help.

But to Church, her investigative work on behalf of the inmates was only a snapshot in the album of advocacy.

She was driven to help the families of the defendants. She called them the forgotten victims. The mothers, fathers, sisters, brothers, wives, and children of the condemned. They were innocent but too often treated as guilty as the killer himself. Tina Church had become a beacon of light in what seemed like an abyss of helplessness to these families.

Holding Colella's letter in her hands, Church read:

> You might be getting a call from an inmate's mother. Ricky McGinn is here on the row and swears he's innocent. I told him to have his family call you. If anyone could help him, I know it would be you. Tina, he's scheduled to die in April.

Church closed her crystal blue eyes momentarily. Her time was splintered into fragments as it was. Her paid work for the public defender of Saint Joseph County took up the majority of her time. She had just completed an exhausting investigation into the shooting death of a South Bend police officer and she was in the middle of a triple homicide investigation. There were always the private-pay clients and, of course, Church's top priority, her family. How could she take on Ricky McGinn's case? What could she do in three months to keep him from the Texas death chamber?

The ring of the phone interrupted Church's thoughts.

"Tina Church," she said briskly.

"Tina, my name is Francis McGinn. My boy is on death row in Texas."

Church drew a deep breath. What were the chances that Ricky McGinn's mother would call at *that* exact moment? She hated to tell Francis McGinn that she couldn't help, but there was so little time before her son's scheduled execution and Church's schedule was as tight as the rubber band that stretched around a stack of file folders resting at her feet.

"Mrs. McGinn, I was just reading a letter from Paul Colella about your son." But before Church had time to tell the elder McGinn that she didn't see how she could possibly help him, Francis spoke again.

"I've been everywhere," Francis said, her voice quavering. "No one will help me."

"Mrs. McGinn, I . . . ," Church began, justifying her rejection of McGinn's case.

"Please help my little boy," Francis begged. "I don't have no money. I can't pay you."

Church felt the familiar tightening in her chest. Francis McGinn was a mother in pain. Church could hear it in the older woman's voice, the tears she couldn't see but knew were falling on her cheeks. This woman loved her son, just as Church loved her own.

Church anxiously twisted the long blond hair that reached to the small of her back. With a sign of exasperation, Church told Francis that if she were to help, she would need to see everything: crime scene photos, court transcripts, motions filed by the appellate attorney, anything that related to Ricky McGinn's case.

Assured that Francis McGinn's daughter Verilyn Harbin would go to Ben Sudderth's office and obtain the needed information and have it sent to her as soon as possible, Church hung up the phone. She massaged her forehead and wondered again what could be done to help with so little time left before McGinn's rendezvous with the executioner.

Within days Harbin was on the phone with Church; Ben Sudderth had denied access to the records. This wasn't the first time Sudderth had stonewalled McGinn's postconviction appeals. Ricky McGinn himself had written three letters to Sudderth requesting that he turn over the case files

to Richard Alley, his appellate attorney. Each time Sudderth had ignored the request.

In a final desperate effort to obtain the files and get
them sent to Church for evaluation, Harbin drove to Sudderth's office in Comanche, Texas, and demanded the records.

"Tina, he won't let me have them," Verilyn Harbin said
angrily as she stood outside the offices of her brother's
trial attorney talking to Church on her cell phone.

"Hold on, I'll get the State Bar of Texas on a three-way
call and see if they can't help," Church said.

With Harbin on one line and a representative of the
Texas State Bar on the other, the private investigator was
assured that the case files would be promptly turned over.

As Verilyn Harbin stayed on the line with Church, she
watched Sudderth pull away from the building. She quickly
slipped inside and the lawyer's secretary handed over the
McGinn case records.

Within two weeks of Church's initial conversation with
Francis McGinn, a brown UPS truck pulled up in front of
her house. As a muscular man began bringing the heavily
taped boxes to her door, Church was dumbstruck at the
sheer amount of information, inside the numerous cartons,
that apparently faced her. Using a sharp utility knife, so
as not to chip her perfectly manicured nails, Church
hacked through the multiple layers of tape that Francis had
used securing the boxes.

"It's like breaking into Fort Knox," Church muttered as
she tugged and pulled at the tape. She had told Francis
McGinn to secure them, not make them impregnable.

Church's frustration at the sheer volume and packaging
of the boxes didn't come close to the sinking feeling she
felt as she began going over the files.

Some folders were empty; multiple folders contained
identical typed police statements—it was a hodgepodge of

disorganization. Immediately Church began to organize the files for review.

"Madness, utter madness," she quipped as she shuffled hundreds of pieces of paper, organizing them into discernible order as she scanned their content.

Church poured a glass of ice tea and moved to her family room and the comfort of an overstuffed blue chair. She turned on the video she had popped into the VCR and began to watch the crime scene unfold.

She sat up on the edge of the chair and looked hard at the screen. She was amazed at the lack of professionalism displayed at the crime scene by the Brown County sheriff's deputies. Stephanie Flanary's hands had not been bagged before her body was removed from the confines of the culvert, her arms dangled off the gurney. Then Church gasped as one of the deputies held up one of Stephanie's hands, displaying one of her discolored index fingers for the camera.

Slowly Church began studying the still photos of the culvert, the truck, the Ford Escort, and the body. She read the synopsis of the events of the case compiled by Francis McGinn; then she reviewed the video and photographs again. In Church's mind there were too many inconsistencies, too many questions left unanswered.

Why had deputies taken a second rape kit from McGinn, when he had already voluntarily submitted to the collection of hair, blood, and semen? Which brought an even bigger question to mind—why take semen? DNA can be determined by the hair and, better yet, the blood. And why take it twice? But the question that plagued Church most: where was the first rape kit? She could trace the chain of custody on the second kit, but no one seemed to be able to tell her where the first kit had been taken or stored. She became almost dizzy from the possibilities that swam in her head like a school of minnows.

Taking a pad from her desk, Church began to write out the inconsistencies of the case as she saw them.

1. McGinn had been charged and arrested on Sunday night. At that point there was no conclusive evidence that the blood in his car was Stephanie's, there was no body, and there was no murder weapon.

2. The condition of the body at the scene. The corpse was not as decomposed as Church imagined it would be for being exposed for three days in Texas's May weather. There was no sign of animal bites and the insect larvae didn't appear to be abundant.

3. Dusty Bilbrey had inspected the culvert on Sunday night, after McGinn was in custody, and had not seen a body in the culvert.

4. From the photographs it looked like someone had thrown blood from the front to the back of the Escort. Splattering would only be consistent if the victim had been killed in the car. They never alleged she was killed in the car. If she was transported in the car, there should have been some puddling of the blood.

5. Lisa drove the car on Saturday without detecting the iron or metal smell often given off by blood.

6. On Sunday morning people looked in the car without noticing any signs of blood.

7. On Sunday morning Randy McGinn stopped Ricky on the roadway. His wife looked into the Ford Escort as she was talking to Ricky and noticed no blood.

8. The blood seemed to have appeared at the sally port of the sheriff's department.

9. The murder weapon was found four days after the murder, in a truck that had been searched a number of times.

10. The DNA results for the semen found on Stephanie Flanary's shorts and the pubic hair found in her vagina were *"inconclusive."*

Tina Church had literally stopped and stared at the DNA

report she held in her hands. The word "inconclusive" had stood out as though attached to a red flag.

The experienced investigator believed that the courts should be 100 percent certain that they had the right person responsible for the rape and death of Stephanie Flanary before they executed Ricky McGinn. She picked up the phone to call McGinn's new lawyer, Richard Alley, in Fort Worth.

After leaving several messages for Alley, with no response, Church contacted Francis McGinn. She learned that Alley hadn't shown much cooperation with the family, and Francis could identify with Church's frustration. And when Church finally managed to talk with the appellate attorney, she learned he knew little about McGinn's case and was unwilling to file a motion for new DNA tests. She decided it was time to get someone else to take action.

The detective's first call went out to the Texas Defender's Service, a nonprofit agency dedicated to the cause of death row appeals. The seemingly tireless efforts of the lawyers at the defender's service had impressed Church when reviewing other cases. She highly respected Maurie Lavine, one of the best of the service attorneys; she talked with her directly about McGinn's case.

Like Church, Lavine was troubled by the lack of cooperation from Alley and even more so about the inconclusive DNA used in the case against McGinn.

"Tina, I'd love to help," Lavine said—Church heard the unspoken "but" in her voice—"but I'm busy with a number of death row cases right now and I just don't have the time needed to devote to McGinn. With his impending death date, you need someone who can get right on it. But I'll be happy to advise you along the way."

With that promise Church began making calls to every prominent attorney in the country, soliciting help. It was imperative to find out, through new DNA technology, if McGinn was truly innocent.

Why not start at the top? Church thought as she dialed 1411 and asked for the number of the Innocence Project. She intended to talk to Barry Scheck.

Scheck, best known for his work with the "Dream Team" on the O. J. Simpson case, began the Innocence Project in 1992 at the Benjamin N. Cardozo School of Law, where Scheck is a professor. The project is a clinical law program for students, supervised by law professors and administrators, that provides pro bono legal assistance to inmates who are challenging their convictions based on DNA testing of evidence. Normally inmates must obtain funding for testing, but when Church approached Scheck, telling him the history of McGinn's case and the financial status of the family, Scheck agreed to pay the $1,400 required to have the tests completed—if the court would agree to order the tests.

On March 28, 2000, a tornado ripped through downtown Fort Worth, Texas, destroying local landmarks, highrise buildings, and killing one man. As the Bank One skyscraper trembled from the high, swirling winds and blowing rain, huge tinted windows popped out of the structure like buttons on a too tight vest. Suction from the twirling currrents pulled papers, computer records, and office furnishings to the concrete walks below.

Richard Alley, along with numerous other tenants, including the Fort Worth office of the FBI, scurried about the area below their shambled offices, retrieving confidential files on many of their clients.

Many of Ricky McGinn's case documents were among those destroyed in Alley's office. Alley had to rebuild his computer database and request replacement documents from the office of the Texas Attorney General.

With Maurie Lavine of the Defender's Service agreeing to pen the motion, Alley made a petition to the district court in Brown County to grant a motion authorizing new DNA testing and to modify McGinn's April execution date. Judge Stephen Ellis in Brown County would hear the arguments.

In the meantime Tina Church had convinced Mike Charlton of Houston to appear at the hearing to present the motion to Judge Ellis, but no formal request to appoint Charlton and dismiss Alley from the case had been filed in Judge Ellis's court. Not from Charlton. Not from McGinn.

Behind the scenes Richard Ellis, a mild-mannered yet passionate criminal defense attorney from California, was directing Church on what steps needed to be taken. He had agreed to come on board and help behind the scenes because he had many of the same concerns as Church when he looked at McGinn's case. Church, instructed by Ellis, would then notify Alley, the attorney of record, of the procedure to follow. But the associations were strained.

Ellis was flabbergasted that Alley would agree to file a motion and would tell Church and Ellis it had been done, but then Ellis would find out he hadn't followed through.

Church later learned that the State Bar of Texas had documents that found that Alley had twice been publicly reprimanded. In 1985 he had knowingly used false evidence and statements of fact; in 1992 Alley had been cited by the bar for failing to properly safeguard the property of a client. The confidence in Alley's ability to help McGinn went from waning to nonexistent.

Alley failed to return Ellis's calls requesting a person-to-person meeting with McGinn, and Ellis, believing it unethical to see another attorney's client, never met with McGinn personally. Ellis did, however, meet with Francis McGinn.

Ellis, who represented five men in Texas, had been on death row to visit another client when he first saw Francis.

He agreed to meet with her in the parking area of a small rural Baptist church just down from the prison.

With a mild spring breeze blowing across their faces as they stood in the gravel parking lot of the little white church, Francis McGinn and Richard Ellis talked about her son. Ellis watched the woman with a sense of awe. She had a love for her son and a faith in him that captured Ellis's soul. She radiated goodness in the face of a horrible tragedy.

Ellis walked away from the meeting believing that he had just talked with one of those people you seldom meet in life, one who profoundly alters your understanding and experience. Through adversity Francis McGinn had grace.

Not long after Ellis's meeting with Francis, Richard Alley, a large, rather unkempt man in his early forties, stood before Judge Stephen Ellis in the very courtroom where McGinn had been convicted. From Lavine's petition he argued that there had been tremendous advances made in DNA analysis over the past five years with a 99.5 percent accuracy. He stated that the new tests could determine once and for all his client's guilt or innocence, rather than relying on the inconclusive evidence presented in his 1995 trial.

Alley claimed that, at the least, new testing of the pubic hair found in Stephanie Flanary's vagina and the semen stain found on her shorts could exonerate Ricky McGinn from the sexual assault of his stepdaughter, thus diminishing his charge from capital murder, which carried a death penalty. He added that the blood evidence from the car, ax, and clothing might establish murder, but only the pubic hair and semen stain elevated the charge to capital murder.

The nervous attorney, whose fingernails were bitten to the quick, shifted his weight from side to side as he addressed the court, while Francis McGinn dabbed a Kleenex to her eyes and wiped her mouth. The attorney she had

had little confidence in and little contact with was before the court pleading for her son's life.

"Mr. McGinn has consistently professed his innocence," Alley stated. "And retesting is not as costly as taking someone's life. The testing will make certain an innocent person isn't killed. This is only a question of time and money to insure accuracy."

Lee Haney, his hair graying at the temples, his mustache and overall appearance neat and trim in contrast to his counterpart across the aisle, stood and addressed the court.

"Stephanie Flanary has been gone for seven years. Twelve carefully selected people determined he was the killer. Over two dozen judges have considered the evidence in this case and have upheld the decision in this courtroom. This evidence has been in existence all the time. Now, in the eleventh hour, they ask the evidence be retested. The state is sure the motion was brought to delay the execution."

In reviewing the latest procedure in DNA analysis, Haney told the court that mitochondrial testing, which wasn't available in 1993, could be taken from any portion of the cell, not only the nucleus. The evaluation could be done without the root of the hair, but results could take anywhere from one month to six months.

In a voice as mellow as any radio personality's, Judge Stephen Ellis announced that Richard Alley, who was on the state-approved list of appellate attorneys, would remain as the attorney of record; then he granted the request for new DNA testing.

"New testing with the advancements in DNA may not change anything," Judge Ellis said. "But then again, there is at least a chance that the defendant might be exonerated. The need for finality in this case, although very important, is not as important as the need to ensure that justice is done."

Judge Ellis set a revised execution date of June 1, 2000.

Church and her band of exuberant attorneys had six weeks to get the testing completed before a man they all truly believed innocent was put to death.

With the test procedures under way, Church decided that if the DNA testing was not complete by the June 1 execution date, Governor George Bush might be called upon to intervene and grant a stay of execution, allowing more time for the test results to be rendered. It was a long shot, at best. Bush had never granted a stay and had repeatedly insisted he was "absolutely confident" that the 127 inmates executed on his watch had all been guilty. Now, with Bush running on the Republican ticket for president of the United States, on a platform that included law-and-order initiatives, Church had little hope that he would grant relief.

She decided what McGinn's cause needed was publicity. She contacted Jonathan Alter of *Newsweek*, giving him a brief rundown on the history of McGinn's case. The well-respected national publication seemed like the perfect venue to bring attention to the plight of one man's attempt to find justice. The story intrigued Alter, and he agreed to run with it.

With McGinn's April death date negated by Judge Ellis and the DNA retests under way, Alter began preparing a *Newsweek* article that would bring the focus of DNA testing in criminal cases to the nation's consciousness. The article did just that, putting Ricky McGinn into the national debate over DNA testing and whether the justice system should guarantee retesting in older cases.

McGinn himself had been scrutinized in some old Brown County cases by the use of the newest DNA procedures.

The first was in the 1989 unsolved death of Sherry Lynn Newman, four years before the murder of Stephanie Flanary. The twenty-nine-year-old's nude body had been found by county mowing crews near the May community.

Now, after eleven years, authorities had hoped that the same DNA the defense was certain would exonerate McGinn from the murder of Stephanie Flanary would help them identify Newman's killer as Ricky Nolen McGinn. But the body had been in a decomposed state that eliminated any possibility of gathering scientific evidence.

A second case, the 1992 unsolved killing of Christi Jo Egger, had been submitted for DNA evaluation in November 1999. The nineteen-year-old had received a number of blows to the head and her body had been dumped in a rural area near Bangs, Texas, near May. She had been raped. Unlike in the Newman case, investigators were able to have DNA collected from the victim, stored, and maintained for future testing in the event a suspect was arrested.

When the results were released in November 1999, the DNA evidence reportedly linked McGinn to the murder of Christi Jo Egger. The DNA profile pointed to McGinn with the accuracy of one in 5.5 billion. Brown County authorities decided not to pursue prosecution since McGinn was already awaiting his date with death for the murder of Stephanie Flanary.

As in the past Francis McGinn refused to believe that her son had committed the murder of the teenager. Ricky McGinn had denied any involvement with Egger or any knowledge of her death.

Convinced that McGinn was the perpetrator in at least two other murders, Mike McCoy traveled to Texas death row in Livingston, Texas, days before what appeared to be McGinn's impending execution. The last-ditch effort to try to get McGinn to confess to the unsolved crimes was futile.

June 1, 2000, was a typical Texas late-spring day. The sun was aglow in the sky and the remainder of the late-blooming wildflowers were a burst of color along the roadsides.

Francis McGinn, however, didn't notice the sunshine or

the flowers. Unless Governor George Bush intervened, her son would die at 6:00 P.M.

Francis and her children arrived early at the Livingston, Texas, prison that housed death row inmates. They had spent a restless night at a low-budget motel in a dormitory-style room, eating homemade sandwiches and bagged cookies.

Visitation at the prison began at 8:00 A.M. and they wanted to spend every moment they could with Ricky. These might be their last.

When Ricky McGinn was taken from the Brown County Jail to the Texas prison that housed those convicted of capital murder, the facility had been located on the outskirts of Huntsville. But on June 1, 2000, the McGinns entered a new high-tech, high-security prison one the outskirts of Livingston.

The new death row affords the condemned prisoners less freedom and fewer privileges. No televisions are permitted. Prisoners are confined to their steel-doored cells for twenty-two hours each day and let out only for solo, supervised periods of recreation in areas enclosed with steel bars. They take all their meals alone in their cells. Each cell is sparsely appointed with a metal bed, one pillow and a thin mattress covered in blue plastic, a metal shelf and a writing table bolted to the concrete wall, a stainless-steel fixture that is a combination sink and drinking fountain, and a commode.

Each time Francis entered the prison she felt a constriction in her heart. It was difficult to see her boy there, to get to talk to him only by phone, looking through a finger-smudged glass. Most difficult of all was never being able to touch him, to hold him as she had when he was a small boy. She hadn't done that since the day he was taken from the courtroom after learning that he had been condemned to death.

Mike McGinn pushed his mother's wheelchair and

walked slowly behind. Francis, who had heart problems
and diabetes, needed the chair to aid in her mobility. Lisa
McGinn was concerned that the emotional stress of saying
good-bye to her son might be too much for her elderly
mother.

At her nearby motel Tina Church rose later in the morning and prepared for a long day of nail-biting anticipation.
She hoped the word would come in early that Bush had
granted the stay. She didn't think her nerves or Francis's
would take a lingering, last-minute announcement.

She was in nearly constant contact with Barry Scheck,
Richard Ellis, and Maurie Lavine. On her way to the prison
she talked on her cell phone to one of the anxious lawyers
as her volunteer driver pulled through McDonald's for one
of Church's "drive-by eating" experiences. She got to
death row about 9:30 A.M.

As Church talked with other clients on the row, she
watched as some family visiting with McGinn laughed and
smiled while others sat at the end of the long visiting room
with tears in their eyes. Sisters and brothers crammed into
the small cubical area, each taking turns talking on the
telephone system to communicate with Ricky. They talked,
prayed, and even sang some gospel hymns as one by one
they said their tearful good-byes.

At noon Francis and her children were told it was time
for Ricky to go. With a smile and a final "I love you,"
McGinn was taken away, hands cuffed behind his back, to
a waiting van that would take him the forty miles into
Huntsville and the death chamber.

Mike McGinn steered his mother's wheelchair out the
doors of the prison, her hands covered her face as she
wept. Her fifteen-year-old granddaughter hugged her neck
and cried her own tears of sorrow.

The young girl had grown up with her uncle Ricky and
loved him. She didn't believe the authorities or the courts;
she had never known her uncle Ricky to be anything but

loving, caring, and kind. He had never touched her inappropriately, had never overstepped the boundaries of their relationship.

The young teen stood by "Granny," as all the grandkids called Francis, and watched for the white van that was carrying Ricky McGinn to his date with destiny.

"There it is," she shouted as she saw the prison vehicle pull past the entrance of the prison and speed toward the Farm-to-Market Road.

"I love you" was shouted by nieces, brothers, sisters, and Francis as they caught their last glimpse of McGinn.

Tina Church got in the car with the driver who had taken her from the hotel to the prison. She talked with Scheck and Lavine by phone, both of whom continued to assure her that George Bush was leaning toward delaying McGinn's scheduled execution. Church knew there were no guarantees. She bit her lip and tried to focus on what else could be done to insure that McGinn got the DNA testing his case deserved. She had done everything she could; it was time to wait.

Bush, who was campaigning for the presidency, in Albuquerque, New Mexico, had told reporters he was "inclined to give McGinn a thirty-day reprieve. By law the onetime thirty-day reprieve was all the Texas governor could do to halt the execution process. For the governor to commute a death sentence to life in prison, he would have to have the recommendation of the Texas Board of Pardons and Paroles, which earlier had voted eighteen to zero to deny McGinn's request for commutation.

In his more than five years in office and after presiding over 131 executions, Bush had never exercised his right to stay an execution. But now, although the Pardons and Parole Board had voted eleven to seven against recommending that Bush grant the temporary reprieve, the governor was considering the move.

"I'm inclined to intervene in McGinn's case because I

want the man to have his full day in court," Bush said. "If there is any doubt, any outstanding evidence that exonerates him from the rape, we ought to look at it."

McGinn, his family, Tina Church, and Janet Talley all waited nervously to hear word of Bush's final decision.

"I never raped my little girl," McGinn had told a reporter during a death row interview the day before he was set to die. "I never killed my little girl. If I could talk to George Bush right now, I would say this: it's been said that an innocent man has never been executed in Texas. That's wrong. There has been and if they execute me, there's going to be another one. All I have is hope. I'll always have hope. Until the last minute I'll have hope."

As Church traveled along Route 190 back to her motel, a debilitating migraine headache drove pain deep into her eyes. Her stomach was nauseous.

"Pull over!" she shouted.

"What?" her driver asked.

"If you value your car, pull over!"

At that moment the door to the four-door sedan flew open and Church began heaving. Her nerves had finally taken hold of her body; she no longer had control.

By the time Tina Church arrived at the motel, Francis McGinn was in her room. As Church lay across the bed and Francis put a cold compress to her head, she was awed by the elder woman's compassion. Her son could be dead in five hours and yet she was concerned for Church.

Church, an outspoken woman known to use rather colorful language, was rendered speechless.

At two o'clock the McGinns and Church moved to the Hospitality House, a refuge for families of condemned prisoners awaiting execution, near the Walls Unit in the center of Huntsville. Every few minutes they asked Church if there was any word, and every few minutes she would call one of the three attorneys who were instrumental in filing the motion for the stay.

Finally, unable to face the anxious faces of the McGinns any longer, Church made her way to the Walls Unit, where a half-dozen media trucks were parked, ready to cover what could be a historical event in Texas history.

At 5:30 P.M. Francis McGinn, Verilyn Harbin, and three other family members arrived at Walls and were taken to a room in the administration building across from the prison facility where they would wait.

On another floor Janet Talley, her new husband Larry Roberts, and their friends and relatives waited as well, equally anxious to hear if the governor was going to stay the execution. Unlike the room that housed Francis, the space where Janet waited was filled with a heightened anticipation that the seven-year ordeal would soon be over.

McGinn consumed his last meal of a double cheeseburger and fries as he watched the hands of the clock tick off the remaining minutes of his life. At six o'clock the lethal injection would begin; he would be dead within five minutes.

Inside the death chamber guards were making certain that the leather straps that would restrain the prisoner were tight, the microphone above his head was working, and the curtains to the viewers' rooms closed. All was set for the 219th Texan to be put to death since 1982. In the past five years, Bush had refused to stop 131 lethal injections, making Texas the national leader in capital punishment. Prison officials had no reason to believe McGinn's execution wouldn't go off as planned.

At eighteen minutes until 6:00 P.M., the warden of the Walls Unit, along with the death row chaplain, entered the cell where McGinn was being held.

"Ricky, the governor has granted a stay of execution."

Tears of relief dampened McGinn's cheeks. His prayers had been answered.

At five minutes before 6:00 P.M., Francis McGinn was told of the thirty-day reprieve. She immediately thanked

God for the gift of her son's life and hugged her children. Outside in the area designated for the media, Francis found Church, wrapped her arms around her, and muttered, "Thank you. Thank you."

Janet Talley Roberts's emotions were anything but joyful. She was angry. Angry at a system that allowed her daughter's killer to live one day longer. Mad that Stephanie had not been given a second chance at life, as McGinn had. She left quietly through a side door of the administration building and drove straight back to Brownwood.

McGinn was quoted as saying, "Thank you for the chance. Maybe they'll see what I've been telling them all these years."

The thirty days allotted McGinn by Governor George Bush turned into three months of waiting for test results.

Meanwhile, in Missouri, the future of someone on death row wasn't hanging in the balance, but a curious footnote in history was. The remains of a man who died in 1951 and who had claimed to be the outlaw Jesse James were dug up. DNA analysis was to be performed to determine if the remains were indeed those of James. Bone and hair fragments from the grave were determined to be those of James and his remains were re-buried.

Both cases—the Jesse James case and the Ricky McGinn case—could have huge impacts on establishing criminal fact and human identification in technological history. The world was watching.

The spotlight also focused on capital punishment itself. Polls showed that a majority of Americans favored capital punishment, but the building distress that just one innocent person could be executed presented a new twist in the debate.

Janet Talley Roberts, appearing on the *Larry King Live* TV show, emphatically said that she believed McGinn killed her daughter. She stated she thought Bush's reprieve was strictly a political move.

"Her blood was on his clothes, his shoes, and in my car," Janet said. "This is an election year. I don't think the state should pay for another thirty days. Why should we support a guilty man?"

Talking about the DNA, King asked, "What if the DNA proves McGinn innocent?"

"It won't," Janet said resolutely.

And Janet was right. At four different testing sites, including the FBI lab and the Texas Department of Public Safety lab, analysis of the semen and pubic hair found during the crime investigation were tested against the samples taken from McGinn. The results, leaked to the media despite a gag order, stated that the male portion in the DNA profiling was identical to McGinn's. The chances of his specific DNA profile occurring in the population was one in 65 quadrillion. The results solidly identified McGinn as having committed the rape of Stephanie Flanary.

McGinn's attorneys questioned the method used to collect the original samples and questioned where the first rape kit was. Francis McGinn questioned the integrity of the Brown County Sheriff's Office, falling short of accusing them of using the kit to plant evidence.

Richard Ellis was disappointed. He had worked tirelessly to assist in the efforts to gain the testing.

"I guess you wonder why someone would ask for that if it's going to incriminate them," Ellis said. "It's not unknown for people to ask for DNA testing and it comes out against them. Maybe they're thinking it's a shot in the dark. It's a one-hundred-thousand-to-one shot, but I'll take it. Some of them have nothing to lose."

One psychologist commenting on the McGinn case thought McGinn had a lot to lose. He could have feared losing the only thing he had left, the love of his family.

"I know he's innocent," Francis McGinn told the press. "You can call it a mother's or God's intuition, but they will be executing an innocent man."

Janet Talley Roberts didn't agree. She was ready for closure.

"I feel like it's been proven," Roberts said. "Listen to the numbers and it's so evident, so let it rest, let it be finished. I never doubted what the results would be."

The debate over DNA testing raged on through national newspapers, magazines, and television programs. Even though Ricky McGinn's DNA tests didn't prove him innocent of killing his twelve-year-old stepdaughter, it did open a dialogue on the possibility of innocent men being incarcerated and executed when advanced testing could prove once and for all the question of guilt or innocence.

Nothing more could be done for McGinn. Church had given him the chance he needed to prove himself not guilty.

Judge Stephen Ellis of Brown County issued a new death date. Ricky McGinn would die on September 27, 2000.

TWENTY-SIX

On September 27, 2000, Francis McGinn and Janet Talley Roberts relived their respective nightmares of June 1.

Francis went to the prison to again say good-bye to her son, knowing for certain it would be the last time she would see him, hear his voice, pray with him.

Janet, along with her family and friends, drove the four hours from Brownwood to Livingston, thankful it was her last trip to the prison capital of Texas. Her emotions and energies were spent. She hoped there would be no last-minute reprieves to stop her welcome closure.

Richard Ellis, believing the common notion that the taking of one life for another would bring some kind of comfort was a lie, doubted that Janet would find the closure she desired.

"You close on a real estate deal; you don't close on death," Ellis said. "It's an inappropriate term and there is no such thing as closure. They're being told a lie by the system. Preparing them for that, for the possibility for closure, is a farce."

The McGinn family once again made their headquarters at the Hospitality House, but this time their trauma was shared with the nation. Surrounded by a film crew from the television program *60 Minutes II,* their raw emotions were captured on film.

The camera focused on Francis as the death row chaplain explained how her son would be strapped to the gurney and the needle inserted into his arm prior to the opening of the curtains to the viewing rooms. Francis and her family would be in one room, Janet and her supporters in the other, the two rooms divided by a solid wall.

McGinn would be given an opportunity to make a final statement; then the lethal injection of three different drugs would begin running through his veins. They might hear a gasping sound coming from Ricky, but the chaplain assured them McGinn would not suffer. It would be the sound of air escaping his lungs.

Francis looked at the chaplain questioningly but remained silent, her thoughts kept to herself. *How can he not suffer, he is being killed for a crime he did not commit,* she thought, still refusing to accept that her son could have killed Stephanie.

Janet Roberts and the ones who waited with her at the prison administration building were given much the same description of what they would see and hear during the execution. However, the mood was more jubilant in anticipation of the long-awaited event.

Groups of people began arriving at the Hospitality House. Mothers, sisters, and fathers who had lost loved ones to the executioner's needle. They were there to support the McGinns, to give comfort.

Janet Roberts had her supporters as well. Mike McCoy, the Brown County deputy who had made numerous attempts to get McGinn to confess to other crimes in the days before his impending death, arrived in Huntsville and visited with Janet. He, too, would be witnessing the execution.

The hushed murmurs of the family and visitors were abruptly interrupted with the ring of the Hospitality House telephone.

"It's Uncle Ricky!" his fifteen-year-old niece shouted.

Prison officials had given McGinn permission to make

one phone call before it was time to enter the chamber. He phoned his mother.

Following the phone call, the group of more than two dozen who had assembled at the Hospitality House clutched hands in a circle of prayer just after 5:00 P.M. At 5:30 P.M. it was time for McGinn's chosen witnesses to leave.

In a floral dress and sitting in her wheelchair, Francis McGinn was pushed to the waiting van by her son Randy. Hugs and kisses abounded, along with words of strength. Many had tried to convince Francis not to attend the execution due to her failing health, but she wouldn't consider it.

"I was there when he came into this world, I'll be there when he goes out," Francis had said.

Francis McGinn boarded the van as those left behind anguished at the sight of the grieving mother. Even Maurie Lavine, who had come in from Austin to be with McGinn earlier in the day, had tears in her eyes. Those who knew her well were surprised to see the emotion from the lawyer who was known for her strength and coolness.

As Janet Roberts and others gathered in one location and the McGinns in another, protesters congregated outside the Walls Unit. Shouts of defiance came from both the pro-death-penalty supporters and the anti-death-penalty protesters. Signs signifying their respective positions cluttered the street blocked off for their demonstrations: GEORGE BUSH IS A SERIAL KILLER!; ABOLISH THE RACIST DEATH PENALTY NOW!!; FROM LYNCHINGS, TO THE CHAIR, TO THE NEEDLE—IT'S ALL MURDER!; EXECUTE RICKY MCGINN. HE RAPED & MURDERED OUR CHILDREN!! STEPHANIE, CHRISTI, SHERRI!; CHRISTI JO EGGER, BORN 12-21-72, MURDERED BY RICKY NOLEN McGINN THANKSGIVING DAY, NOV. 1992.

Shouts were bantered back and forth between the two

factions. The anti-death-penalty coalition outshouted the others through use of a portable microphone system.

Verilyn Harbin arrived, dressed in a black suit, white shirt, and heels. She calmly took the microphone and attempted to educate the rowdy crowd on specifics of her brother's case, but no one wanted to listen. Angry shouts of "Let him die!" and "He killed our children" became too much for Verilyn and she retreated to the sanctuary of the waiting room and her family.

A few minutes before six o'clock, Janet Roberts, her family and friends, and the family of Christi Jo Egger were escorted to one of the two glassed-in viewing rooms. They waited there while Francis and her family were brought to a neighboring room.

The curtains were opened, revealing McGinn stretched out on the gurney, his arms extended out from his sides and strapped down to cloth-covered boards. He turned to look where Janet stood, along with Robin Sirois and others, then began to speak.

"Robin, you know this ain't right," McGinn said before looking to his mother. "Mama, Adam, Mike, Sonny, Michelle, y'all know I love you. Tell everybody I said hi and that I love them and I will see them on the other side. Okay? And now I just pray that if there is anything against me that God takes it home. I don't want nobody to be mad at nobody. I don't want nobody to be bitter. Keep clean hearts and I will see y'all on the other side. Okay? I love y'all, stay sweet. I love you."

McGinn smiled at his family, many of whom were sobbing. Francis placed her hands on the glass that separated her from her son and cried, "Jesus, Jesus, Jesus. . . ."

As McGinn drew in his last breath and then sputtered as the drugs began taking effect, he became the thirty-third person executed in Texas that year.

The victims' families were quiet as they were taken into a room where they would have time to gather their thoughts before facing the press, just as they had been during the execution. The McGinns left, immediately going to the Huntsville Funeral Home; Francis would be able to hold Ricky for the first time in five years.

As Francis was being wheeled to the waiting van, Mary Mapes, the *60 Minutes II* producer, approached her with condolences.

"Oh, honey, I understand your sweet mother passed a few weeks ago. I'm so sorry," Francis said.

Mapes was stunned. Francis McGinn had just witnessed the death of her son and she was thinking of Mapes's grief. *An amazing woman,* Mapes thought.

In the small room that Janet Roberts later described as the "let's talk room," Steve Flanary approached his ex-wife.

"Well, you moved away from Houston down there where your girls would be safe," he said bitterly. "Well, look what happened. You're just as guilty as that mother-fucker we just fried."

Janet's temper erupted. "Don't tell me I'm as guilty as he is, cause that don't happen!" she shouted.

She was mad, disgusted that Flanary would accuse her of any wrongdoing. After all, he was the one who owed her about $60,000 in back child support, and he was the one that had molested his own children when they were younger. She wasn't about to put up with any lip from Flanary, especially on that day.

Minutes later Janet Roberts stood before a bevy of press who waited for her reaction to the execution of her ex-husband. Dressed in jeans and a bowling shirt, Janet seemed to revel in the attention.

"I feel a lot of relief. I know she's [Stephanie] shining down on us today and McGinn will not breathe our air anymore."

The relief for Janet came from knowing there would be no more trials, no more stays of execution, no more tests.

The death of McGinn wouldn't bring her little girl back, but Janet had an inner peace that came with knowing Stephanie was with God and that she herself wouldn't have to relive the horrors of the past ever again.

Steve Flanary stepped forward and said, "This is a time to close a painful chapter in my life. This execution was for all other victims who have lost children. One more person who thrives on killing young children is gone. I believe in the death penalty one hundred percent."

Christi Egger's grandmother also addressed the press. "There is never going to be any closure, but there is satisfaction that he cannot get out and kill any more little girls," Moselle Ham said. "This man got a humane way out and he beat these girls to death. It was proven over and over."

Across town, at the Huntsville Funeral Home, Francis McGinn hugged her son, patted his cooling face, and kissed his cheeks. Surrounded by his siblings, McGinn's body, in the navy blue shirt and pants provided by the prison for his execution, lay on a rolling gurney. His brothers and sisters took turns holding his hands, touching his chest. Tears flowed like tributaries feeding into a sea of grief.

Tina Church stood back and watched as the family mourned. After several minutes she decided it was time to leave them alone with their sorrow.

Climbing into the car with her driver, Church was physically and emotionally spent. As the driver started the car, a loud explosion took place. Church hit the floorboard of the front seat.

"What the hell was that? Where did it come from?" Church asked, believing someone had taken a shot at them.

Smoke came from the hood of the car and the driver began to laugh. "Feel like a sitting target, do you?" she asked. "It was just the battery."

After replacing the exploded battery and calming Church's

nerves, the duo was on their way. Church would be home soon, back in Indiana working on the next case, hoping to stop another execution and perhaps save a life.

On Friday, September 29, 2000, in the Higginbotham Chapel in Rising Star, Texas, Ricky McGinn's body lay in a gunmetal gray casket lined in white. The casket flower spray of white spider mums, maroon mums, yellow daisies, purple accents, and one red rose rising from the center lay at the foot of the coffin. Verilyn, who had been the strength of the family, the one who had visited Ricky nearly every week, driving ten hours from Granda, Mississippi, to Livingston, stood over her brother's body. He looked at peace and handsome in his light gray suit. The inmate whites had emphasized his prison pallor; the silverish gray gave him a glow she remembered from years before.

For seven years Verilyn Harbin had been the rock for both her mother and her brother. During the events of June 1 and September 27, she had held her emotions intact, but Ricky was dead; she could no longer keep herself together.

With a burst of passion, Verilyn leaned forward, took Ricky in her arms, and hugged him tight. She couldn't let go. She was afraid to let go. Her viselike grip caused embalming fluid to seep from the corners of Ricky's mouth, burning the skin. Finally her sister Lisa pulled her away and convinced her to go home and rest before coming back to the funeral scheduled ninety minutes later.

The funeral director tried his best to dab the fluid from Ricky's mouth, but the damage was done. Funeral guests would have to view the marred body as it was.

At 2:00 P.M. the small chapel was filled to capacity—except for one important person. The McGinns had refused to allow Latasha McGinn or her mother, Imogene Bible, to be present at the service. The girl had called the night before, requesting to attend.

"Absolutely not," Francis had said, adding that it was one of Ricky's final wishes that Latasha and her mother not be at the funeral. There had been so many hurt feelings. Francis still felt like Latasha's courtroom testimony was a determining factor in Ricky's penalty. She'd vowed to have nothing to do with her granddaughter. Her name had even been omitted on the program as a survivor of McGinn's.

Lisa and Randy McGinn sang gospel songs and the Reverend G.W. Wheeler officiated.

At the end of the service, before the guests filed by the casket to pay their final respects, Reverend Wheeler read a letter written by McGinn that he had requested be read at the funeral. The farewell note said:

Hello to all my family and friends,

I just want Brother Wheeler to read this short letter. It won't take but a minute, so please bear with us, ok.

I just want to thank my family and friends for standing with me over the last seven years. Really for my entire life. We have a big family. There has to be one with rambling fever. Well, I had a lot of it in me, and while it had to be one of us, it was a hard job, but I done the best I could, to do it right. Ha!

Really, I want to say I love all my family, each and everyone of you. I love and appreciate you all, and all my friends that have stood with my family through their terrible nightmare. I love and appreciate everyone of you.

I hope that my family will grow closer and help each other. Please stand by one another and be there for each other, no matter what. Family is very important. If family isn't important to you, than you better make it that way because you never know when it will be ripped away and taken from you. Like telling your mother I love you and hugging her neck. Telling your brothers and sisters you love them and hug their necks once in a while too. I have lived this last seven years in a place where I had to fight just to die with a mustache. In a place where you were lucky if roaches weren't in your cold dried up meal trays. There isn't much family love and loyalty where I have been, so take advantage of every minute you can with your family. Let them know that you love them and care about them.

Mama, I love you more than life itself and want you to know that I appreciate you being there for me all my life. It never mattered, you were always there. You are the very best mama in the whole world and I was lucky enough to have you as mine. Now, I need you to be strong, as all my brothers and sisters and nieces and nephews need you so much more that they will ever admit, so stay strong, ok? I love you.

I want to say to all my family and friends, please have no bitterness or anger toward the ones who have hurt us and been our enemies. Just pray for them, that they will be all right in the end. Bitterness just brings unhappiness and misery to ones life and then you lose all meaning of life after awhile so never be bitter. Be happy for me that I no longer have to suffer. God said it was time for me to come home, and so now I'm with my daddy again. So keep a clean and peaceful heart and smile and let the whole world smile with us. I love you all and hope to see you in heaven. Never give up hope and always have faith. I don't have time to name off everyone, but to all that has helped me in the last seven years, I love and appreciate you.

Kids, please take care of our little mama. Help Lisa to take care of her. Make sure they have all they need. Brother Wheeler, I want to thank you for all your help and you seem to come when I needed to see you the most. Thanks for being there, I appreciate it very much. I love you.

I'm not saying good-bye, but just that I will see you all at our great big family reunion in heaven. I love you all.

Go to the family reunion this year at Mike's. Help him get ready for it and please everyone be there and make it the very best ever. Thanks, I love you.

Mom Marge, I will help you build your mansion in heaven and eat the candy there with you someday. I told you I would never say bye, and told you I would tell you I would see you later. I love you much, and thanks for all you have done.

Verilyn, I can't say enough how I appreciate all the money you have been out over these years, but always know I appreciate everything. I love you dearly and I hope you will be happy always.

Everyone, thanks for being the most wonderful family in the whole entire world.

I love you all

Ricky

EPILOGUE

The case of Ricky McGinn has had far-reaching implications, well beyond the execution of a convicted man. The significance of DNA testing and the determination of guilt or innocence by scientific means were brought to the national consciousness, plus a renewed debate over the validity of the death penalty was set in motion.

Cases once built on sound police work alone are now aided by DNA technology. And it will be an increasingly important component of the justice process, when appropriate.

In the same week Ricky McGinn's capital-murder conviction was upheld, Roy Criner, a fellow Texas inmate, was freed after spending ten years in prison for a rape he did not commit. One man executed and one man exonerated by the same scientific means.

Unlike McGinn, who had to seek outside sources of funding for DNA testing, other inmates who make claims of innocence where there is a scientific basis will have their requests paid for by the state.

Thanks to more than $7,000,000 in grants to be divided among seven states by the U.S. Justice Department, over 145,000 claims out of an estimated 750,000 will be cleared. These are DNA samples from convicted criminals that have never been analyzed. In addition, the money will pay for entering the analysis results on the FBI's Combined

DNA Index System, a computer network that allows comparisons with samples in other states.

Texas, along with a number of other states, is now systematically taking DNA samples from certain classes of offenders. The DNA from convicts can then be compared with DNA found on evidence at crime scenes and can help convict or, in some cases, exonerate suspects.

But many prosecutors are still reluctant to free those, like Criner, exonerated by DNA evidence. Those hard-core prosecutors are one of the reasons why Governor George Ryan of Illinois imposed a moratorium on executions after thirteen inmates, one of whom came within two days of execution, were proved innocent.

As difficult as the deaths of both Stephanie Flanary and Ricky McGinn have been for their families, their own lives have gone on.

Francis McGinn: Francis continues to believe in her son's innocence. In poor health she spends much of her time sitting, praying, and looking at photographs of Ricky.

Janet Talley Roberts: Janet remarried not long after McGinn's incarceration. Her new husband is the son of the first Brown County deputy at the scene of Stephanie's disappearance. They are both members of the volunteer fire department in their community.

Janet was thrilled when students from the high school that Stephanie would have attended planted a tree in her memory.

Denise Flanary: Denise has graduated from high school and is also a member of the volunteer fire department.

Verilyn McGinn Harbin: Verilyn has moved back to Rising Star, Texas, and is caring for her mother. She became close friends with a death row inmate she met while visiting her brother and revisits the prison frequently.

Glen Smith: The former deputy is now the sheriff of Brown County.

Mike McCoy and Valten Posey: The two deputies continue their work with the Brown County Sheriff's Office.

Lee Haney: The Brown County district attorney was defeated in his bid for reelection and is now in private law practice.

Ben Doyle Sudderth: Like Bob Spence, Ricky McGinn's first trial attorney, Ben Sudderth was killed in a one-car accident before McGinn's execution.

Tina Church: Tina continues her work as "the other victims' advocate," helping death row inmates and their families.

ACKNOWLEDGMENT

No book ever becomes reality without the assistance of a variety of sources. Some provide technical support, while others offer legal assistance. And some contributions to the work come from the hearts of people.

I thank Mike McCoy for opening his files and offering his recollections; Valton Posey for his candor; my friend James Cron, crime scene investigator, for his expert analysis and opinions; Jan Blankenship, L.P.C., for her thoughtful insights, as well as her friendship; and Richard Ellis for his legal knowledge.

The story of Ricky McGinn is filled with a myriad of emotions experienced by those closely touched by the loss of Stephanie Flanary. These people exposed their hearts and souls to the world by allowing me to gain entry into their darkest days and deepest sorrows. My sincere appreciation is extended to Janet Talley Roberts, Denise Flanary, Francis, Verilyn, Lisa, Mike, and Randy McGinn, along with other members of the McGinn family. They each showed great courage and dignity in the face of incredible scrutiny and loss.

Many thanks to Tina Church for her dedication to the work she so selflessly performs on behalf of others, for her tirelessness in assisting me in this project, and for occasionally offering some much needed comic relief.

I am grateful to my good friend LaRee Bryant for her encouragement and expertise in the preparation of the manuscript, and Karen Haas, who put up with my constant ramblings and tardiness. Both are wonderful editors and welcome supporters.